PROTESTANT
WORSHIP
MUSIC

CHARLES L. ETHERINGTON

pROTESTANT
woRship
music

ITS HISTORY
AND PRACTICE

HOLT, RINEHART AND WINSTON, NEW YORK
CHICAGO SAN FRANCISCO TORONTO LONDON

To the memory of
WILLIAM THEODORE THOMPSON,
beloved friend and teacher

"The golden evening brightens in the west."

❖

May, 1965

PREFACE

There is no dearth of books on church music. Many organists and choirmasters, including myself, have derived great benefit from the writings of their distinguished colleagues, whose wisdom and experience have qualified them to write with authority.

Most writers, however, insofar as they deal with its practice, concern themselves chiefly with music as applied to those churches which have liturgical forms of service. The invaluable books by English writers, which have a wide circulation on this continent, deal, not unnaturally, with the music of the Anglican Church. Many American churchmen also write from the liturgical point of view; and even those with less interest in liturgy support and subscribe to most of what has been said by their Episcopalian and Lutheran colleagues.

No one can afford to ignore the development and influence of liturgical music—from which all church music stems. On the other hand, to confine one's writing to that particular phase of worship music is to leave the nonliturgical church musician with many questions unanswered and many problems unsolved. It is the Protestant, nonliturgical point of view that is taken in this book.

A reviewer of my earlier book, *The Organist and Choirmaster,* good-naturedly accused me of making concessions to popular taste.

In the realm of church music, I am as idealistic as the strictest purist, but I try to be realistic as well. I do not believe that it is of much value simply to point out to one's readers how things *ought* to be done, especially when conditions under which they work sometimes make the fulfillment of ideals difficult or impossible. One has to recognize conditions as they are, and to suggest to his readers methods of improving those conditions or making the best of them.

If only musicians were concerned with church music, there would be little difficulty in raising the standard. We could afford to concentrate on ideals. But worship music, like worship itself, concerns the whole body of worshippers. Some of them may have an appreciation of music, but most of them neither know nor care what the music of the church should be like. The practical point of view must take that condition into consideration.

The church musician must begin his upward climb towards the idealistic from the state of music as it exists in the church where he is active. This book is written to help him in that ascent, and to prepare him for the rebuffs that he will encounter on the way.

I should be very disappointed if I thought that any reader might accept my statements and opinions at their face value. This book is not intended to be dogmatic or pontifical. It is hoped that the views expressed herein may be subjected to thought, criticism, and comparison with the views of other writers whose works are listed in the Bibliography.

Since church music is the concern of all church people, I have tried to make my writing intelligible to the clergy and laity, as well as to musicians, by avoiding technical language as far as my subject will permit.

I acknowledge with gratitude the help and influence of the many people who have unwittingly contributed to the preparation of this book: my teachers, my friends, my family, the writers of reference books which I have consulted, and the many clergy and choristers who have been patient subjects of my experiments. More specifically, I mention three men who, in my most impressionable years, awakened and encouraged my interest in the church and church music: Alfred Budd, my Sunday School teacher at St. George's, St. Catharines; Canon Fred C. Piper, my rector at Thorold; and William Theodore Thompson, my choirmaster and teacher for many years.

Thanks are also due to Novello and Company, Ltd., London and the H. W. Gray Company, New York, for keeping me abreast of developments in church music for many years; to the Boston Music Company, Boston, G. Schirmer Inc., New York, and Carl Fischer Inc., New York, for their ready and generous response to my appeal for copies of the latest and most modern examples of choral music.

CHARLES L. ETHERINGTON

Fergus, Ontario
February, 1962

CONTENTS

I

MUSIC
FOR WORSHIP

✤ IN SEARCH OF A DEFINITION

The usual method of beginning a book on church music is to pose the question, What *is* church music? Although many attempts have been made to answer it, the question remains as pertinent today as it was to our forefathers half a millennium ago, for a satisfactory, unqualified definition of the term has never been agreed upon.

That is not to say that individual writers have failed to arrive at definite conclusions or to reach some measure of agreement among themselves. But writers are not the only judges of what constitutes church music, nor are their opinions considered authoritative by all those who regulate its practice.

The arbiters of the music that shall be used for services of worship are clergymen, organists, and choirmasters. They may consult books on the subject; they may be guided to some extent by the vague, general directions issued by church governing bodies or contained in the prefaces to hymnals; they may simply follow their own likes and dislikes, or fall in with any suggestions advanced by members of their congregations. Whatever their methods or qualifications may be, the decision is theirs.

1

This freedom of choice is admirable in principle, but the results are confusing to one who seeks a definite standard of music worthy of a place in public worship.

One may visit a church where the music consists of plainsong and Elizabethan motets and assume that, since it has been chosen by a cultured, scholarly minister and a doctor of music, it must be the type considered most suitable for a church service.

Down the street one may find another church with an equally distinguished minister and an equally qualified organist using a totally different type of music. Visits to half a dozen churches, where the equipment and facilities make possible any kind of music the minister and organist prefer, may reveal few or only superficial similarities.

Discounting the preferences of those who have little musical or church background, and of those who regard music as an ear-tickler rather than an integral part of public worship, we are faced with the problem of deciding which clergyman and which organist and choirmaster have hit upon just the right type of music as part of the church's worship. The priest who recently introduced a jazz mass to his congregation has exactly the same official status as his ecclesiastical brother who can tolerate nothing written after the sixteenth century and the minister who can abide nothing composed before the 1890's.

One would suppose that the office and training of a clergyman would qualify him as an authority on any phase of public worship; yet it is no mark of disrespect to suggest that, as far as music is concerned, some clergymen must lack good judgment, since obviously they cannot all be right. The same may be said of organists and choirmasters, who share the responsibility for the wide variety in the types of music heard in our churches.

Our search for a definition of church music becomes more involved as we realize that we are not merely seeking a type of music that meets a definite standard. We are seeking the standard itself.

Music is used in churches for one of two purposes: either as an aid to and a part of the act of worship or as a means of entertainment.

I suppose few clergymen or organists would admit that the music in their churches, apart from the hymns, possibly, is designed to entertain the congregation. Yet, much so-called church music in current use is obviously intended to be something apart from the actual worship. When the choir rises to sing the anthem, when a soloist carefully chooses a conspicuous position which will leave the congregation in no doubt as to his identity, or when the organist begins what is aptly termed an "organ interlude," there is a temporary cessation of worship. Experience has taught the congregation that the dignity and reverence which have marked other parts of the service are to be suspended. There is no actual applause, but the expressions on the faces of the congregation indicate that their thoughts are not turned inward or Godward, but directed towards the musical performance.

Probably few clergymen are happy in such a situation. Some may tolerate it because it is the only kind of music their organists are able or willing to prepare or because they feel that it satisfies their congregations. Many organists, alas, are quite happy with this situation; but many others would serve up better musical fare if their ministers and congregations would stand for it.

Music used as interludes between parts of the service proper cannot be called worship music, for it is performed in the same spirit as it would be performed in any place of entertainment. Those who prepare it need no other standard than the likes and dislikes of their congregations.

Considered as part of the act of worship, music must meet a high, if as yet indefinite, standard. It must satisfy the ideals of both the churchman and the musician.

I have heard it argued that an organist and choirmaster should be a churchman first, a musician second. Actually, there is no more need for him to subordinate his musicianship than there is for the preacher to subordinate his scholarship. Like the architects and the builders or the decorators and the designers of the church furnishings, he uses his art to the best of his ability, having regard to the purpose for which it is intended. The forms he uses may be different from those of secular music, but they fall short of their purpose if they are inferior.

For those who agree that it should be part of, rather than apart from, the act of worship, church music is not an end in itself. As with anything else in connection with the church, it should contribute to the purpose for which the congregation is assembled, a multiple purpose set forth in the Book of Common Prayer as the confession of sins, the obtaining of forgiveness, the rendering of thanks, the setting forth of God's praise, the hearing of God's Word and, finally, the asking for those things which are necessary for the bodily and spiritual welfare of the people. To justify its place in the service, music must assist in turning the hearts and minds of the people towards God.

Pure music, that is, music which has no association or appeal to the listener beyond the actual sounds he hears, can achieve this result for only rare individuals. A person very sensitive to music, in whose soul something of the inspiration that moved the composer finds response, may for a time be transported emotionally and even spiritually. Whether he is turned Godwards or not depends partly on the nature of the music, partly on the individual's peculiar response.

Obviously he will not be brought to a devotional frame of mind by a waltz, a polka, or other forms of music written for the sole purpose of entertainment; but he can, and often does, come closer to a realization of God's presence through hearing serious music at home or in the concert hall than he does in church. This statement may be incredible and even shocking to people who are not musically sensitive, but a moment's reflection should persuade them that there is nothing strange in the thought of God making Himself felt through any medium that will awaken a response.

If we are asked just what music has this uplifting power, we can give no definite answer. One person may be so moved by the slow movement of Beethoven's "Emperor" concerto; another may be left cold by that movement but transported by a Chopin nocturne; still another, not greatly affected by either, may find inspiration in a Bach fugue. No one of them can be classed generally as music that will raise man's thoughts to God, since each affects different individuals in different ways. None could be regarded as suitable church music, for whatever exalted mood they may induce, they do not dispose one's mind towards confession, thanksgiving, praise, and prayer.

The church organist, choosing a voluntary which he hopes will create an atmosphere of worship, cannot be sure that a piece with a nonsuggestive title such as *Prelude* will suitably affect all, some, or none of the congregation.

There is no pure music that can arbitrarily be classified as "sacred" or "church" music. In considering the suitability of music for an accompaniment and aid to worship, more than combinations and successions of sounds must be taken into account.

✤ ASSOCIATION

Most people like music of one kind or another, but except for those who have an intellectual grasp or a genuine appreciation of pure music, it is little more than an aural exercise unless it is artificially related to something else which the mind can comprehend. This relationship or association may be suggested by the composer himself, by someone seeking to interpret the music in familiar terms, by the provision of words to be sung, or by the circumstances under which one first hears a particular piece. In any case, it ceases to be pure music for those who rely on such relationships for their enjoyment.

Association by Suggestion

The composer may furnish the association by giving his piece a suggestive title. If he calls it *Morning*, for instance, we are partially prepared before a note is sounded. (We assume, of course, that he has in mind a pleasant, sunny morning when one feels right with the world; not a foggy, sleety dawn when we awake feeling cross and bilious.) The composer may have wished only to create a mood, but to the imaginative listener the music becomes descriptive of the rising sun, the twittering of awakening birds, and all that he finds pleasant in a morning scene. It matters little whether he relates the music to daybreak over a Canadian lake, the Maine woods, or the Grand Canyon, provided he really enjoys it. Perhaps the piece might just as well have been called *Evening,* for the average listener would have as easily accepted the impression, supplied appropriate imaginative details, and heard the music with equal enjoyment.

Titles such as *The Music Box, Marche Militaire, Funeral March,* and *Cradle Song* make it even easier to understand what the composer is driving at and to feel that one is sharing an experience with him.

Sometimes, when the title is related to something outside our experience, we are aided by a "programme," a story which enables us to follow the composer's design, as in Saint-Saëns' *Danse Macabre,* Gounod's *Funeral March of a Marionette,* and Rimsky-Korsakov's *Scheherazade.* Often our appreciation depends on familiarity with a play to which the music is related, as in Grieg's *Peer Gynt Suite,* or Mendelssohn's incidental music to *A Midsummer Night's Dream.*

But there are countless pieces of music—symphonies, sonatas, suites, preludes, etudes—whose titles give absolutely no clues as to the composers' intentions or emotions, no suggestions of familiar scenes or experiences or emotions of our own with which to relate the work. Two such compositions bearing the same label may be as different from one another as day is from night. Unless we have heard the work before, we do not know what to expect; we cannot prepare ourselves for it as we can in the case of a piece with a descriptive title or a programme. For that reason, the untrained listener is apt to be bored by pure music except for occasional melodic fragments that tickle his ears or strongly rhythmic passages that set his foot tapping.

The vastly increased attendance at symphonic concerts, the nationwide interest in symphonic and opera broadcasts, and the tremendous sales of "classical" records are attributable only in small part to increased facilities for musical education. The chief reason lies in the fact that all efforts to instill an appreciation of music are accompanied by the presentation of artificial relationships.

Programme notes at concerts, commentators at lectures and broadcasts, descriptive material on record jackets, all are designed to inform the average listener what he should hear and feel and imagine when listening to a piece of pure music.

Sometimes the emphasis is placed upon the composer, his nationality, his career, his chronological place in history—all of which, while interesting enough, should have nothing whatever to do with one's enjoyment of the music. The piece would be better judged on its merits. If it conveys something to the hearer, it matters not whether it was written by Beethoven in Vienna in the nineteenth century or by Bill Smith in Battle Creek the week before last.

Commentators often draw attention to certain passages—a motif for horns, an ethereal string passage—with the result that some people are so intent upon listening for these parts that they give insufficient attention to the rest of the work. The form and instrumentation are meant by the composer to be means to an end, not ends in themselves.

Perhaps the most harmful aspect of attempting to thrust appreciation on the lay public is in the presentation of ready-made interpretations. We are told that this or that passage depicts grief, joy, or some other particular state of mind in which the composer is supposed to have found himself. Very seldom have we any authentic record of the state of the composer's feelings: the whole description is of the interpreter's private reaction to the music; and it may be totally different from, and less enjoyable than, the lay listener's response would be if he were left alone to form his own impressions.

Occasionally, when no programme has been provided or suggested by the composer, some well-meaning person will invent one. The reaction to certain pieces of music has often been predetermined by fanciful stories or absurd fables, from which they become inseparable.

Tedious as these verbal aids become to one who likes to listen to music for music's sake, it would be wrong to disparage methods by which great numbers of people have been drawn to serious music. (After all, it is better to walk with a crutch than not to walk at all.) It is intended only to remind the reader that the average listener requires some association of the music with an extraneous image or idea.

The organist lacks the advantage enjoyed by other musicians in that, when he plays a piece with a nondescriptive title, he has no means of awakening in the congregation's minds an association of ideas. He must trust to luck that the music itself will create an atmosphere of worship.

Association with Words

When music is wedded to words, there seems to be no doubt as to its character and purpose. Yet the words, rather than the music, determine whether the piece is sacred or secular, a song of thanksgiving or a prayer.

Some of the dignified Lutheran chorals, which people of all denominations regard as sacred music because they seem to belong so completely to the sacred words to which they are sung, were originally used for secular songs.

Much of the early polyphonic music is so similar that, if he did not catch the words, one might wonder whether he was listening to a madrigal or a motet. Even hearing the words of a sixteenth-century motet, one may be struck by the fact that words expressing joy and praise are often sung to exactly the same kind of music as passages that express lamentation and penitence.

Thirty years ago Arthur Sullivan's part song *The long day closes* was considered capable of changing its appeal sufficiently to be used to the words "Savior, Thy children keep." Compilers of many modern hymnals assume that music which made *John Brown's Body* a marching song will be rendered sacred by setting it to "Mine eyes have seen the glory of the coming of the Lord," and that the lilting character of the *Londonderry Air* will be somehow softened or disguised when it is used for a hymn.

There is no music more lively and piquant than Bach's background to the choral *Jesu, Joy of man's desiring,* yet it is considered sacred music because of the words with which it is associated; and the same may be said for *Sheep may safely graze,* actually an aria from a secular cantata which has become hallowed by English translations and the name Bach.

On the other hand, lovely fragments from the great composers, which organists sometimes introduced into their playing, have to be avoided because they are so strongly associated in the minds of the congregation with soap operas for which they have been used as "theme songs," or trashy words for which the melodies have been pillaged. This, of course, is the great harm done by the indiscriminate use of good music—the impairing of its inspirational qualities by associating it with something cheap and tawdry.

It works the other way as well. Poor music can be, and often is, used and sanctified by association with words of a sacred character. Let the organist make it known that he is playing a choral-prelude based on sacred words, or a piece with a suggestive title such as *Prayer* or *Meditation,* and he can almost feel the congregation straining to achieve the mood that the words—not necessarily the music—suggest. He can get away with almost any kind of music, provided it is not conspicuously incongruous, if the extraneous association is sufficiently strong.

Sentimental Associations

Finally, we come to perhaps the strongest source of association—the circumstances under which a piece of music is first heard. If it recalls a pleasurable occasion, one may retain a sentimental fondness for that particular music, regardless of its intrinsic worth. A hymn one's mother used to sing, or learned at Sunday School or as a choir boy, retains a place in one's affection because of its pleasant association with happy, carefree childhood and because the hearing of it was shared by people of whom one was fond. The realization, later on, that the words are poor and the music worse will not totally suppress a shamefaced, sentimental response to the hymn. If it is neglected by the choirmaster, or if it is combined with a different tune, one has a vague feeling of being cheated.

Music heard on important occasions in one's life—at a dance one has attended in particularly pleasant company, at one's wedding, at the funeral of a friend, at one's first symphonic concert—will always have the power of bringing back those moments and will be cherished for this if for no other reason.

Even plainsong and polyphony are called the perfect musical expressions of worship because they are heard only in combination with sacred words and in religious settings. They have not been desecrated and associated with profane uses in our time. If some perverted genius were to succeed in popularizing Gregorian chants and Palestrina motets by using them for sentimental ditties with catchy rhythms and instrumentation, our notion of them as purely religious music might be seriously disturbed.

✣ DIVERSITY OF RESPONSE

The question arises whether all this music which creates its effects because of suggestive titles, the association with words, and the revival of memories turns people Godwards and, to that extent, may be considered as sacred or worship music.

Who can tell? The same piece of music may affect any two people in different ways. To awaken an identical response in both, music of different types and associations might be required.

The problem arises every week in every church and in the church at large. Were a committee empowered to declare arbitrarily that only this or that type of music was suitable for the accompaniment of worship, what type would be chosen? Must people who like gospel hymns be bored by plainsong? Must lovers of plainsong sing Victorian hymns? Must those who prefer Victorian hymns sing Negro spirituals?

Perhaps one clue to the solution may be found in a brief survey of the policies of the primitive Christian Church in adapting its dogmas, doctrines, and practices to embrace "all sorts and conditions of men"— policies which were a condition of survival and expansion.

❖ THE EARLY CHURCH'S GENERAL POLICY
OF ADAPTATION

Had it been their intention to confine the new faith to their own kind, the disciples of Jesus Christ would have been spared many problems. He had told them: "I am not come to destroy the law or the prophets, but to fulfil." (Matt. 5:17.) Any suspicion that He might have been tearing down a religion to which they were bound by every conceivable tie would have aroused instant and bitter opposition on the part of the crowds He addressed. That His teachings were consistent with Judaism was proved by the facts that He persuaded many devout Jews, including the disciples themselves, and that His philosophy did not interfere with His own observances of the Jewish religion.

But Jesus also said: "Go ye into all the world, and preach the gospel to every creature" (Mark 16:15), and this meant not only the teaching of fellow-Jews with whom the disciples had a great deal in common, but missionary work among peoples whose philosophy and customs were totally foreign to Judaism and what was later to be called Christianity.

Simon Peter, chided for consorting with uncircumcised men and eating ritually unclean food (Acts 10:1–11:18), justified himself by pointing out that only by departing from the strict Jewish code was he able to approach Cornelius and his household and effect their conversion.

About five years later, some of the stricter Jews were to be found following in the wake of Paul and Barnabas and telling the Gentile converts that, in spite of the missionaries' leniency on the subject, they must submit to circumcision in order to be saved. (Acts 15:1–31.) As a result of the protests of Paul and Barnabas, a hearing was held at Jerusalem. The issue was whether the observance of the meticulous laws of Judaism must be made a condition of conversion to the faith of Jesus Christ, or Christianity made comprehensive enough to embrace those who refused to become proselytes to Judaism. The wrong decision would have spelled the end of the movement. The agreement to adapt the new teachings to the customs and environment of the Gentiles set a precedent for adaptation that has worked for the continued progress of the church through the ages.

It was not long after that the apostle John, recognizing the need for a written record that would awaken a response in the minds of the Gentiles, particularly the Greeks, reconciled the life and teachings of Jesus with certain aspects of Greek philosophy—the Word, the Logos, the Godhead. To put it mildly, Christianity lost nothing in the process.

The later adoption of certain pagan festivals and observances, transferring to them Christian significance, not only made the conversion of the pagans easier but gave us many of our most cherished rites and holy days.

It was the need for adaptation and the inflexibility of the Church at that age that precipitated the Reformation. It will be remembered that one issue was services in the vernacular, a means of making the Word and the worship of God comprehensible to the people.

Protestant bodies have ever recognized the inevitability of adaptation without the compromising of essentials. A stiff, unyielding insistence upon petty observances seldom fails to provoke a schism. It is doubtful that a man can truly worship by hearing or uttering a patter of unintelligible words. He must approach and be approached in terms which he understands at least in part.

The modern missionary is as keenly aware of the need for adaptation as were Paul and Barnabas. He can get nothing at all across to the heathen unless he learns their language; and as he accepts their speech, he must also accept many of their customs. To "civilize" them overmuch may give them the impression that the missionary represents the white man's God. They must be made to feel that they are God's children, not His stepchildren.

Even among people who speak the same language some variation of approach and response is to be expected. The Salvation Army, for instance, reaches people who would be uncomfortable and bewildered in a fashionable Anglo-Catholic church. Some of us might be embarrassed if we were asked to don a uniform and beat a drum, but who dares deny that the Army's particular approach has borne fruit among types of people to whom it makes Christianity something real and understandable?

✤ ADAPTATION IN CHURCH MUSIC

The official attitude of the church towards worship music has been, with rare exceptions, extreme—extremely strict or extremely lax.

Even in pre-Reformation times, when an authoritarian Church had a reasonable hope of controlling its music, little trickles of innovation escaped the dam of authority; and the Church Fathers repeatedly found it necessary to repair the breaches and dry up the errant channels. Cautious, conservative, fearful of worldly influence, the Church countered musical excursions into the strange and unknown by retreating to a safe past, and striving to hold a position that had become or was becoming archaic.

With the Reformation and the removal of strong, central ecclesiastical government, the dam of restriction weakened, cracked, and finally burst, loosing diverse currents that gained force, spread, and sometimes mingled. Periodically certain Protestant groups have sought to check or control this current or that: some have even returned to the original basin and endeavored to reconstruct the crumbled walls that once defined the limits of the whole body of church music.

Since people are so variously affected by music, something of the same policy of adaptation which has marked periods of the church's greatest progress would seem to be applicable to the practice of worship music.

If music is to serve any good purpose in the services of the church, it must be of a type which the people will understand and to which they will respond favorably. If it leaves them cold and unmoved, it will do more harm than good, despite its excellence from the standpoint of the musician and churchman. Boredom can be as distracting as frivolity.

It may well be argued that lack of firm direction has already resulted in much unworthy music being heard in our churches, but this lack of firm direction is not the offspring of official tolerance but of official indifference.

✤ LESSONS FROM HISTORY

A book on church music must either presuppose a knowledge of the general background of the subject on the part of the reader or undertake to supply that background.

Present problems cannot be resolved intelligently without reviewing the past. The real value of history lies in its being a record of experiences as well as a chronicle of facts. The accumulated experiences of our forefathers, which history enables us to share vicariously, helps us to form our judgments.

The purpose of this preamble—the posing of the question, What is church music? and leaving the answer very much up in the air—is to prepare the reader for the outline of the history of church music which is to follow.

Our purpose will be not only to consider the development of church music as a science and an art, which can be interesting enough in itself, but to observe the reactions of ecclesiastical authorities and people to problems which that development created. We will find that the problems and reactions and general chaotic states of church music that existed in the past were much the same as we have to face today. While past generations never did arrive at a permanent or altogether satisfactory solution, their partial successes and failures may serve as guides as we seek to arrive at a conclusion regarding the present state and future possibilities of Protestant church music.

2
Jewish music

❖ EARLY JEWISH MUSIC

The earliest followers of Christ were Jews: therefore, their ideas regarding the appropriateness of music as an accompaniment to worship would be derived from the Temple and synagogue.

Music had had a long and honorable tradition among the Jews. It was a form of expression used on every important public occasion. Since every aspect of Jewish life was inseparable from religion, all the music of the Jews was, in a sense, "sacred."

Their first recorded song of triumph, in Exodus 15, followed their successful flight from Egypt and the destruction of Pharaoh's hosts.

One is tempted to speculation regarding the origin of the music of that song. Had Jacob and his followers any background of music when they went to Egypt? If so, how pure had it remained during their centuries among a strange people? There seems to have been no desire for assimilation on the part of either the Egyptians or the children of Israel, for the latter remained a distinct tribe or race at the time when Moses offered them deliverance. Nevertheless, it is inconceivable that two peo-

12

ples living in such close proximity should fail to influence each other's customs and culture. One may assume that the Song of Triumph contained some elements unknown to Jacob, and that the children of Israel carried out of Egypt musical instruments which they had not brought in.

The song was a spontaneous one: it could not have been prepared before an event the exact outcome of which none could foresee. It seems possible that Moses, or someone acting for him, extemporized the words to a sort of chant or singsong, the inflections of which were familiar.

There is a strong suggestion that it may have been sung antiphonally. Certainly the people could not have sung *with* the leader, since they had no foreknowledge of the words. A careful examination shows several passages that could be sung on any occasion for prayer and thanksgiving (verses 2, 11, and 18, for instance). The leader might extemporize the narrative and the people, at a given signal, respond with some well-known ritual words of praise.

> LEADER: I will sing unto the Lord, for he hath triumphed gloriously: the horse and his rider hath he thrown into the sea.
>
> RESPONSE: The Lord is my strength and my song, and he is become my salvation: he is my God, and I will prepare him an habitation; my father's God, and I will exalt him.

Besides the fact that the whole passage lends itself so well to antiphonal treatment, we have evidence that antiphonal singing was well established among the Jews early in their history—considerably later than the Exodus, it is true, but certainly early in the history of the kingdom of Israel. It must have begun sometime, and it is just possible that it may have been the survival of a custom that began during the years of bondage.

As part of the celebration of thanksgiving, the women danced, tapping the rhythm with timbrels; and Miriam repeated the narrator's opening words and probably any other snatches of the song that she could remember (Ex. 15:20–21).

It is possible, of course, that an historian may have invented the Song of Triumph in order to lend color to his record; but the fact that he considered this particular form as tending to lend authenticity to his history argues that it was typical of the expression of praise of the children of Israel at that time.

Few further references to dancing and music are found until the books of Samuel, the Kings, and the Chronicles, but there they abound. Evidently these arts had not been permitted to languish, for they were integral parts of religious observances. Festivals, coronations, triumphs in battle, weddings, the delivery of prophecies, worship, and even funerals were occasions for music. Even such a solemn ceremony as the

return of the Ark of the Covenant to Jerusalem was celebrated by music
and dancing (I Chron. 15:15–28).

✤ THE DAVIDIC TRADITION

About 1040 B.C., King David, himself a musician (I Sam. 16:23),
appointed "certain of the Levites" to provide music for the liturgical
services (I Chron. 16:4–7), and a later chapter lists the number and offices of the musicians (I Chron. 25). This number was increased when
the Temple was built and dedicated.

Some three hundred years later, in Hezekiah's reign, we find the
Levites still supplying music for the temple worship "according to the
commandment of David" (II Chron. 29:25).

Still another three hundred years later, after the Babylonian exile
and the restoration of the temple order in Jerusalem, the Levite families
which had been traditionally charged with the liturgical music had resumed that office. The record is careful to state that the traditions of
David were preserved (Neh. 12:35–36, 45–46). They were probably preserved until the destruction of the Temple in A.D. 70.

When we remember that the evolution of our modern music from
the first tentative attempts at polyphony has been accomplished in something less than a thousand years, it is rather hard to realize that a like
period (from David to the beginning of the Christian era) produced no
radical changes. It is well known, however, that the development of
music began much later than that of the other arts. It was long confined
to what nature made obvious—that short pipes and strings produced
higher sounds than long ones, that certain successions of sounds were
more pleasing and aroused different emotions than others. Perhaps it
could scarcely be called an art; certainly it was not a science. Until
music was considered a subject worthy of man's intellectual powers,
rather than merely something to provide pleasant aural sensations and
appeal to the emotions, little real progress could be made.

Probably the Jews, especially those Levites whose responsibility it
was, were as curious about music as were later generations of Europeans
in the Christian era. There were several factors that prevented them
from carrying their curiosity to the point of further study; but the chief
handicaps were the evanescence of that which aroused their curiosity,
and the conditions under which they lived.

Unlike the products of other arts—buildings, paintings, sculp-
tured figures, even literature—which have more or less permanence and
can be studied and examined over and over again, music ceases to exist
almost as soon as it is produced. It is as elusive as a breeze. Once the
brief moment of its existence is past, it remains only a memory until it

is re-created. Without a system of notation by which to record what was heard, the Jews could only pass their music on by repetition, much as folk tales were perpetuated. While many minor variations would be introduced, due to faulty transmission or slips of memory, the music would remain substantially the same. If occasional innovations were introduced, they would die quickly. Innovations in music are never favorably received, even in our times, and they would stand even less chance of survival among a conservative people such as the Jews. Moreover, there was no method of preserving new musical ideas for the consideration of later, and possibly, more enlightened generations.

Learning and the arts flourish in times of peace; and the history of the Jews reveals no long, untroubled periods when, undistracted by wars and national unrest, they might have made significant cultural advances. Perhaps the period of their captivity in Babylon offered as good an opportunity for learning as any other: certainly the contributions to Jewish literature during the exile were as important as at any other time. One institution connected with Jewish worship, the synagogue, had its origin in Babylon.

It is safe to assume, then, that the liturgical music to which the first Jewish followers of Jesus were accustomed was much the same as that of David's time some eleven hundred years earlier and was perhaps rooted in even more ancient usage.

✣ MUSIC IN THE TEMPLE AND THE SYNAGOGUE

The music of the Temple at Jerusalem was probably very elaborate, being performed by a large choir of Levites and an orchestra composed of many and varied instruments. The ceremonial trumpets were not for accompaniment, but heralded certain parts of the service with fanfares. Cymbals, which had once played an important part in religious music, were not used in the Temple after its restoration, perhaps because of pagan associations.

Because the tradition of Temple worship ended abruptly with the fall of Jerusalem in A.D. 70 and no authentic records exist, we cannot know the exact nature of the music.

The features of the musical portion of the service were the singing of the *Shema* ("Hear, O Israel"), the singing of the daily psalm (in which the people had a part), and the cantillation of the Scriptures.

Cantillation was the reading of the Scriptures to modal inflections which had become more or less traditional. It was not so much a tune as a musical reading. It may have had its origin in the declaiming of the Scriptures at higher than normal pitch, resulting in a sort of singsong of artificial inflections. (It is said that in recent times certain Welsh preachers, carried away by their own eloquence, used to raise the pitch of their voices and deliver their sermons in an extempore semi-chant that was half speech and half song.)

The synagogue bore much the same relation to the Temple that the parish church does to the cathedral. It was the usual place of worship and instruction for all Jews who did not attend the Temple services oftener than the prescribed three times a year. There were synagogues in every village and in the cities as well. In Jerusalem alone there were about four hundred.

Music in the synagogue probably depended upon local conditions. Singers and instrumentalists would be pressed into service if they were available, but there must have been many small communities unable to muster a choir and orchestra. Even the larger synagogues would scarcely be able to rival the splendor of the Temple service, nor would it have been considered fitting to do so.

The music of the synagogue was continued after the fall of Jerusalem and the dispersion of the Jews, although without instrumental accompaniment. Because it seems to have been preserved pretty much in its original form by certain groups of oriental Jews, especially in Yemen and Iran, musicologists have been able to form a fair idea of the type of music familiar to early Jewish Christians.

Ex. 2:1. The sounds represented are only approximate.

It is from this source that we learn more about the cantillations. They were based on certain melodic forms, subject to some improvisation. The scale foundation was pentatonic (although the Jews, of course, did not recognize that), a foundation which characterizes nearly all primitive music (see Ex. 2:1).

Melodies founded on the pentatonic scale—almost always unconsciously—are common in such widely separated areas as China, Japan, India, Africa, and in American Indian tunes and Scottish folk music. The fact that this scale was also the basis of early Greek music, a forerunner of our modern system, leads some people to jump to the hasty conclusion that some of our plainsong is derived from Jewish music. That there would be a similarity between the melodies of two peoples using the same limited musical resources is inevitable, but the similarity is more likely to be coincidental than the result of deliberate imitation. There is a possibility that some Jewish melodies survived unchanged by later Greek influence on church music, but it is no more than a possibility.

Prayers and psalms were chanted. Perhaps the melodies were less subject to improvisation than the cantillation, but the range of chants was wide and may have included folk music, as in the Temple worship.

✤ INSTRUMENTAL MUSIC

It would be difficult to form an estimate of the music of any people without taking into consideration their instruments. An instrument, unlike the music it produces, has substance and some degree of permanence. It can be observed, studied, and made the subject of experiment. As a result of experiment and accidental discoveries, many improvements can be made.

The children of Israel would almost certainly possess primitive wind instruments when they went down into Egypt. The reference to "organ" in Genesis 4:21 probably means a pipe, either of the flue or reed variety, which has always been popular among oriental peoples. From the primitive pipe developed a number of improved wind instruments mentioned in the Bible: the flute, the reed pipe, the shawm, a type of bagpipe, cornets, trumpets, and the long, straight ceremonial trumpets. Later there was an organ-like instrument, the magrepha, used in the Temple worship.

Stringed instruments are generally found among settled peoples with a comparatively high standard of civilization, and it is more likely that the children of Israel borrowed them from the Egyptians, who had long used strings, than that they developed them themselves. The harp, the psaltery, the lute, the viol, the dulcimer, and the gittith were stringed instruments of various sizes and shapes, having few or many strings of various lengths. The strings were plucked, of course; and it would be interesting to know if the Jews discovered the effect of reducing the vibrating length of a string by stopping it with the finger.

Percussion instruments included tabrets and timbrels, varying in size from tambourines to good-sized drums, cymbals, castanets, and the shalishim, a metal bar struck in the manner of our triangle.

We gather from this catalogue of instruments that Jewish music was shrill. Being essentially melodic, the chief supporting instruments would be those capable of sustained sound—the wind instruments—and since there could be little modification of sound, the music was probably loud as well as shrill.

Although melody was the chief element, the fact must not be overlooked that the stringed instruments could produce sounds above and below the compass of the human voice and could produce several sounds simultaneously. It is hard to believe that a player would pluck out the note of the melody on one string at a time: the sound would be lost in the general din. No one with a spark of imagination and a harp in his hand could resist drawing his fingers over the strings and producing chords of sorts. Therefore, it seems likely that something of what we would call harmony was present, although cautiously and crudely used.

In stressing the features of the cantillations and the singing of the psalms, there is a tendency among modern writers to overemphasize the freedom from strict rhythm that marked much liturgical music. One cannot ignore the instruments of percussion, whose functions were solely rhythmic; or overlook the fact that dancing, which accompanied so many Jewish ceremonies, demands strong rhythm.

The Jews, then, possessed in crude form all the principal elements of music: melody, harmony, and rhythm. While modern music has derived its development of these elements from other sources, we do owe at least something of the tradition of chanting, free rhythm, and antiphonal singing to the Jewish liturgy.

Traces of Temple and synagogue music may be difficult to find in present-day church music; but if it were possible to retrace our steps to the first mission fields of the apostles, particularly Greece and Rome, we would no doubt find that it played its part in influencing the trend of liturgical music, although early Jewish ritual music itself was lost in the process of evolution.

3

THE INFLUENCE OF
EARLY GREEK MUSIC

✤ ENVIRONMENTS OF GREEK AND JEWISH MUSIC

About five and a half centuries before the first Jewish Christians worshiped in Temple and synagogue, at the time when the Jews had just ended their exile in Babylon and were rebuilding the Temple, a development which was to have a profound influence on the music of the Christian Church was taking place in faraway Greece.

We say "faraway" Greece because, although the geographical distance between Jerusalem and Greece is short in terms of modern transportation, it represented a long and arduous journey twenty-five hundred years ago, a journey undertaken by few. And if the distance between the two lands was great, the differences in thought, culture, and condition between the peoples were even greater. The environment and philosophy of a Greek would be as mythical and incomprehensible to a Jew as the daily life and thought of a Guarani Indian are to the average resident of North America.

The Jews as a nation were on the downward path. Defeated, dispersed, born in captivity, their glories in the past, their future based on

19

optimism rather than hope, they had nothing to bequeath to the world but their religion. The unrest which had prevented significant cultural advances (most of their learning was borrowed from other peoples) was to continue during their last struggle for survival as a separate political group.

The Greeks, on the other hand, were on the upgrade. Already possessed of a military, political, and cultural history which had brought them to an advanced state of civilization, they were a forward-looking people on the threshold of an even greater artistic, philosophic, and scientific era whose glories would persist long after their political and military importance had faded.

In such widely diverse environments, the traditional and the intellectual, are to be found the progenitors of our modern church music. Although they long remained separate, they were eventually to merge, producing a type of music that preserved elements of both.

✣ DEVELOPMENT OF GREEK MUSIC

The beginnings of Greek music were lost in antiquity, even at the time of which we are writing. The Greeks themselves believed that it had been gathered from all parts of the then known world, which is quite possible. But music did not exist as an independent art. It was incidental to other arts—drama and dancing, chiefly—and its characteristics depended largely upon the mood or "mode" called forth by words and actions.

The music was monodic, probably very much like other oriental music based on the pentatonic scale or something close to it. It is not to be inferred that the ancients recognized any scale or system. The pentatonic scale was reconstructed much later from the five sounds that were used *intuitively*, rather than systematically, by primitive peoples. Certain successions of sounds gained wide usage because they were pleasant and familiar to oriental ears, not because of planning or logic.

But the Greeks had reached a point where intuition was giving way to inquiry. While some valuable preliminary work had been done, notably by Terpander (670 B.C.), it was Pythagoras (582–507 B.C.) more than anyone else who developed the science without which music could never have become an art.

It had been discovered that the shortening of the vibrating portion of a string to one half its original length doubled the frequency of the vibrations and produced the sound which we call the octave. By further experimentation it was found that in addition to the simple ratio of vibrations that produced the octave (2:1), other simple ratios, 3:2 and 4:3, produced the sounds which we know as the fourth and fifth. These

sounds formed the basis of the Greek musical system and even today are indispensable to our system of tone relationship.

In its early form, the principal stringed instrument, the kithara, had only four strings. The outer strings were tuned to a fourth (say E and A), and various tunings were used for the inner strings. This group of sounds was called a *tetrachord* and comprised an important unit in Greek music.

Later, as strings were added, it became possible to extend the range to include another tetrachord, say B and E.

What came to be known as the Greater Perfect System was a combination of conjunct, or overlapping, and disjunct tetrachords extending over a range of two octaves and accommodated by a fifteen-stringed kithara. Since such a succession would produce only fourteen sounds, an extra sound, A, was added at the bottom.

Any segment of eight sounds could be used as a scale or mode; that is, any sound could be used as a starting point and its octave as the opposite limit of the scale. This meant that all modes consisted of the same sounds, but the differences in their starting points resulted in a different arrangement of tones and semitones for each mode.

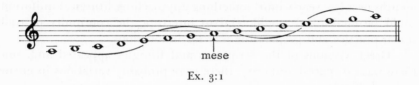

mese

Ex. 3:1

The point of departure, with its octave, had not the significance of the tonic or key-note of our modern scales. The *mese,* which appears in Example 3:1 as note A, was the central tone of the whole system around which the music revolved. It was the principal sound, whatever the mode. The sound on which the scale began derived its importance from the facts that it defined the limits of the mode, and determined the mode's peculiar succession of tones and semitones and its relationship to the mese.

Playing the notes on a piano will not reproduce exactly the sounds of the Greek system. The relationships of sounds other than the fourth, fifth, and octave were to undergo many refinements, and modern notation can convey no more than an approximate idea as to how the Greek scales sounded. Nor was the pitch fixed, as the illustration might suggest. The whole system could be raised or lowered to suit the range of voices as long as the relationships between the sounds were maintained.

Lacking authentic music of this period, we cannot give examples of music based on these modes; but examples of plainsong in the Ambrosian and Gregorian modes, which will be found in the next chapter, follow to some extent the practices of the Greeks.

✤ GREEK MUSIC AND CHRISTIAN LITURGY

When Paul and his fellow-Christians made their first missionary journeys, Greece had been for nearly two centuries subject to Rome. But although Greek military might had succumbed to the Caesars, Greek culture flourished and awaited, like a finely wrought vessel, the inpouring of the precious gift of Christianity.

No doubt the Jewish Christians used their own language and traditional chants when preaching to and worshipping with the dispersed members of their own race; but the success of their mission to the Gentiles demanded the adoption of the Greek language and later, Greek music. This was especially true after the devastation of their homeland left Greece the chief hope for the preservation and growth of Christianity.

Music was probably a secondary consideration for a time. Preaching and teaching were the chief tools of conversion, and details regarding forms of worship would come later. The lapse of time—even a few months or a few years—until something approaching liturgical uniformity could be established would tend to interrupt the continuity of traditional practice and prepare the way for innovations.

Greek versions of the Scriptures and liturgies appeared and, since there was no central authority, there were probably variations in greater or lesser degree.

There was no instrumental accompaniment to the liturgy, but whether the absence of instruments was due to an objection to their use or merely to the fact that no performers were available among the early congregations is not known. Certainly instrumental music was not contrary to Jewish religious tradition, which leads one to suspect that it was abandoned for practical reasons. Its omission retarded the general development of music as an independent art; but, on the other hand, it resulted in the gradual development of choral music to a point which might never have been reached had church musicians not been forced to depend solely upon the resources of the voice.

Since the monodic music of the liturgy was so closely wedded to words and inflections, music suited to the language of Jewish worship would seldom be suitable for translations. More or fewer syllables would be required for expression in the Greek tongue, points of stress would differ, as would the positions and nature of the inflections.[1]

---

[1] A similar situation arose at the time of the English Reformation, when music written for the Latin liturgy had to be adapted to the vernacular. Indeed, any at-

If the liturgy was to be sung in Greek, then, it must be to music that would accommodate the language. The Jews would be reluctant to break with tradition and probably they made attempts to reconcile Jewish and Greek monody wherever it was feasible. But it would seldom be feasible.

The adoption of Greek music was practical from another standpoint. We have seen that it was the policy of the Jewish missionaries to pour the new wine of Christianity into the new bottle of Greek civilization, to refrain from forcing converts to accept Jewish rites and customs and language that might prove stumbling blocks in the work of evangelization. In keeping with this policy, it was only natural that the Greeks be permitted and encouraged to use their own music.

It must be remembered, too, that the use of music required the participation of the Greek congregations. There were no groups of trained Levites in the mission field as there had been in the Temple. Responsorial parts of the liturgy would have to be sung by the people in their own language and to music with which they were familiar. Perhaps even from the very first those parts customarily sung by the priest or cantor would often have to be sung by Greeks, for a Jew might possess the gifts of preaching and teaching and still lack the ability to sing. Later, most leaders in the services were Greeks.

It seems fairly obvious that if the Jews had barred everything but their own traditional monody, music would soon have ceased to have a place in Christian worship. That it survived and flourished is proof enough that it followed an idiom familiar to the Greeks.

In assessing contributions to church music by musicians of various periods, we are apt to underestimate the foundation laid by the Greeks, not only in the first two or three centuries of the Christian era but also during the half dozen centuries that preceded it. Without this important basic contribution, all that has followed would have been impossible to achieve.

tempt to translate from one language to another involves difficulties of meter and stress, and it is rare that the music is as effectively combined with the translation as it is with the original words.

4

MUSIC IN
THE EARLY CHURCH

✣ THE ERA OF PERSECUTION

Two periods of church music which we can consider with a fair degree of certainty are that of the primitive Church of the apostles, when the seed of Christianity was being planted in Greece, and the Greek Greater Perfect System was the familiar mode of musical expression of congregations made up largely of Greeks; and that of Ambrose, Bishop of Milan in the fourth century A.D., when the first of the church modes was established as the standard of worship music.

Of what happened during the three hundred years between Paul and Ambrose we have only hints. In order to partially fill out the gap, it becomes necessary to make deductions based on what we know of the general state of the early Church and the modification of Greek culture.

Even in its early days in Greece, the Church did not enjoy a completely peaceful existence; but as long as Christianity remained an obscure sect, active chiefly among poor and middle class Greeks, opposition was unorganized and sporadic. If the authorities were aware of the cult at all, they probably regarded it as a passing fad which could be disposed of by the legionaries if it threatened to get out of hand.

It was the extension of the Gospel to the seat of the Empire that

24

placed the lives and the religion of Christians in peril. They could not long remain obscure in Rome. The increasing number of converts and their refusal to conform to Roman rites which were contrary to their faith soon brought them to the attention of the authorities, even of the emperor himself. Scorning compromise which might have brought about a mitigation of their cruel treatment, they suffered violent persecution with very short respites for nearly three centuries.

Whatever was taking place to affect music generally, certainly there could be no development of Christian church music under conditions as they existed.

That music as an accompaniment to liturgy survived at all is a matter of wonder. We must not forget that the Church was anything but a local or closely-knit organization. It was spread far and wide throughout the Empire, and little groups of secret worshippers were meeting everywhere. When it was safe to do so, they sang.

There is evidence that music continued to be sung during these three terrible centuries, the strongest evidence being that Ambrose, when the Church at last found surcease from persecution, had the materials and traditions at hand upon which to base his liturgical modes. Had music disappeared from the services, it would have been necessary for him to start from the very beginning, which was certainly not the case.

If there was little uniformity in the primitive Church, there was less during the years that followed.

Among Jewish Christians there might remain traces of the traditional Temple chants, although changes of environment and faults of memory could not fail to modify them. The Greeks, with less tradition and, therefore, less sentimental attachment, would be more liable to changes and innovations and might, in their worship music, be influenced to some degree by the secular music of the day. Near the eastern extremities of the Roman Empire, the liturgical music may have acquired a distinctly oriental flavor that was not far removed from earlier Jewish music.

The Roman Christians (and these interest us most, since our music came to us through the Western Church) used a borrowed musical idiom —the Greek—to clothe their native Latin. Probably some of them, too, preserved relics of the old Jewish chants which had been passed on from generation to generation with the inevitable changes and inaccuracies that befall folk music. More common would be the music of the Greek liturgies, music that would be more familiar to Roman ears. In either case, modifications would have to be made to adapt the melodies to the Latin tongue. Doubtless, as Latin variations of the liturgy increased, the Romans would invent new melodies in the general style of the old in order to accommodate the new words.

There were no means of comparing musical usage. The members of one congregation had few opportunities to communicate with other Christian groups. Many groups would have not only their own versions of older melodies but a number of tunes that were peculiarly their own. The situation was chaotic. The best that can be said is that there was a similarity in the general style of singing, since all groups were familiar with Greek modal music, although they did not necessarily adhere to it strictly, and the tradition of certain forms, such as chants, remained strong.

✤ MUSIC IN A ROMAN ENVIRONMENT

Music, apart from that of the Church, had undergone many changes since Greek culture was at its height.

Greek music had never been as simple as one might suppose from examining the structure of the Greater Perfect System. The use of a segment of the system, with the mese as the principal sound, does not seem complicated in theory, but the selection of any particular segment was not made solely for the purpose of satisfying the ear. Each mode had a certain *feeling* consonant with the effect that was intended to be made by the words, dance, or drama which it accompanied. The choice was made from a sense of propriety, an instinct for rightness.

The Romans, with little culture of their own, adopted that of the Greeks even before Greece became a colony. But the adoption was far from being an assimilation. Whereas the Greeks were inherently aesthetic the Romans acquired culture from without, donning it like an ill-fitting garment that had been designed for others. They failed to appreciate the subtleties, the shades, the overtones that were so obvious to the Greeks.

Nor did closer contact with the Greeks after they became subjects of the Empire make the Romans more sensitive to the arts. The two peoples were cast in different cultural molds, determined by generations of their predecessors.

Music, like the other arts, declined in a Roman environment. Nothing was added to it, and much was lost. Grace, beauty, subtlety of thought and speech were not conspicuous among the Romans, and there was no place for music that reflected those qualities. Power, manliness as exemplified in military prowess, and the rude and often brutal entertainment of the Colosseum formed the social background that music served.

The Greeks had experimented with other than the diatonic intervals of the tetrachord. They had toyed, not altogether successfully, with a succession of sounds which included what we would call a quarter tone. Some distinct progress had been made with a chromatic tetrachord.

Their stringed instruments, particularly the kithara, encouraged experiment, for the pitch of the strings could be adjusted easily.

Characteristically, the Romans preferred the robust tones of brass instruments, which were incapable of chromatics. This limitation tended to restrict the usefulness of the diatonic system and ruled out the possibility of expansion.

Meanwhile, music had declined among the Greeks themselves. A people subdued tends to lose something of its intellectual and artistic virility, and the forward movement of Greek culture slackened. As far as music was concerned, there was a slipping back.

We learn something of the changes that had taken place by the middle of the second century A.D. from a treatise by Ptolemy, the mathematician and astronomer of Alexandria.

Ptolemy describes modes exactly the same as the old Greek modes as far as the actual sounds were concerned, but with this important difference: the mese, instead of being a fixed sound for the whole system, was always the fourth above the hypate, or starting note, of the mode. The tonal center, which had formerly been immovable, now shifted with each change of mode.

This change may seem of little importance to one whose ears are attuned only to modern music. It made a tremendous difference in Greek music, however. Each mode retained certain peculiar characteristics; but, regarded as an entity rather than a segment of the whole tonal system, it lost much of its original meaning and power of expression.

Whatever happened to music between the writing of Ptolemy's treatise and the stabilizing of the church modes was largely a matter of chance. There was no place in society for the professional musician or artist, Greek science waned, and the Romans had neither the fundamentals nor the interest to advance science and art. Music survived much as folk music survives, subject to the memory, the whims, and the imagination of those who passed it on.

✣ FORMALISM

The Edict of Milan, issued by the emperor Constantine in 313, marked the beginning of a new era for the Christian Church. Persecution ceased. There was nothing now to prevent what had been a spiritual fellowship from becoming a corporate unity. The task of establishing uniformity of doctrine and practice was urgent, and for that purpose the Councils of Arles (314) and Nicaea (325) were convened.

It seems scarcely likely that any step was taken towards establishing a uniformity of music at those councils, since there were several major issues to test the patience and tempers of the Church Fathers. Neverthe-

less, the structure of the liturgy and the elaboration of the priestly functions that emerged from the discussions started a trend that was to influence the development of church music.

During the time of persecution, meetings for worship must often
have been marked by informality. What singing had to be done was
done chiefly by the congregation. The music was familiar and relatively
simple.

After 313, sanctioned by authority, the Church itself became authoritative. Practice and liturgy were those prescribed by the governing clergy,
rather than chosen by individual congregations. Much of it would be
unfamiliar to many groups, and voices that had been raised spontaneously
would become hesitant and silent.

As worship became more formal, the clergy took over more of the
music that had formerly been sung by the congregation. In order that
the officiating clergy might not be forced to monopolize the music, choirs
were formed, composed largely of the lesser clergy and, perhaps, some
members of the congregation who showed special aptitude for learning
and singing music. It is believed that Pope Sylvester established an official school in Rome for training in the singing of church music.

Some writers tend to overemphasize the part played by the congregation in the liturgy. In truth, it was very small. Whatever changes were
made were by the clergy or under their direction, with no thought of
congregational participation. The people were left behind, deprived of
much of the musical function that had previously been theirs.

There is no doubt that the entrusting of the music to persons who
were more or less skilled led to a healthy development of the art. Nevertheless, the neglect of the congregation, the altering of its role from that
of active participant to passive onlooker, was to have grave repercussions
in the centuries that followed.

❖ THE AMBROSIANS

To Ambrose (333?–397), during his later years Bishop of Milan, is
generally given the credit for bringing about something approaching uniformity in church music by establishing the first of the church modes
which were to provide the basis for plainsong.

Whether Ambrose undertook this work on his own initiative or at
the invitation of the Church Fathers is not known. Nor do we know how
far the good bishop's personal contribution extended. The reforms may
have been largely his own work, or they may be Ambrosian only in the
sense that they were carried out by others under his authority.

The church modes were bereft of the mathematical basis that
marked the Greek scales. They were probably the result of an effort

to combine the best features of ancient chants, the adaptations that had acquired the authority of wide usage, and the principle of the Greek eight-tone scale.

They resemble the Greek scales, as did those of Ptolemy, in that they are made up of the same sounds. As Ptolemy described a movable mese, so did Ambrose (or his musicians) ; the difference being that, whereas Ptolemy's scale placed the mese on the fourth above the hypate, or starting note, in Ambrose's the mese was on the *fifth*. Again the change may seem slight on paper, but in practice it was startling.

The four modes of Ambrose, which came to be known as *authentic,* are shown below. Since the terms "hypate" and "mese" have lost their original meaning, they are replaced by *final* and *dominant,* which serve the same functions. It might be mentioned that, in the Ambrosian system, the definiteness of the dominant was often lacking, other notes being given more prominence in recitations.

DORIAN MODE	d (final)-e-f-g-a (dominant)-b-c-d
PHRYGIAN MODE	e (final)-f-g-a-b (dominant)-c-d-e
LYDIAN MODE	f (final)-g-a-b-c (dominant)-d-e-f
MIXOLYDIAN MODE	g (final)-a-b-c-d (dominant)-e-f-g

Another great contribution of Ambrose was the metrical hymn. Hymns had always been popular with worshippers, Jewish and pagan as well as Christian. They had been in use for centuries in Asia Minor and probably retained more of their original form than other types of music as they spread to the west. But they were prose hymns. Those of the early Christian Church were chiefly the psalms, the New Testament canticles (*Magnificat, Nunc Dimittis,* and *Benedictus*) and portions of the liturgy commonly sung by the whole congregation.

They were probably more melodious and easier to sing than chants. They had "tunes" of their own, much more flexible and more easily remembered than the long recitations and fixed inflections of the chants. Although they were in prose, they were not unrhythmical. The natural stresses falling upon certain syllables made for a strong although irregular rhythm.

Ambrose wrote his hymns in meter. They became poetry rather than prose, with all the lines having the same number of syllables and the stresses evenly spaced.

> Splendor paternae gloriae,
> De luce lucem proferens,
> Lux lucis, et fons luminus,
> Dies dierum illuminans.

Ambroses's hymns were expressions in poetry of ideas that his predecessors would have expressed in prose.

While the rhythm of the words was measured, the music was not. Plainsong never did achieve measured time, and the rhythm of metrical hymns, like that of prose, depended upon the natural stresses of speech. Perhaps this was one reason for the omission of instruments from worship music. The freedom of what we call today "speech rhythm," the scarcely perceptible lengthening of certain syllables and the shortening of certain others, is not easy for the performer on a musical instrument to follow; and the somewhat crude instruments of the fourth century did not lend themselves to such accompaniments in any case.

Ambrose may have written his metrical hymns because the form appealed to him, but it is not unlikely that he intended to compensate the people for the musical parts of the liturgy of which they had been deprived. We have mentioned that the trend of the day was to exclude the congregation from participation in the service. In the Western Church, the music was becoming so specialized that it was sung chiefly by those trained for the purpose: the Greek church, at the Council of Laodicea (367), frankly ruled against the congregation taking a vocal part in the service lest they corrupt the ancient Byzantine plainsong.

Perhaps Ambrose sensed the danger inherent in the practice. At any rate, his metrical hymns, and those of his successors, were primarily for congregational use and constituted the most interesting parts of the service from the standpoint of the laity.

✤ THE GREGORIANS

Extension of the church modes and important developments in the art of plainsong are attributed to Gregory I (called "the Great"), Pope from 590 to 604. Considering his other accomplishments, it is incredible that he could have spared much time for music during his fourteen years as pope. If he contributed anything to the reforms of church music for which he is given credit, it must have been before his election to the papacy. More probably the reforms are known as "Gregorian" for the same reason that the reforms two centuries earlier are known as "Ambrosian": they were brought about chiefly during Gregory's term of office and, therefore, may be considered to have had his tacit if not his expressed approval.

The development of music has always been gradual; and there were no more sudden, drastic changes in Gregory's time than there had been in the eras of Ptolemy and Ambrose. In each case there was a summing up and sorting out of the modifications in thought and practice that had accumulated over the years. What we know as Gregorian music consists of a codification of the changes that had taken place since the Ambrosians set the musical house in order, some additions original with the Gregorians, and further modifications that were probably made quite a long time after Gregory.

While the Ambrosian, or authentic, modes provided the material for a great deal of plainsong, there was need for even greater variety. Four new modes, known as *plagal,* were added. Each consisted of the same sounds as its corresponding authentic mode; but, whereas the authentic proceeded from the final to its octave with the dominant in between, the plagal began and ended on the dominant with the final between.

AUTHENTIC

d - e - f - g - a - b - c - d - e - f - g - a

PLAGAL

At first, the difference between the authentic and its plagal mode was simply a matter of compass. However, since it was hampering to have the dominants, generally used for recitations, at the top or bottom of the scale, new dominants were set for the plagal modes. These were originally a third lower than the dominants of the authentic modes, but some were altered later. The finals retained their original function in both the authentic and plagal modes.

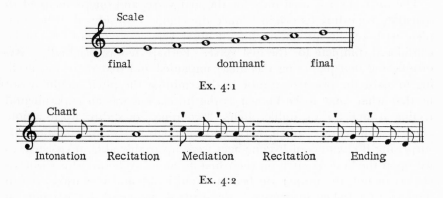

Scale

final   dominant   final

Ex. 4:1

Chant

Intonation   Recitation   Mediation   Recitation   Ending

Ex. 4:2

Examples 4:1 and 4:2 are in the Dorian mode. The compass and dominants of all modes are shown in the table on page 32.

Although the pitch indicated conforms with the written scales in order that the principles may be clearly understood, any of the modes can be transposed to pitches more suitable for singing.

The changing of the pitch does not destroy the character of the mode, since each sound retains the same relation to the other sounds.

Plainsong chants were (and are) sung in free, flowing style without

MODE	COMPASS	FINAL	DOMINANT
1 Dorian (authentic)	d - d	d	a
2 Hypodorian (plagal)	a - a	d	f *
3 Phrygian (authentic)	e - e	e	c *
4 Hypophrygian (plagal)	b - b	e	a *
5 Lydian (authentic)	f - f	f	c
6 Hypolydian (plagal)	c - c	f	a *
7 Mixolydian (authentic)	g - g	g	d
8 Hypomixolydian (plagal)	d - d	g	c *

* Denotes altered dominants

time values as understood in modern music. The length of a syllable was determined by its importance in speech, not from the value of a note written above it. (There were no written notes at all for a long time, and for a much longer time there were no notes written in a manner that indicated time values.)

The two or three notes with which a chant began were known as the *intonation*. Although they are written as eighth notes (quavers) in Example 4:2, they derived their time values from the syllables to which they were sung and, therefore, were not necessarily of equal length.

The intonation is used only for the first verse, and one is tempted to speculate regarding its origin. Since the chant is considered to be complete without the intonation for all other verses, why should it not be considered complete for the first verse? Perhaps it was, originally. Remembering that plainsong was unaccompanied and that there was nothing to assist the priest or cantor in determining the pitch, might it not be that what came to be known as the intonation was an experimental feeling around for a suitable pitch? "Scooping," or sliding up to a note from a slightly lower pitch, is common enough today; and it would be surprising if chanters of bygone ages were invariably able, unassisted, to hit upon the desired pitch on their first attempt. Whether this theory is correct or not, the intonation became traditional, and it is used even in modern times when instruments are available to sound the first note of the chant proper.

The *recitation* was always on the dominant. It is shown as a whole note (semibreve) in Example 4:2 because its normal use for several syllables caused it to be prolonged. It might be quite short, however, if few syllables were chanted to it.

The first part of the verse ended with the *mediation*. The chant in the example shows four notes in the mediation, but the last was omitted in verses which provided no syllable for it. The mediation sometimes consisted of only two notes, the second of which could be omitted if it was not needed. It is probable that at one time the mediation offered an opportunity for extemporization, perhaps as far back as the Jewish liturgical chant, and that it assumed a fixed form much later than the other parts of the chant. In later usage, the points over the notes correspond to similar points over the syllables to which they are sung.

The second *recitation,* again on the dominant, opens the second part of the verse.

The several notes forming the *ending,* pointed to coincide with the pointing of the syllables, worked down to the final of the mode. Endings, which are inflections, early became traditional and more or less classified. Singers accustomed to plainsong can identify the ending by the numeral which follows the mode identification: thus, tone V:2 indicates that the chant is based on the Lydian mode with what has become known as the second ending.

Ex. 4:3

Chants are, of course, the simplest form of plainsong. Psalms, canticles, hymns, and other parts of the liturgy were often sung in more elaborate form. The dominant might be less prominent, but the melody tended to return to it often, clearly marking its importance. Example 4:3 is in mode 3. Joined notes are sung to one syllable. Note the recurrence of the dominant, indicated by asterisks.

✤ IDENTIFICATION OF CHURCH MODES

The layman who wishes to examine and become familiar with modal music may find the following suggestions helpful.

Since plainsong is now often written with key signatures, the first step towards identifying the mode is to transpose the notes to pitches that will permit the music to be played on the white keys of the piano. If the signature contains flats, the last flat will have to be rewritten or

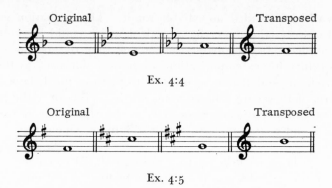

Ex. 4:4

Ex. 4:5

mentally considered as the note F (Ex. 4:4). If the signature contains sharps, the last sharp must be read as B (Ex. 4:5). If we were dealing with modern music, we would say that we were transposing to the key of C major.

Having so arranged the notes mentally or on paper, the next step is to examine the last note, or *final,* which will generally narrow our search to two modes, one authentic and one plagal. For instance, if the final is D, the mode will be either 1 or 2. If the compass lies between the final and its octave (D–D) we are safe in assuming that the music is in mode 1; if the notes go far above or below D (between the dominant A and its octave), we are in mode 2. A note or two beyond the compass of the octave will not affect the mode.

The difference in compass will be accompanied by a difference in the oft-recurring dominant: mode 1 has A for its dominant, mode 2 has F.

Mixed modes that extend far beyond the compass of an octave are often encountered. If, for instance, the melody ranges from C to the octave above the nearest F (an eleventh), it is a mixture of modes 5 and 6, although the dominant of one may be more prominent than that of the other.

The dominant by itself is not a reliable guide to the mode. The recitations for chants in modes 3, 5, and 8 would all be on C; for modes 1, 4, and 6 the dominant is A. Only the final can determine which of the modes is in use.

In later plainsong, the awkward interval between B and F was overcome by substituting generally B flat, but often F sharp. This information is given here, before treating it in its chronological place, in order that the reader who examines plainsong melodies may not be mystified by appearances of these altered notes.

Accompaniments for plainsong, which appear in many modern editions, are foreign to the Gregorian period and will be considered more fully in their proper place.

✤ REFERENCES

Excellent material for the study of plainsong will be found in Roman Catholic service books.

The chant books of some liturgical Protestant churches contain plainsong chants. Some good examples are to be found in *The Hymnal* of the Protestant Episcopal Church.

The following plainsong hymns are in many hymnals, even of non-liturgical churches. They are representative of several periods, but are Gregorian in structure, if not in time. The names generally associated with the tunes are in italics, the first lines of the English verses to which they are usually sung are in roman type. (This practice will be followed throughout the book.)

Mode 1

Christe Redemptor: Jesu, thou Joy of loving hearts.
Sancte Dei: Saint of God, elect and precious.
Veni Emmanuel: O come, O come, Emmanuel. (Transposed to the white keys of the piano, it will be necessary to substitute B flat for B, a circumstance reflected in the signature of modern versions.)
Vexilla Regis: The royal banners forward go. (B flat substituted for B.)
Christe Sanctorum: Christ, the fair glory of the holy angels. (B flat substituted only when there is a descent to F.)
Splendor Paternae: O splendor of God's glory bright. (B flat substituted.)

Mode 2

Urbs Beata: Blessed city, heavenly Salem.
Rector Potens: O God of truth, O Lord of might.
Audi Benigne: O kind Creator, bow thine ear.
Quem Terra: The God whom earth and sea and sky.

Mode 3

O Solus Ortus: From east to west, from shore to shore.
Aeterna Christi: The eternal gifts of Christ the King.
Pange Lingua: Sing, my tongue, the glorious battle, or, Now my tongue the mystery telling. (F sharp substituted for F only when there is a descent from B.)
O Lux Beata Trinitas: Be present, holy Trinity. (B flat substituted.)

Mode 4

Rerum Deus: O God, creation's secret force.
Conditor Alme: Creator of the starry height.

Ecce Jam Noctis: Ah, holy Jesu, how hast thou offended.   (B flat substituted.)

Stabat Mater: At the cross her station keeping.   (B flat substituted.)

Mode 5

Adore Te: Jesu, Son of Mary, Fount of life alone, or, Thee we adore, O hidden Savior, thee.

Divinum Mysterium: Of the Father's love begotten.

Tantum Ergo: Therefore we before him bending.

(Note that all these examples end on the dominant, not unusual in mode 5.)

Mode 6

Nocte Surgentes: Father, we praise thee, now the night is over.

Martyr Dei: O saving Victim.   (B flat substituted.)

Splendor Paternae: O splendor of God's glory bright.   (B flat substituted.   A different version from that in mode 1.)

Mode 8

Veni Creator: Come, Holy Ghost, our souls inspire.

Iste Confessor: Only Begotten, Word of God eternal.

Jam Lucis: Now that the daylight fills the sky.

Aurora Lucis: Light's glittering morn bedecks the sky.

5

The

post-gregorian era

❖ THE CHURCH AS A TEMPORAL POWER

The character and position of the Christian Church in the west after its favorable recognition by the Roman rulers would have been a matter of wonder to the primitive Christians had they been able to foresee it. The toleration and privileges granted by Constantine I in the early fourth century were but indications of greater changes that were to follow.

Before the end of the fourth century, Christianity had assumed the status of a state religion in Rome. The supremacy over all other bishops, for which the bishops of Rome had long striven, was legally established in 445 by a declaration of the emperor. All citizens were required to be members of the Church, and punishment for heresy became increasingly severe. When the Roman Empire finally collapsed in the fifth century, the pope became the authority not only in the Church but in temporal matters as well.

Christianity had developed from a small cult of scattered, meek, persecuted, outlaw groups into a sovereign power, the successor to the Roman Empire. Meekness had given place to authority over men's lives

37

in this world and in the world to come. Even kings were to become subject to the pope. Poverty was succeeded by almost fabulous wealth, humility by arrogance, simplicity by grandeur.

The development of the Church as a temporal force had its effect upon church music. The elaboration of the ritual and the ostentation of the services were probably no more precious in the sight of God and no more inspiring to the souls of men than the simple liturgies used by the very early Church, but they were part and parcel of the pomp and circumstance surrounding an ecclesiastical organization ambitious for the worldly prestige that had been attached to the imperial courts.

It would be unkind and untrue to suggest that the extensions of the liturgy and music were prompted wholly by worldly rather than by pious motives. Devout men, whose sole aim was the enrichment of the services for the glory of God, made valuable contributions to both liturgy and music; but there is no doubt that the nature of their contributions was influenced by the emphasis that was being placed upon the temporal functions of the Church.

✤ OUTLETS AND RESTRAINTS OF AUTHORITY

Music flourished in an authoritarian church in the sense that the possibilities of plainsong were explored (within certain limits), and schools existed for the purpose of instructing boys and men in the correct manner of singing the liturgy.

There is no intention of going into detail here regarding the development of the mass. That subject belongs more properly to a history of the Church than to a history of church music. Suffice to say that there were many additions and elaborations, all tending toward increasing the need for trained singers and depriving the people of active participation.

Simple chants continued to be used in places where the singers were not capable of singing complex melodies and in larger churches for the occasional use of the congregation; but the increasing skill and numbers of trained singers made possible the invention of more florid melodies. (The examples of plainsong tunes recommended for reference at the end of Chapter IV would have been considered very advanced in, say, the sixth century.)

The limitations imposed upon church musicians forbade any experiments beyond the formulas set forth by the Gregorian modes. This restriction had the merit of insuring that the resources of plainsong were thoroughly explored, but it curbed at that time and for centuries to come any tendency on the part of church musicians towards inventiveness.

It would be strange, for instance, if it occurred to no one to combine voices in parts, yet plainsong remained monodic for a long time.

It is hard to believe that no one thought of using musical instruments for certain parts of the liturgy, but ecclesiastical opposition to instrumental music bordered on the fanatical.

It has been suggested in an earlier chapter that instrumental music, a feature of Jewish Temple worship, may have been abandoned first, because musicians were not available among the early Christians and second, because the simplicity of the early services made the use of instruments unnecessary. Indeed, the very simplicity of the liturgy, with its irregular rhythm and stresses, made instrumental accompaniment anything but a simple matter.

Their absence from church music does not mean that instruments were not in use, however. They had been so long associated with secular and licentious practices, with the military and the Colosseum, that they had acquired a bad reputation. St. Jerome is supposed to have said, early in the fifth century, that a Christian maid should not even know what a lyre or a flute was like, the implication being that she should shun the worldly pleasures with which those instruments were associated.

The nature of plainsong was still such as to make accompaniment difficult and, perhaps, undesirable; but imaginative musicians must have seen opportunities for heightening the effects of certain parts of the ritual by the introduction of instruments. Nevertheless, the prejudices of the Church prevented such an innovation.

Too much credit cannot be given the Church for organizing, codifying, and preserving music, but the preservation was such as to discourage expansion. Who can guess how much the progress of music might have been hastened had restrictions been relaxed even a little? Considering the strides that have been made in the past three and a half centuries since Palestrina, it is hard to believe that there were not men in the ten centuries between Gregory and Palestrina capable of carrying music much farther forward than was actually the case. In music, as in so many other fields, the Church preserved and defended the status quo against deterioration and progress alike.

✤ MUSIC IN THE MONASTERY AND MISSION FIELD

If any slight, forward movement in church music was made, it was outside the realm of ecclesiastical officialdom.

It was in the quiet of the monasteries, rather than amid the pomp and splendor of the city churches, that learning and research were carried on. Here were the atmosphere and the leisure for study and contemplation; here, too, in time, the collected records of the thoughts of bygone scholars.

During the period which we are now considering, monasticism was growing and spreading. Benedict of Nursia, early in the sixth century, founded the order which bears his name; and the movement was given impetus by the election of the Benedictine monk Gregory I to the papacy.

The offices and mass were sung in the monasteries, but the excellence of the music varied, depending upon the musical training of the community. The plainsong was simple. The monks had not the facilities, and perhaps not the desire, for elaborate music; and their seclusion did not enable them to keep in touch with what was going on in churches served by trained singers.

Small variations would creep into their liturgical music through faults of memory, and there would be no one to correct them. The remembering of the ever-increasing amount of plainsong was a feat in itself, for there was as yet no recognized system of notation by which it could be recorded.

While no staggering advances in music were made in the monasteries, perhaps their very inaccuracies, the departures from form that would not have been permitted elsewhere, laid the foundation for improvements that were to be made later.

And there were, no doubt, experimenters in a small way. Far from being a law unto themselves, they were, nonetheless, removed from the keen ears of their bishops and from the rigid restrictions that governed liturgical music. If their abbot happened to be lenient about such things or not well informed about music or tone deaf, slight changes might occasionally be introduced by design as well as by accident. If one of the brothers dared not make his vocal trials in chapel, there was nothing to prevent him from making changes to a tune as it ran through his mind. One cannot believe that the people of that period were so basically different from later generations as to have as little musical imagination as the paucity of recorded results seems to suggest.

Perhaps several individual monasteries made small contributions to the system of notation that evolved eventually. Whoever was in charge of the music would require a remarkable memory to carry all the details of liturgical music in his head, and it is known that some attempts were made to keep notes as aids to memory.

As far as music was concerned, the missions served the same useful purpose as the monasteries. Christianity was taken to the pagans by competent men well versed in the liturgy and ritual as well as in the doctrines of the Church. It may be assumed that the services were carried out as nearly in accordance with Roman practice as facilities permitted.

As long as the missionary effort was confined to capitals and kings' courts, the liturgy and music remained pure. But the missionary leaders could not be everywhere. As the Gospel spread and converts in outlying districts required continued ministrations, lesser priests would have to carry on without much direction from their superiors. Some of them may not have been musically gifted and, like their brethren in the monasteries, committed errors simply through faults of memory. Others may have been recruited for missionary work from the monasteries, in which case they would be more familiar with music as sung in their own chapels than with the splendid liturgical settings of Rome.

Separated from central authority and from each other, these missionary parishes and dioceses often developed little trends and peculiarities of their own. After a few centuries these peculiarities, or "uses" as they were called, were so pronounced as to be recognized. In England alone there were several such "uses": the Sarum, the Hereford, the Lincoln, and others.

None of these became great independent movements, and no doubt they were considered provincial by the Romans, but each modification as it became accepted provided the gifted and adept composers that were to come with just so much more scope.

❖ THE CONTINUING DEVELOPMENT OF MUSIC

It has been remarked that the development of music was a gradual process, baffling all attempts to docket it neatly in dated compartments. The assigning of a date to some particular phase of music simply means that at that certain period some particular advance, some new method, thrust itself upon the awareness of musicians in general. The idea may have been conceived centuries before, been subjected to experiments and rejections, perhaps developed in some obscure community and, eventually, through the interchange of ideas, made known to the world at large.

Perhaps nothing illustrates this better than the evolution of the organ. No one can set a date for the invention of the organ. It has not been mentioned previously in this résumé of church music because, at the period of which we are writing, it was scarcely a serviceable instrument from a musician's point of view. Yet it had its beginning when some prehistoric creature discovered that a pleasant sound could be produced by blowing air through a tube. And if we postponed mentioning it until it reached perfection, we should not mention it at all; for it is still being improved.

While it is very easy to get the impression that the two or three centuries which we have chosen to call the post-Gregorian era were barren of results, such was not the case. It was a period of sending forth tender shoots from the lusty plant of church modal music, shoots that would leaf, bud, and blossom in the centuries to come.

It is customary for historians, especially for those dealing briefly with their subject, to turn immediately from the Gregorian era to the age of polyphony. Insofar as recorded significant facts are concerned, they are justified in making the leap of several centuries. But comparing the one period with the other is like comparing the seed to the flower. One must remember the many stages of growth that intervened.

Without the slow, hesitant, unspectacular advances of the post-Gregorian era, some planned, some the results of accident and what official church circles would have called error, the transition from monody to polyphony would never have come to pass.

6

THE INFLUENCE OF
THE CELTIC CHURCH

✤ INDEPENDENT DEVELOPMENT

That missionaries of the Gregorian and post-Gregorian periods were not the first to carry Christianity to western Europe is a fact sometimes forgotten or ignored.

The Church was active in both Britain and Gaul during the Roman occupation, which ended early in the fifth century. Since the supremacy of the Bishop of Rome had not been established at that time, the Celtic church was more or less independent, although its bishops are known to have attended councils in Rome.

It may be assumed that, during the occupation, the liturgy and music of the Celtic and Roman churches were similar, although not identical. These were the days before Ambrose undertook to reduce church music to an orderly system, and there was no uniformity even in Rome. The influence of folk and secular music was strong, and the folk music and traditions of the Celtic races were vastly different from those of southern Europeans, who had borrowed most of what culture they possessed from the Greeks.

The withdrawal of the Roman legions led to almost complete independence of the Celtic church in Gaul and, coupled with the Saxon invasions, to its extinction in Britain. But one young Briton, Patrick, the son of Christian parents, was to become a power in the Celtic church; and his successors were to kindle the flame of Christianity anew in his native land.

Patrick studied in Auxerre, a city in northern Gaul with a strong Celtic tradition, from 419 to 431. Neither he nor his teacher Germanus was in close touch with Rome. If they were acquainted at all with attempts to reduce liturgical music to something resembling a system, the last development which could possibly affect them would be that of the Ambrosians, whom they followed by less than half a century.

Patrick began his missionary work among another group of Celts, the Irish, in 431. Much of his success was due to the fact that he pursued what we have chosen to call, in the first chapter of this book, a "policy of adaptation." The customs and social structure of the people were respected, and we may assume that they were encouraged to use their native music in the service of God. There was no reason why they should not have been, since Patrick and his fellow missioners had no satisfactory substitute to offer.

Learning flourished. The Irish church became noted for its monasteries and scholarship. By the middle of the sixth century, the great school at Aranmore was attracting scholars from all Europe.

Specialists believe that Irish church musicians were at least as active and inventive as those in other parts of Europe, but their isolation made it necessary for them to work independently. Probably unacquainted with the modal system of Ambrose, almost certainly unaware of the later changes that were taking place in liturgical music in Rome, their work would have a distinct Celtic flavor.

The Celtic became an evangelizing church. Columba founded the Ionian church in Scotland in 563. Columban (or Columbanus), with twelve followers, preached and established monasteries in what are now France, southern Germany, and Switzerland. (One of his companions, later known as St. Gall, founded the famous monastery in Switzerland which bears his name.) David, who converted the Welsh, probably came from the Irish church. In 635, at the invitation of the king of Northumbria, Aidan came to England and built a monastery on the island of Lindisfarne.

Kindred to the peoples whom they were seeking to convert, sharing much the same tradition (and much the same type of music, incidentally), the Irish probably found their task easier than would have missionaries of an alien race and culture.

There seems to have been no conflict between the Roman and Celtic churches as long as their ways remained separate. Patrick and Columban are known to have been welcomed in Rome and to have received the approbation of the pope.

✣ SUPPRESSION OF CELTIC RITES

It was in the mission field that conflict developed. There, differences of rite became apparent. During its long isolation, the Celtic church had failed to keep pace with the changes that had taken place in Rome and had made some changes on its own account.

Although differences in music never became a main issue, they did exist; and there are indications that the Roman ecclesiastical authorities found them displeasing.

The differences between Celtic and Roman usage would be far greater than the variations that crept into the Roman liturgy due to local monastic customs, and it was the Celtic version that was in use in parts of England, Scotland, Wales, and western Europe when Augustine arrived in Kent in 597.

It is not hard to believe that, under the supervision of a capable priest like Augustine, newly arrived from Rome, every detail of the liturgy, including the music, would be carried out in the best Roman tradition. It is claimed, indeed, that the English tradition of plainsong inaugurated by Augustine long rivalled that of Rome.

Augustine's activities were confined chiefly to Kent, whose king, Ethelbert, extended him every encouragement and assistance. Canterbury, then, became the center and fountainhead of liturgical learning; although its influence would tend to weaken somewhat as mission priests became thinly spread over a wide area whose facilities of communication with the center of authority were few and difficult.

The Venerable Bede, to whom we are indebted for most of what scanty knowledge we have of the period, does not mention the use of the Roman liturgy in the north of England until 669. Bede as a boy sang in the monasteries of Jarrow and Wearmouth in about 680, which must have been soon after the establishment of the abbey of Wearmouth. He expresses some concern about the threatened deterioration of the music (even at that early date!) blaming it upon neglect and the tendency to admit elements of secular music. The founder of the abbey, Benedict Biscop, considered the state of the music serious enough to justify bringing an expert, John, Archcantor of St. Peter's, from Rome.

It will be noted that Jarrow and Wearmouth were in Northumbria, the scene of the activities of Aidan and the center of strong rivalry between the Celtic and the Roman churches. Although the supremacy of the Roman church was established in 664, the Celtic church had been under the aegis of King Oswald for thirty years, enjoying all the advantages that Augustine enjoyed in Kent. The Celtic liturgy and music were predominant in Northumbria and, being familiar to the people, threatened to persist in spite of all efforts to supplant them with the Roman use.

Admitting that two centuries of separation from Rome must have resulted in major divergences, one is led to suspect that the reformation of the liturgical music was primarily a measure to combat Celtic influence. After all, the Roman authorities had dealt often enough with the intrusion of secular music to make unnecessary the bringing of a musician all the way from Rome for that purpose alone. The deterioration which Bede mentions may not have been as much actual deterioration as divergence from Roman practice—which would have been quite enough to damn it in the opinion of the Roman clergy.

We see then, early established, the Church's newer policy of suppressing anything that did not stem from ecclesiastical authority. The necessity for discipline and guarding against error cannot be denied, but praise of the church fathers for maintaining the purity of liturgical music is too freely and thoughtlessly bestowed. Who can say what harm may have been done by the stifling of Celtic church music, or by the stubborn refusal to examine thoughtfully the developments that were taking place in secular music?

✳ LATER SUPPRESSION OF CELTIC SURVIVALS

Charlemagne, king of the Franks, very soon before or after his coronation by Pope Leo III in 800, brought musicians from Rome to establish a school of church music at his capital, Aix-la-Chapelle (or Aachen) ; and in 803 the Council of Aachen decreed that all monasteries use the Roman plainsong. This move may have been merely part of an exchange of favors between the Pope and Charlemagne, or the king may have had a genuine interest in standardizing liturgical music.

If it was considered necessary to go to such lengths to insure the use of Roman plainsong, some other form or forms must have existed and, to some extent, flourished. Since this region was one in which the Celtic church had been active, it seems reasonable to suppose that the Celtic use, or some trace of it, survived, and that it was this, as well as local usages and inaccurate versions of the Roman use, that Charlemagne intended to suppress.

It is interesting to note that among the monks sent from Rome to Aix-la-Chapelle at Charlemagne's request was one who fell ill while crossing the Alps and stopped to recuperate at the monastery of St. Gall in Switzerland. He must have been interested in what he found there, for he asked and received from his superiors permission to remain. Since his mission was music and he was not likely to have been swerved easily from his purpose, it may be that the music as much as anything else influenced his decision. It will be remembered that the monastery of St. Gall was founded by one of the Celtic monks who set out with Columban over two centuries before Charlemagne's campaign to Romanize the music of the Frankish church. The Celtic tradition would be strong there, and its continuance would be encouraged by the Irish monks and scholars who came to St. Gall to partake of its learning. It became an important center of plainsong.

Certainly musicians of an inventive turn of mind in western Europe did not have to rely solely on musical ideas imported from Rome. Although other elements may have fallen into disuse in churches and monasteries, they could not be removed from people's memories, but would be passed on from generation to generation in the manner of folk music.

Since we have no clear picture of what was going on at the time, we cannot know how strong these survivals were or compare the continuing strain of Celtic influence with other non-Roman elements; but it may be significant that, when plainsong finally blossomed into polyphony, it was from this region that the greatest composers of their day came.

Attempts to standardize plainsong were evidently not altogether successful. After the Norman conquest of England in 1066, the Normans tried to force many of their customs upon the English, including the French manner of singing the liturgy. *The Anglo-Saxon Chronicle* tells us that, in 1083, the Abbot of Glastonbury posted archers in the clerestory with orders to shoot down the stubborn monks who persisted in singing the office in the English manner which they considered to be proper. (This must have been just about the ultimate in ecclesiastical discipline!)

Whether the Normans or the English were closer to the Roman use, and what departures had been made from the officially approved manner of singing, we cannot tell. Certainly variations had crept in, either in France or in England, perhaps both, in spite of the Church's efforts to keep plainsong "pure" by excluding outside influences.

7

Church Music in the Middle Ages

❖ EMBELLISHMENT OF PLAINSONG

Early plainsong was anything but elaborate. It was almost, if not quite, mandatory that no more than one note be sung to a syllable lest the text be obscured or the continuity of the words interrupted.

As choristers became more proficient and the appropriateness of florid passages for festal occasions was recognized, an exception was made in the case of the *Alleluia,* the last syllable of which was considerably prolonged and embellished.

To the florid passage which closed the Alleluia, words were later added, first prose, then verse. This interpolation was called a *sequence.* It may have been introduced because of the abuse of the privilege of embellishment, the distaste of some clerics for music sung without words (the final *a* of the Alleluia was so prolonged that it almost ceased to be part of the word), or the desire to add meaningful words to the liturgy.

In some places the verse of the sequence was sung in addition to, rather than in place of, the added notes of the Alleluia. In the eighth century, in France, added melodies were sung without words, but these gradually developed into sequences.

48

There seems to have been much more freedom permitted in this than in any other part of the liturgy. Perhaps the abuses that crept in were tolerated because the florid Alleluias and verses were traditional from the time of Pope Gregory I. At any rate, the rhymed sequences served as a method of developing hymnody.

Tropes are said to have come into existence in the ninth century. They resulted from florid treatment of parts of the liturgy other than the Alleluia (the *Kyrie eleison* was a favorite subject). A lengthy passage was sung to one syllable, and that not necessarily the last one. In an attempt to make tropes more palatable to church authorities, words bearing on the original subject were interpolated for the extra notes.

Although Tutilo (or Toole), an Irish monk at St. Gall, is often given credit for originating them, tropes developed gradually and independently in several localities in the ninth and tenth centuries and became very popular. Never admitted into the Church's official service books, collections of them existed as auxiliary or supplemental to the Gregorian plainsong. One such collection, used at Winchester Cathedral and known as the *Winchester Troper,* still exists in manuscript form.

The toleration of tropes led to their abuse, and they were abolished in the fifteenth century. A few survive in the form of hymns.

✤ ORGANUM

Whatever crude and unorganized attempts at harmony may have been made in secular music, where instruments of various types and sizes would invite experimentation, the intention was to keep plainsong strictly monodic.

Singing of plainsong in parts, a sort of harmony in the rough, crept in as the result of error rather than of design.

Singers of the Schola Cantorum would have no difficulty in singing in unison (in octaves when both men and boys participated); but untrained singers, such as might be found among the lower clergy, in the monasteries, and among the laity, might find parts of the plainsong beyond the range of their voices. Some of them might follow the exasperating practice that still survives among unmusical men of dropping an octave lower when they could not reach the notes and returning to the correct pitch when it came within their voice range. Others were quite capable of singing the melody without swooping up and down from one octave to another, but chose a pitch which would enable them to sing all the notes with ease, regardless of the fact that it did not agree with what the others were singing.

Modern people who are at all musical would probably attempt to sing in thirds, or even sixths, with the original melody, but either procedure would have sounded extremely bad to the people of that time if anyone had dared sing such intervals. As a matter of fact, it would never have occurred to anyone to sing in thirds or sixths, because ears were not familiar with them and would not have tolerated them. Instead, the singer who could not reach the proper pitch but sought a comfortable range for the melody in Example 7:1 would begin a *fifth* lower.

Ex. 7:1

Played over on the piano, this succession of fifths sounds unpleasant to most ears. Even allowing for slight differences in tuning, it would still sound harsh to many people if they could hear it as sung by early churchmen. It sounded quite plausible in those days, however. The fifth and the fourth, the latter an inverted fifth, had long been important intervals in the musical system, the only intervals at which simultaneous sounds were heard.

Even the early churchmen shuddered a little at those points (marked by asterisks in the example) where diminished fifths occurred, and it was some time before they learned how to overcome this unpleasant effect.

Church musicians were not particularly happy about the addition of a second, improvised part to plainsong; but people would sing it, not with the intention of departing from tradition, but simply because they could not sing at the proper pitch. The Church bowed to the inevitable and accepted the custom. They called the original part *vox principalis,* the added part, *vox organalis,* and the combination of the two, *organum.*

Very soon organum ceased to be confined to the men and was sung by the boys as well, producing four parts or, more properly, two parts, each doubled at the octave. The vox organalis could be higher or lower than the principal part: if higher, the movement was in fourths (inverted fifths).

Ex. 7:2

In Example 7:2, using the same melody as above, but transposed, the principal voice is the lower one. This version is not authentic and probably never existed, but it shows the method of turning monody into organum.

The augmented fourths (inverted diminished fifths), at the points marked by asterisks, served to emphasize rather than lessen the harsh effect. The *tritone,* as the augmented fourth was called, long continued a vexation. Sometimes singers would soften the harshness by flatting the note of the vox organalis, thus producing a perfect interval; but they could not be relied upon to do so, and it was not considered correct in any case.

Free Organum

It was to avoid the tritone that the strict rule requiring parts to move in parallel fourths and fifths was relaxed, and the organal voice ceased to follow slavishly the principal voice.

Ex. 7:3

The first device was to keep the organal voice stationary on the note previous to that which would produce a tritone; then, when the danger was past, the movement in fourths and fifths could be resumed. The third section of the tune in Example 7:2 might be treated as it is in Example 7:3.

It will be noted that instead of the tritone at the points marked by asterisks, a sixth and a third appear. These intervals were not considered good, but only as lesser evils to the tritone. It will be noted, too, that oblique motion occurs at these points, and the parts move momentarily in contrary motion after the first asterisk. These evasions—for they were little more—prepared the ear for further developments which soon followed.

Because the repetition of a note in the organal voice resulted in less motion, it became customary to make that the lower part, and to restrict its downward range to bass C.

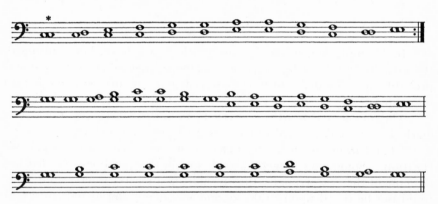

Ex. 7:4. ✻ Ambros: *Geschichte der Musik,* Vol. II. Quoted by Theodore M. Finney in *A History of Music* (New York: Harcourt, Brace & World, Inc., 1947), p. 64.

It is interesting to note that, in Example 7:4, the voices begin each line in unison, the organal voice remains stationary until the principal voice reaches the interval of a fourth. At the end of a line where the singing of a fourth would take the organal voice below bass C, both voices sing in unison. At the close, the voices are again in unison, this time for effect rather than because of limitations of range.

There is a great deal of oblique motion and some contrary motion. The voices are often singing in seconds and thirds. There is considerably more behind this style of organum than the avoidance of the tritone. It would appear that musicians were making tentative attempts towards an independent second voice in place of one that had long been an appendage to the principal voice.

One may wonder why the effect of the third did not lead to an increased use of that interval; but it must be remembered that the third in those days was neither major nor minor, but tuned according to the Pythagorean theory, which would scarcely be acceptable even to our modern ears.

How long it took for organum to develop to this point we do not know. Strict organum was sung quite early, and some slight modifications may not have been long in following; but the type of free organum of which we have given examples was not widely known before the late tenth century.

❖ FURTHER STEPS TOWARD POLYPHONY

History is silent regarding church music during the century between 1050–1150, but a great deal happened in the century and a half that followed.

For much of our information we are indebted to a Paris musician, Franco of Cologne. Paris was an important musical center and, although theorists were often mathematicians and astronomers, placing emphasis on science rather than art, there were many practical musicians as well. Three of them who contributed greatly were connected with Notre Dame: Léonin, Pérotin, whose compositions are still available, and Robert de Sabilon.

It is suggested that French music may have received an impetus at this time from British students who were in Paris: Giraldus Cambrensis, Walter of Odington, John Garland, and others. Certainly there were surprising developments in Britain. Singing in two parts, often in thirds, was known in several districts in England, and particularly in Northumberland. The Welsh sang in several parts. It was during this period that the famous rota *Sumer is icumen in* appeared—a truly remarkable composition compared with other music of that period.

It may be more than coincidence that singing in parts, particularly in thirds, was most common in those parts of Britain that had once been served by the Celtic church and exposed to Celtic music.

In spite of ecclesiastical prohibitions and disciplinary edicts, the music of the church was being influenced strongly by the music of the world. Travelling musicians, known variously as jongleurs, minstrels, troubadours were welcomed everywhere. Kings and great nobles had their own jongleurs. The lesser nobility extended hospitality to wandering minstrels at their castles that the tedium of the long evenings might be relieved by music. These itinerant musicians may not have been well versed or particularly interested in the theory of music, but they had some facility in song, a gift of improvisation, and the desire to please.

Their songs had many verses, and it is not hard to imagine the assembled company roaring the catchy refrains after a few repetitions.

In contrast to the gay songs and the convivial atmosphere of the great hall, the plainsong and the cold, bare churches would seem austere; and it is not surprising that some attempts were made to enliven church music a little. The clergy might have qualms, but their superiors were often far away, while the lord of the manor, whose favor they cultivated, was close at hand and exerting pressure for a relief from austerity.

While the more learned musicians made significant contributions, many changes were improvised by wandering musicians and, as their use spread, regularized by the theorists.

The new freedom found several modes of expression, but the basis of a composition was always a melody, now called *cantus firmus,* but serving the same purpose as the vox principalis in organum. This melody, generally in the tenor, was sung to long notes in order to allow time for florid treatment of the accompanying part or parts. Originally the cantus firmus was a plainsong melody, but since it was often sung so slowly as to be unrecognizable, composers did not scruple to use secular melodies, a practice which brought censure from the church authorities. (By "secular melodies" it is meant tunes associated with secular songs. As was pointed out in Chapter I, no melody is sacred or secular in itself, but only because of such an association.)

The *discant,* or descant, was one form of florid treatment described by Franco of Cologne. It was an improvised melody, sometimes very elaborate, sometimes fairly simple, sung against the cantus firmus. The singer of the discant could do almost anything he liked provided that his part and the cantus firmus sounded consonant intervals at those points where the cantus firmus advanced to a new note. As long as the discant was improvised, it was, of necessity, sung by a solo voice. Later, the part was predetermined and sung by a group of singers. Usually no words were allotted to the discant.

The *conductus* was distinguished from other forms chiefly by the fact that the use of a plainsong melody as a cantus firmus was frankly abandoned. Secular tunes were often used and, quite as often, the melody was original with the composer who could extend it as much as he saw fit. Only the cantus firmus had words: the other parts, which were smooth and flowing, were sung to vowels. One form of embellishment that intrigued composers and delighted singers was the *hocket,* or *ochetto,* which was the division of a melody between two parts, each of which sang alternate words. This device lent itself admirably to frivolity, and Pope John XXII forbade its use as early as 1322.

Franco also speaks of the *rondel,* the forerunner of our round or canon, in which the same words and melody are sung by two or three alphabet to represent sounds. Boethius gives the following names to the sounds in use in his time (fifth century) :

A B C E H I M O X Y CC DD FF KK LL

In the tenth century, the following indications of pitch were current:

G A B c d e f g a b c′ d′ e′ f′ g′ a′

The letters probably served the purpose of the mathematician-musician, but did not lend themselves readily to sight-reading.

Easier for the eye to follow were the earlier forms of *neumes,* which are believed to have been borrowed from the Byzantine, or Eastern Church. They were suggestive rather than exact, indicating the rise and fall of the voices but not the pitch. It was the duty of the choirmaster to set the pitch and interpret the neumes for the singers.

/ \ — ✓ ⁊ ! /: ⌒ ⼉

Since these signs did not define pitch, they were merely aids to memory. They told the singer when to proceed to a higher or lower note, but not how much higher or lower. It would be impossible to read a melody written in neumes, impossible even for the person who made the notes unless the outline recalled the melody or unless he added private signs of his own.

			mun				
t		lis pec	ta	di,	mise	re		
t		tol	ca			re	no	
t								
s	Qui							bis
t								

Ex. 7:5

This defect was partially remedied by the use of the staff, a series of lines and spaces which, at first, made neumes unnecessary. How soon experiments were made with the staff we do not know, but in the time of Hucbald (c. 849–930), the spaces between six lines were used to represent the strings of an instrument (Ex. 7:5). The lines meant nothing in themselves. The letters *t* or *s* at the beginning of the staff showed whether a space represented a tone or a semitone from the one above it, and the voices in turn, each part overlapping the one that preceded it. T greatest value of this type of composition lay in the fact that it challeng the ingenuity of composers.

The *motet* had words for each of its two, three, or four parts, whi were skillfully interwoven. Some of the rules given for the constructic of a motet would be quite familiar to a modern student of strict counte point.

There was a great deal of contrary motion in part singing at th time, a much freer use of thirds and sixths and what we call passing note Much experimentation was being done; rules were being formulatec Composition resembled the fitting together of a jigsaw puzzle: notes an combinations of notes had to be fitted against a cantus firmus in such way that they violated none of the rules. Sometimes, when satisfactor combinations and successions of sounds could not be achieved, the cantu firmus would be altered for the sake of the other parts. Beginning stu dents in counterpoint today, working by trial and error, go through mucl the same experience as the musical experimenters of the late twelfth anc thirteenth centuries.

The advances in this century and a half were remarkable for the times, and, although composers did not quite succeed in writing great music, they helped to set the stage for the great polyphonists who were soon to appear on the scene. Very few of them stand head and shoulders above their fellows, although one must mention Adam de la Hale (c. 1240–1285), a native of Arras, some of whose works were republished as late as 1872. His compositions were chiefly secular, but they had a pro- fo nd influence upon later church composers.

All this was done without the encouragement or even the grudging approval of the Church, although some churchmen had a hand in the forward movement. The Church would have preferred an adherence to the old plainsong. Innovations were regarded with suspicion and hostil- ity. New forms were admitted reluctantly to the services only when it became apparent that they would be used with or without official sanction.

❖ NOTATION

From very early times there seems to have been a desire to make notes which would enable musicians to recall melodies without having to depend entirely upon the memory. No doubt many people, especially those charged with the teaching of plainsong, devised private systems of their own. Perhaps, if it were possible to discover them, we might find that some of these systems were quite ingenious.

Recorded methods of notation begin with the use of letters of the

Qui tol-lis pec-ca- ta mun - di,   mi – se – re – re no - bis.

Ex. 7:6

syllables sung at those pitches were written in the spaces. The same tune
written in modern notation is shown in Example 7:6.

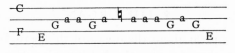

Ex. 7:7

Guido d' Arezzo, the great theorist of the early eleventh century,
was familiar with, and may have invented, a four-line staff, both lines and
spaces of which represented definite pitches. At the beginning of the
staff the top line was designated as C, the second from the bottom as F
(the origin of our modern clefs). Example 7:6 on Guido's staff would
appear as in Example 7:7.

A little later, the F line was drawn in red and the C line in yellow.

The process of combining the neumes and the staff was a long one
extending over some four centuries, during which time the neumes assumed the forms of black squares which were more easily read on and
between the lines.

✤ CANTUS MENSURATUS

As long as melodies were sung in unison or strict organum, there was
no necessity for signs that would define time values. The rhythm of the
words, the values and stresses of ordinary speech, were enough to keep
the singers together. The "feeling" of the rhythm was the same as it is
today when a group of people read or repeat a psalm or prayer in their
natural speaking voices.

When voices were allotted parts more or less independent of the cantus firmus, the matter of time became important. To put it simply: if
one was improvising a discant, he would have to have some means of
knowing how long the principal voice was going to hold a note in order
to time his ornamental part accordingly.

As the number of parts increased, a great deal of attention to the
time element was necessary if the singers were to keep together.
Neumes, or early forms of notes, began to assume proportional values,
the *brevis* being one half or one third of the *longa,* according to a complex set of circumstances determined by the rhythmic modes, which in
turn were designed to accommodate syllabic rhythms.

No conscious effort seems to have been made to create divisions such as measures, phrases, and sections of modern music. The intention in assigning time values to the neumes was not to create a form, but simply to devise a means whereby singers of various parts might keep together. There was no standard. Many copyists used signs of their own, and it might be difficult to read even a familiar part from the notes of a copyist whose methods were unfamiliar.

✱ THE ORGAN

Not much is known about the organ of this period, but it seems desirable to mention that, in spite of the Church's early prejudice against it, it was being used here and there.

A type of organ known as the hydraulus, in which water pressure was used to regulate the wind supply, is known to have existed as early as the third century B.C., and it was this type of instrument which was popular at the Roman games in the time of Nero. Because of its raucous tone and its pagan associations, the Western Church would have nothing to do with it. In the Byzantine East, however, it continued to be used and developed, and some time before the end of the fourth century a purely pneumatic organ was in use there.

The first real evidence of organs in western Europe dates from the close of the eighth century. For a while they were to be found only in the palaces of some kings and in some very large churches.

By the end of the tenth century, however, organs were becoming more numerous, especially in England and Germany, although by no means common. A famous one was that of Winchester Cathedral, built about 950. It had two manuals of twenty notes each, and each note had ten pipes, making a total of four hundred pipes. There were twenty-six bellows, the working of which required seventy blowers.

In central as well as western Europe organs were in use. We know that a new organ (presumably replacing an older one) was built at the cathedral of St. Vitus, in Prague, in 1254.

Some organs were played by means of sliders, lengths of wood which, when pulled out, uncovered the bottom of the pipes and permitted the entry of wind. The sound would cease when the sliders were pushed back. Playing by such means must have been slow and cumbersome, however skilled the performers might be.

Other organs were played by means of keys wide enough to accommodate the players' fists, for a great deal of force was required to depress them.

There were probably no stops as we know them. All pipes controlled by any particular key sounded when that key was depressed.

There was no way of modifying the sound, which was always *fortissimo*.

No music was written for the organ. It was purely and simply for the accompaniment of plainsong, and the player pounded out the melody in unison with the singers.

Probably the singing of organum led to the early use of what we now call *mutations;* that is, the tuning of ranks of pipes to pitches other than normal. Since organum was sung in perfect fifths, mutation pipes of that day were generally tuned a fifth higher than normal. Thus, if the performer depressed the key for C, pipes tuned to G would sound along with it, thus enabling the player to sound both parts of the organum.

Quite apart from its connection with organum, the principle of mutations was a sound one, strengthening the natural harmonics of the fundamental sound and adding brilliance to the tone. Most modern organs of moderate size include *twelfth* or *quint* stops, although, since successions of fifths are less acceptable to our ears, our mutation stops are proportionately much softer than those of early organs.

8

ARS NOVA

By the early fourteenth century, the gradual evolution of music had reached a point at which it could be referred to as *ars nova*—"the new art."

There was no sudden, sharp division between old forms and methods and the new, but many streams of thought and invention that had long moved sluggishly and independently were merging, finding direction, and moving forward with more speed and purpose.

Ars nova was marked by greater freedom in composition: the discarding of the confining influences of organum and conductus, more graceful and melodic lines, increased independence of parts, and the abandonment of the old rhythmic modes.

That so many radical changes were made in such a comparatively short period was due largely to the weakening of ecclesiastical authority, which had always been conservative and opposed to change. Like the Roman Empire, whose prestige and power it had inherited and whose authoritarian policies it sought to perpetuate, the Western Church faced a crisis which demanded that all its energies be bent towards its survival.

The preoccupation of the pope with temporal affairs that rendered his position in the Eternal City untenable, the removal of the papal seat to Avignon, the Great Schism of 1378 which resulted in two and, at times, even three rival popes, diverted the attention of the ecclesiastical governing bodies from the outposts of the Church.

If developments at the papal level brought disillusionment regarding the invincibility of the Church's temporal position, the profligacy of many local clergy undermined its respect at the diocesan and parochial level. Self-seeking priests, no longer able to depend upon strong backing from Rome, curried favor with kings and nobles to whom, in many cases, they owed their preferments and appointments. The activities and ambitions of many bishops and abbots were more worldly than spiritual. The obedience they enforced was no longer the result of awe for their spiritual powers, but of fear of the force of arms which they commanded themselves or could obtain from their patrons.

While general open revolt against the Church was still a long way off, the temper of the people was changing. Life was becoming more secularized in the sense that many of the arts and sciences that had long been almost exclusive possessions of churchmen were now being practiced by laymen, who were not hampered by the necessity of reconciling their findings with the traditional views of the Church.

Musicians, among others who had ceased to regard the Church's decrees as the last word, threw off the authoritarian shackles and took cognizance of what was happening to music outside the Church.

As early as 1324, Pope John XXII recognized the trend and tried to stem it by issuing an edict from Avignon. He directed his displeasure towards "certain disciples of the new school, much occupying themselves with the measured dividing of the *tempora* . . . preferring to devise methods of their own rather than to continue singing in the old way." He deplored the use of discants, hockets, the introduction of secular melodies in parts accompanying the cantus firmus, and all the variations and ornamentations that had been added to plainsong. He expressed a fear that the old ecclesiastical modes might be forgotten, since in many instances they seemed to be ignored.

After issuing a prohibition which he could not enforce and threatening a penalty which he was in no position to mete out, Pope John provided a convenient loophole for those who might have had qualms about defying the papal edict. "Yet for all this," he decreed, "it is not our intention to forbid, occasionally . . . the use of some consonances, for example the eighth, fifth and fourth, which heighten the beauty of the melody. Such intervals, therefore, may be sung above the *cantus ecclesiasticus*, yet so that the integrity of the *cantus* itself may remain intact, and that nothing of the authoritative music be changed."

There could not have been much doubt about the decorous additions to the plainsong that the Pope had in mind; yet, because he failed to define precise limits, even those musicians who professed obedience to the Church chose to interpret "some consonances" and "the integrity of the *cantus*" a great deal more freely than was intended.

But a new movement was afoot. Musicians persisted in using new techniques without caring much whether the ecclesiastical authorities approved or not. If their work was not acceptable to the Church, they could turn to secular music, which presented an ever-widening field for their talents.

It is difficult to trace the development of secular music up to this time. Historians do not record the trivial; and since most early historians were churchmen, and music was considered important only in relation to the Church, the worth of worldly music was not admitted. Nevertheless, refinements had been taking place. The increased interest in secular forms by theorists, the establishment of tentative rules of composition, and improved methods of notation that made possible a somewhat freer circulation of intelligible manuscripts, all served as an impetus for musicians who would carry their art forward.

Pope John's edict reveals not only the continued inflexibility of the Church towards music but also the great strides that had been made in the development of music during the half century since the Franconian period, mentioned in the last chapter.

The interest in secular forms that had succeeded mere curiosity was now, in turn, succeeded by enthusiasm. Ars nova was a secular movement, but its influence upon all music of succeeding periods makes it of vital importance to the student of church music.

✢ NEW RHYTHMS

One of the most important features of ars nova was the recognition of other than triple rhythms.

One cannot believe that music for songs and dances in duple and quadruple time had not long existed, but it was not considered as serious music and so was not included in any learned theoretical systems. It must be recalled that rhythm, as such, had been but lately recognized by musicians; and then chiefly because the rhythm of prosody, which served so admirably for unadorned plainsong, was inadequate for the needs of discant and conductus. Perhaps duple rhythm had been ignored for the very reason that it was widely used in popular forms, for the cleavage between sacred and profane was sharp. The fact that accepted rhythmic modes in triple proportion were named *modus perfectus* argues that a *modus imperfectus* must have existed. The belief that triple modes reflected the perfection implied by the doctrine of the Trinity was also a strong factor in their exclusive use.

As with many other prejudices, that against duple time was weakened during the period of ars nova, although it was still known as modus imperfectus.

❖ FORMS

Compositions in which the voices imitated each other at regular intervals of time became very popular. In their simpler forms they had been known as rondels, the word "canon" being used in its literal sense as a rule or direction for the entry of the parts. Later, as the imitations became more skilled and complex, they became known as *canons*. Then, as now, the pattern of the theme was more strictly followed in canon than in imitation, which is a more comprehensive term. The writing of canons was fascinating as well as affording exercise and instruction to composers, and they were no less enjoyed by groups who sang them. In France the canon was known as the *chase,* in Italy as the *caccia,* and in England as the *rota,* from the manner in which one voice followed another; and it is this form that is meant by the contemptuous term "chasing tune" as used by church authorities. The principle of the canon is perfectly exemplified in our present-day rounds or catches, such as *Three blind mice* and *Row, row, row your boat.*

In France, which was the chief center of musical culture from the twelfth through the fourteenth century, there developed several forms: the *lai, ballade,* and *rondeau,* chiefly secular. Church music was more influenced by the *isorhythmic motet,* based upon a cantus firmus in the tenor but employing longer melodic patterns than had been the case in the past.

The chief development of Italian musicians who, next to the French, were the most active in the ars nova period, was the *madrigal,* a purely secular form which had a lasting effect upon choral composition. Indicative of the changes that had occurred is the fact that very little church music was produced in Italy at this time.

❖ INCREASED HARMONIC RESOURCES

Gymel and Faburden

A device that was retrogressive in form but of great value in promoting freer use of the third and sixth, which had long been considered dissonant, was the *gymel*. Towards the end of the fourteenth century, a variation of the gymel was known as *faux bourdon, or faburden,* meaning "false bass." (The term has quite a different connotation in modern music.) "Gymel" and "faburden" are not, as a matter of fact, strictly synonymous; but their principle is the same.

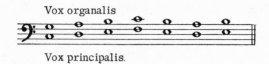

Ex. 8:1

The basis was plainsong in organum (Ex. 8:1).

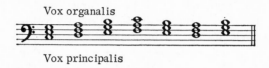

Ex. 8:2

To this was added a part between the two voices, at the interval of a third above the lower note, resulting in a triad (Ex. 8:2).

Ex. 8:3

Thus far, the vox principalis or the vox organalis (whichever happened to be the lower) had served as the bass part. Now, however, this lower part was transposed an octave higher, leaving what had been the middle part in the bass, hence the term "false bass," or faburden (Ex. 8:3).

Ex. 8:4

When the vox organalis was omitted altogether, the added part and the vox principalis were sung in thirds or sixths (Ex. 8:4).

(The second form is gymel rather than faburden, since the principle of false bass is lost.)

Theoretically, the gymel is a by-product of the faburden, although it is claimed by some that singing in thirds was practiced in parts of England as early as the tenth century.

It may be imagined what the free use of thirds and sixths did to a system of music in which both those intervals had formerly been considered as necessary evils, to be tolerated when they could not be avoided, but to be avoided as much as possible. Particularly as the melodic lines became more flexible, less dependent upon the form of the cantus firmus, the value of thirds and sixths as a relief from the austerity of the strict rules of early modal composition became evident.

Musica Ficta

In Chapter IV we noted that source of irritation to early musicians, the tritone or augmented fourth, represented in our musical system by the notes F and B. Its inversion, the diminished fifth, was considered only slightly less objectionable.

We have seen that in free organum these intervals were avoided by altering the vox organalis in such a way that it need not follow the principal voice strictly in fourths or fifths, but might retain its note in the last previous consonant interval until the danger of producing the tritone was past.

This device served its purpose for the simple harmony of the day, but more difficult was the problem of dealing with the tritone in melodic passages. It was quite feasible to include both F and B in the melody as long as they were widely separated, but an ascending or descending passage that included both these notes was ugly. Very early, even before the days of free organum, some singers arbitrarily sang B flat instead of B or, less frequently, F sharp instead of F. The custom then arose of indicating on manuscript copies the places where such alterations were to be made. Modern editions of plainsong often have the altered note designated at the beginning of the staff, where it sometimes confuses students who mistake it for a key signature. (In the examples for examination at the end of Chapter IV, the use of these altered notes is mentioned.)

Much the same problem had to be solved again with the free use of sixths and thirds, since the minor forms of those intervals were not considered consonant. These intervals were changed to major by the alteration of one of the notes. The rules governing sharps and flats were so complex that they would bewilder us, even if we knew them all. The interesting fact is that all the chromatics within the octave were brought into play, theoretically at least. They were not used with great facility, but their recognition and admission to the musical system provided new material for experiment.

Counterpoint

While medieval musicians had gradually abandoned the approved church practice of writing obviously in fourths and fifths, a series of those intervals had long provided the basis of their compositions. Regardless of ornamental and passing notes that tended to disguise what amounted to organum, fifths formed the skeleton of their work, and to that interval they returned again and again. The ornamental notes, whose function was exactly what their name implies, were subject to no very definite rules except that, at certain points, they had to carry the voice towards a consonance with the cantus firmus. The effect was often extremely harsh, but what occurred between the matching of point against point to form consonances (*counterpoint*) did not matter as long as the musician had a chance to display his ingenuity. It is hard for us to understand how ears that could not recognize thirds and sixths as being consonant could tolerate some of the discords which occurred in the ornamental treatment of discant and motet.

Thirds and sixths had appeared, of course, but only as passing notes and subject to no rules. Thanks chiefly to the devices of gymel and faburden, these intervals came into their own and were regarded as quite legitimate in counterpoint.

With this new resource at hand, it was no longer necessary to return constantly to the unison, the fourth, the fifth, and the octave; and the use of consecutive perfect intervals of the same kind was forbidden. To us who have grown up with this prohibition, it seems scarcely worthy of comment; but it was a revolutionary step at the time and a departure as radical as any made during the period of ars nova.

The torturous method of combining two or more tunes to form a motet in such a manner as to produce a satisfactory number of consonances and as few dissonances as could be managed gradually fell into disuse. Composers still retained the cantus firmus as a basis for their counterpoint, but they learned to treat the other parts independently and with some regard to contrast and a flowing effect.

It must be emphasized, however, that many of the musicians of this period were theorists rather than artists. Their pleasure lay in overcoming technical difficulties within the framework of the rules, rather than in producing music that would be attractive to the ear. Their music had an indefinite quality. It meandered along without any real form as we know it and without anything like the key tonality to which we are accustomed. It was far from insipid; on the other hand, it was greatly lacking in vitality—but only, of course, compared with modern standards. In comparison with what had gone before, it was new and splendid.

✤ COMPOSERS

Very few composers of the fourteenth century are known by name, in spite of the greatly increased activity among musicians. There are several reasons for this. Printing had not yet been invented and thus compositions could be recorded and preserved only in manuscript form. The Church remained the chief repository of manuscripts and records; and, while many of the chief dabblers in ars nova were churchmen, they composed independently of and without the sanction of the Church. Consequently, we know more about the important developments made possible by their work than we do of the work itself.

Philippe de Vitry (c. 1291–1361), French bishop and composer, has left few traces of his work beyond his valuable treatises on ars nova, from which much of our information is gleaned.

Guillaume de Machaut (c. 1300–1372) composed at least one setting of the mass (there were few great contributions to church music in this period) and a great many secular works.

In Italy, *Francesco Landini* (c. 1325–1397) was the most prominent musician of his day. He was a renowned organist, although just what qualifications a renowned organist of the fourteenth century would possess is left to conjecture. He was a skilled composer, probably for the organ as well as for voices.

9

THE AGE
OF POLYPHONY

✣ THE CULMINATION OF PURE CHORAL MUSIC

The end towards which music had been moving from its beginning was achieved in the fifteenth and sixteenth centuries.

The seed that found lodgment in primitive Christian worship, took root in Rome, sent forth shoots at various times and places throughout Europe, underwent frequent and severe prunings at the hands of the ecclesiastical authorities, and budded in the period of ars nova, now reached its florescence, attaining its fullest flower with Palestrina and his contemporaries.

It was choral music that engaged the attention of serious musicians, and this for several reasons.

First, there was the matter of tradition. The Church, which had long been the custodian of music as well as all other arts and sciences, had tolerated only music for voices, making a single, grudging exception in the case of the organ. While the Church dominated the scene, a composer's only hope of having his work recognized and performed widely lay in his conformity with official practices. The influence of the Church remained strong long after its authority had weakened. The prestige which ecclesiastical sponsorship had lent to choral music made it the only medium acceptable to musicians who sought to develop their skill in composition. Moreover, they were familiar with the possibilities as well as with the limitations of human voices, and there existed many carefully trained choirs capable of singing almost anything that was written for them. With so much still to be done in so fruitful and familiar a field, few composers were tempted to stray to the less familiar and unrewarding field of instrumental music.

As a result of neglect by serious composers, instrumental music had made no great demands upon instruments or performers. Consequently, the instruments of the fifteenth century had developed only to a point at which they were capable of providing simple accompaniments to the popular tunes of the day. Nothing more was required of them. They had no qualities to attract the attention of composers whose interest lay in the further development of a field of music already far beyond the scope of instruments.

This combination of factors resulted in the entire study of musicians being concentrated upon pure choral music, and no age has produced as much fine music of this type as that now under discussion. It is not to be supposed that the composers of these two centuries were musical giants compared with those of earlier periods. Had they lived and worked under the same conditions as their predecessors, they would probably have produced much the same type of music. They began their forward movement from an advanced position that had been attained by the labors of their untiring and, for the most part, anonymous predecessors. All the harmonic resources, all the accumulated experience of the past were theirs. Although they were responsible for many refinements and increased skill in the use of their facilities, the tools that they inherited were serviceable.

Whereas in the past, emphasis had been placed upon the technical aspect of music, in the polyphonic era (when so many of the technical possibilities had been explored), music began to be regarded in an artistic sense. Composers became increasingly aware of the variety of effects to be obtained by the combinations of certain sounds (chords), by the different arrangements of the notes of the chords, by the contrasts made possible by allotting passages to voices of certain registers, and by the closer relations of the various melodic parts to one another.

No more were the parts accompanying the cantus firmus merely ornamental, having little meaning of their own. Composers strove to make each part interesting in itself, possessing some individuality, yet yielding something of that individuality in its relation to the whole composition. It was not sufficient that the various voices combine only here and there to form consonances: the combinations throughout, both singly and in conjunction with what preceded and followed, must be pleasant to the ear. The skill acquired in creating such melodic lines led, in time, to the abandonment of the cantus firmus as the center around which the other parts revolved.

The music remained indefinite; indeed, the musicians of the time were content to have it so. The influence of the old, unrhythmic plainsong melodies was still strong, and there was none of the orderly structure or form which is considered indispensable to modern music.

A system of note values had been devised, as we noted in Chapter VII, but they determined only the duration of each note as compared with the others. Essential as this was for keeping the voices together, its value was momentary, and there was no thought of using it for regular, measured time that would have produced rhythmic order. Indeed, the mode of writing could not have been accommodated within the framework of regular form. The independence of each voice was not confined to its melodic line, but extended also to the duration of its phrases. Thus, while one voice may have reached a point of repose or climax, another voice had passed such a point and was pressing on to a fresh one. This alternation of accents and climaxes between voices, combined with an absence of regular, measured rhythm in any of the parts, made for a steady but indefinite flow of intermingled melodies whose only unanimity, as far as time was concerned, came at the close.

Later in this period, a simpler method of composition gained favor, although it by no means displaced the elaborate contrapuntal style. The desired effect was achieved by writing simple harmonies in which the voices moved in successions of chords, somewhat similar in general style to our modern hymn tunes. There were, however, important differences: the movement of melody and chord were based on modal harmony, our sense of key tonality being entirely absent; and the rhythm was still irregular.

This chordal method of composition not only focused attention on the effect of chords as such but it also paved the way for the adoption of those elements whose lack was mentioned above.

Successions of chords inevitably suggested regular rhythm. While composers continued to use the irregular stresses of prose texts, they did on occasion adopt regular time, leaving excellent examples for later writers who would carry the device farther.

It was early realized that the chordal form of writing deprived composers of many artifices upon which they had relied to sustain interest in extended compositions. The monotony caused by the absence of anything approaching what we call modulation was, in contrapuntal writing, avoided by the interest which the independence and interweaving of the voices created. This diversion was wholly absent from chordal writ-ing. Even satisfactory cadences were denied him who would adhere strictly to the church modes. Sharps and flats were used, it is true, but for the purpose of avoiding unpleasant intervals rather than with any thought of modulation. Once the danger of harshness was past, the sharpened or flattened note was replaced by the diatonic sound it had altered, without any preparation or thought of changing key.

Composers now began to use sharps and flats not merely to avoid harshness but to obtain certain harmonic effects for their own sakes. Moreover, chords containing F sharp and F natural, C sharp and C nat-ural, were used close together, producing a chromatic effect that must have been at once delightful and strange to ears accustomed chiefly to diatonic intervals. Some composers, overanxious to make use of all re-sources, went too far with unpleasant results.

From the use of chromatics, composers began to have an inkling of the important relationship between the chords which we know as the tonic and dominant, and to develop new notions regarding scales. The modal system was gradually breaking up, simply because it did not afford the resources necessary for the development of chordal harmony.

The tonic-dominant relationship was but seen through a glass darkly. It was sufficiently understood to enable contrasts between what we call a major key and its relative minor (several chords of which are common), but there was lacking a system which permitted free and easy modulation. One may distinguish the mode in which one of these old compositions begins, but it soon progresses to a bewildering maze of chords that defy classification, and only after much seemingly pointless meandering does it return, at its close, to its original mode.

Criticism of the music of this period can be made only in its com-parison with later developments. Actually, much of the fifteenth- and sixteenth-century polyphony was great music by any standards. It is quite capable of appreciation by modern ears that have had opportunities of becoming accustomed to it. Indeed, it has become almost a fetish with certain schools of admirers.

✤ THE AGE OF FREEDOM AND DISCOVERY

Musical genius was not alone responsible for the transition from the comparative crudity of gymel and faburden to the glorious polyphony of Palestrina and Lasso.

A new spirit was abroad among men, a spirit of freedom and adven-ture. The bonds which had kept them close to home, tied to the old and tested things of the past, were thrown off.

Men sought out worlds beyond the narrow existence that had been theirs. It was an age of discovery, of reaching out, of ever-increasing initiative.

Magellan, Columbus, Cabot, Diaz, pushing out the boundaries of the known world to fabulous limits, typified the visionary and venturesome men in all fields of endeavor. Philosophy, art, science, and literature were no longer closed chapters to which "finis" had been written by the great ones of the past. The known whetted men's appetites for the unknown.

This new outlook was largely the result of the weakened position of the Church in civil affairs. While the Church possessed the power and prestige to make and unmake civil rulers, and to set arbitrary standards for unlearned men of humble and high degree, initiative and research had been stifled. The centralization of the secular authority, formerly thinly distributed among feudal barons, strengthened the hands of kings, who had never enjoyed being subject to the dictates of Rome. The increase of royal power and the corresponding decrease of ecclesiastical authority served to lessen men's awe of the pronouncements of the Church. Stirred by a divine discontent with the restraints under which they had labored, they looked to secular rulers for a patronage which the rulers were only too willing to extend. Initiative in the arts and sciences passed from the Church to the world.

Musicians were not slow to take advantage of royal patronage. They wrote a great deal of church music, as they had done in the past, but with a freedom encouraged by their patrons. Moreover, they could and did turn their talents more and more to secular music, certain of its acceptance among nobility and commoners alike.

Kings and nobles had long maintained choirs in their private chapels (we have mentioned Charlemagne's school of church music at Aix-la-Chapelle in the ninth century), but they governed their chapels as they governed their lands—with the sanction, and largely under the direction of, the ecclesiastical authorities.

About the beginning of the fifteenth century, these royal chapels increased in number and importance, setting their own standards to a large extent.

Membership in the chapels royal was much sought after for three reasons: because it offered opportunity for study and collaboration with the greatest musicians of the time, because it lent prestige to the musician and his work, and because it enabled one to pursue his art while being assured of his subsistence.

Enthusiasm was not solely on the side of the musicians. The royal patrons were much interested in their chapels, often authorizing representatives to visit churches and cathedrals throughout the country for the purpose of impressing especially good singers for service in the chapel royal. (This privilege was also extended to St. Paul's Cathedral, London, at one time.)

These royal schools—for they were as much institutions of education as they were chapels—serving as gathering places for the best musicians, led to the formation of geographical groups or schools, each school displaying certain characteristics which distinguished it from others. Thus, when we presently consider the works of individual composers, we shall find it more convenient to place some of them in national groups than to deal with them in strict chronological order.

Finally, royal patronage enabled musicians to travel and to exchange ideas with colleagues in other countries. It is unlikely that composition proved lucrative for the independent musician, but kings encouraged (and paid for) periods of study abroad in order that their composers might keep abreast of the latest developments of the times.

Thanks partly to the interchange of thought among musicians of various nationalities, there were no sharp differences in the general style of their compositions. Distinguishing features were to be found in each school, but fundamentally all schools developed along much the same lines.

✷ EARLY ENGLISH SCHOOL

John Dunstable (c. 1370–1453) may be considered the first great composer of the new school of polyphonic writing. An Englishman by birth, he seems to have spent much of his life abroad. It was not unusual for English musicians to visit that part of France which was under English rule, and it was a comparatively short step from the provinces to Paris, and from Paris to the Low Countries where music was developing quickly. Dunstable's travels took him even farther, and most traces of his work have been discovered in Italy.

His ability to move his parts freely, avoiding the harsh harmonies that had marked earlier music, made him famous in his day. Thirds and sixths, with which his predecessors had experimented, were used suavely by Dunstable, although there were still many chords that sounded empty because the third was lacking.

His treatment of discords was new in his day and remains good practice in modern times. He confined his discords to passing notes (the progression from one note of harmony to another through a dissonance), and suspensions (in which the dissonance is prepared as part of the previous chord and, immediately after its sounding, proceeds to a concord).

Although little more than fragments of Dunstable's music remain, much of the work of his successors stands, to some degree, as a monument to his genius. His fame spread throughout Europe, and his style was closely studied by musicians of his own and later days.

Lionel Power may have been as famous as Dunstable, whose contemporary he was, but his reputation has long survived his work. He is known to have been an outstanding theorist, and to have written an important treatise.

Henry Abyngdon (1420–1497) deserves mention as the first master of the children at the Chapel Royal, his appointment coming in 1455 after he had served as succentor at Wells Cathedral.

This is one of the rare periods in history when English musicians gave leadership to their colleagues in Europe. There have been times since when England boasted fine composers, but in nearly every instance they have followed paths defined by pioneers of other countries.

That Dunstable, Power, and their contemporaries took the initiative in musical composition in the early fifteenth century is due largely to the interest and encouragement of the royal house. Henry V and Henry VI (whose reigns covered the years 1413 to 1461) are believed to have been not merely passive patrons but active collaborators. How far their composition extended we cannot tell, but certainly some worthy music inscribed "Roy Henry" is the work of one king or the other. Their compositions are not in themselves as important as the fact that they were actively occupied with music to some extent, thus lending support to musicians who might otherwise have succumbed to the discouragement of laboring in obscurity.

✤ THE EARLY NETHERLANDS SCHOOL

The group of composers dispersed through what are now northeastern France and Belgium are variously known as the Early Netherlands, the Burgundian, the Early Flemish, and the Gallo-Belgic school.

They might be termed loosely disciples of Dunstable, since they were greatly influenced by his work and sought to emulate it. They wrote chiefly for three voices, interest often being focused on the highest voice rather than upon a cantus firmus in the tenor. The use of the third in melodic lines is a characteristic, but they used many chords without their thirds. Consecutive fifths and octaves in parallel motion are abandoned, but there is considerable parallel motion in the form of faburden, with the third of the chord in the lowest part (consecutive chords in the first inversion).

Guillaume Dufay (c. 1400–1474) is the only composer of the Early Netherlands school whose later compositions rivalled those of Dunstable —the only member of this group, indeed, whose work has survived.

More than Dunstable he experimented brilliantly (for his time) with canon and imitation, carrying out these devices not only in short passages but in extended form. His achievement in this direction was a distinct step towards the later development of the fugue.

Dufay wrote several settings of the ordinary of the mass, and of hymns and antiphons, a fact which argues the admissibility of the newer style of writing by the church authorities.

It is probable that the Church was cautiously relaxing its rules under the sheer weight of contemporary musical trends. Had concessions not been made, no worthwhile church music would have been written. The old, austere forms had nothing more to yield to inquiring minds and were already archaic. Moreover, many of the objectionable features of experimental composition had been overcome. There was really nothing for the Church to object to in this newer, flowing polyphony that was emerging from the chaos of the last few centuries.

On the other hand, caution on the part of the Church engendered caution on the part of composers, restraining them from liberties that might result in an ecclesiastical ban. A nice balance was preserved. When composers wished to write something gay or lively which would not fit within the framework of the liturgy, they turned to secular music, of which much was written, even by those who are now remembered only as composers of church music.

Gilles Binchois (c. 1400–1460), whose name is often coupled with that of Dufay, has left fewer works by which to be judged. It is interesting to note, however, that he wrote Passion music "in the new style" for the Duke of Burgundy, whose chaplain he was; and that, in doing so, he was keeping alive an old tradition. From as far back as the fourth century the Passion of Christ had been dramatized during Holy Week under the careful supervision of the Church. Where it was feasible, some music was introduced; and by the time of Binchois, the Passion was entirely or almost entirely musical, something on the style of present-day cantatas.

✤ ENGLISH TUDOR MUSIC

In England, the group of composers who assumed the mantles of Dunstable and Power, while active during the two short reigns that followed those of the musical Henrys mentioned above, reached their maturity after the establishment of the Tudor dynasty in 1485, and may well be included in the Tudor school.

Gilbert Banestre (dates of birth and death uncertain), Robert Fayrfax (c. 1465–1521), Laurence Squire, John Hothby (d. 1487), William Cornyshe (c. 1465–1523), Richard Davey, and Richard Pygott, all of this generation, failed to achieve the stature of their illustrious predecessors; but they produced much good music that served as a bridge between

Dunstable and Power on the one hand, and the more advanced Tudor composers who were soon to arrive upon the scene.

The composers of this early Tudor school were conservative rather than progressive. Willing and competent to make good use of the ideas and style of Dunstable, they added few innovations of their own. Perhaps there was no need for innovations. Dunstable had opened such a vast field of possibilities as to absorb the skill and imagination of musicians for two or three generations to follow. They may be said, then, to have worked on a level attained for them by Dunstable.

We sometimes fall thoughtlessly into the error of thinking of this period as one of general advance in music. In royal chapels, colleges, and cathedrals, where competent musicians were employed and well-trained choirs maintained, and in the homes of the nobility where an interest in the arts was becoming a mark of the gentry, recent developments in music would be familiar; but the people at large would know very little about them.

Even in this mid-twentieth century, when news may spread throughout the world in a matter of a few hours, the general public does not become aware of new and radical styles in music until years after they have become familiar to an inner circle of musicians and, perhaps, people who frequent those cathedrals of music, the opera house and the symphony hall. It should not be difficult, then, to realize that the rural folk of Europe, and even urban dwellers who worshipped in less fashionable and wealthy churches, might not be even vaguely aware of the musical revolution that was taking place so near at hand.

Parish church music was, in some cases, a century or more behind the new school. The facts that few small churches had choirs and that the contemporary choral music was written for skilled singers were obstacles to progress. The plainsong liturgy and perhaps a few simple plainsong hymns, all sung in unison, organum, or occasionally, in thirds, constituted the music. A parish priest or musician who had been exposed to good music and wished to introduce new methods into his church would be opposed by tradition, suspicion, and stubbornness.

The congregation was led or supported in the singing and responses by an organ or a clerk. Organs existed even in many village and rural churches. Small and clumsy, they were used only to accompany the plainsong and in most cases sounded only the melody. The "organist" was anybody willing and able to pick out the tune on the crude keyboard.

✳ THE LATER NETHERLANDS OR FLEMISH SCHOOL

While the English composers of the last half of the fifteenth and early sixteenth centuries plotted a course that had been pretty well charted by

Dunstable, their colleagues in the Low Countries pushed on to even greater achievements.

Although we must consider them as successors to Dufay, some of the earlier composers of this school lived during his lifetime. Nevertheless, they were of the following generation, and their accomplishments after Dufay's death warrant their being placed in another group.

Jean Ockeghm (c. 1430–1495) was born somewhere in eastern Flanders. It is not generally agreed that he was a pupil of Dufay, but it is almost certain that he was acquainted with the work of the older man, and it is hard to believe that, living and working in the same region, they were not associated in some way.

Ockeghm, although he wrote some beautiful music, is known chiefly as an explorer of polyphonic resources. Some of his compositions remind one of mathematical problems, ingeniously worked out but lacking spontaneity. One is more aware of the orderly mental processes of the composer than the flow of music. It is, in short, music for the intellect rather than for the ear; and, as such, it lacks music's most important quality.

Nevertheless, Ockeghm's writing possesses great value. His painstaking work in developing melodic phrases—canon, imitation, inversion, augmentation, diminution—saved his successors this labor and left them free to clothe the somewhat stiff technical framework with grace and beauty. His greatest glory, like that of so many creative men, shone in the work of his pupils.

Jacob Obrecht (1430–1505) was a native of Utrecht. He served in churches in that city, and in Cambrai and Antwerp, all important centers of music. Like many of his countrymen, he spent much time in Italy, where he died. Some of his music has been published in recent years.

Josquin des Prés (c. 1450–1521) was the most eminent musician of his time. Born in Conde, and a pupil of Ockeghm, he went to Italy as a young man and remained there until he was fifty.

A brilliant young man could have found no more favorable place and time to prove his ability than in Italy at the height of the Renaissance. Josquin's fame spread quickly throughout Europe, and he was honored at the courts of kings and princes.

Josquin wrote fine music judged by any standards. He was a master of every technical device used by his predecessors; but whereas even so great a composer as Ockeghm could not escape from stiffness, Josquin achieved ease and animation that charmed the mind of the theorist and the ear of the listener alike.

Although there was a tendency on the part of composers to abandon the cantus firmus, Josquin continued to make use of it. More and more frequently the cantus firmus was drawn from a secular song rather than from the traditional plainsong. In order that it might not be too obvious, and also to afford ample opportunity for the elaboration of the accompanying parts, the secular cantus firmus was sung very slowly to long notes, and slightly altered when the composer deemed it advisable.

The ecclesiastical authorities seem to have raised no strenuous objections to the use of secular canti firmi as long as they were carefully obscured. Later on, when little attempt was made to disguise them, a ban was placed on the obvious use of secular songs as themes for church music.

Josquin's fluency in polyphonic writing was not surpassed even by the great Palestrina. He seems, at times, to be striving for the establishment of a tonal center (what we might call a definite key) and, while he was not altogether successful, his intuitive resolutions of discords tended towards that end. In this respect, it was the ear rather than mathematical formulas that achieved the desired results.

In the early sixteenth century, the goal of serious musicians from all Europe was study with Josquin des Prés. His pupils were active in every musical center on the continent, and those who were not fortunate enough to study with him studied his work and were thus influenced by him.

Heinrich Isaac (c. 1450–1517) was a worthy contemporary of Josquin. He, too, was Flemish and spent part of his life in Italy.

His later years were spent in Germany in the service of Maximilian, the last of the Holy Roman Emperors. Isaac had great influence among the active German musicians of his time, not only because of his favored position in the emperor's court but also because of the respect commanded by his very fine work.

Jean Mouton (d. 1522) in Paris, *Eleazar Genet* (c. 1470–1548) in Rome, and *Nicholas Gombert* (c. 1495–1570) in Madrid were among the many pupils or disciples of Josquin des Prés who carried his methods to all corners of Europe. No composer since Dunstable had exerted such wide influence as Josquin.

✤ THE VENETIAN SCHOOL

Adrian Willaert (c. 1480–1562) is one of those composers who may appropriately be placed in either or both of two schools.

Born in Flanders, he studied music in Paris with Mouton and Josquin des Prés and was later at Rome, then Ferrara, then at the court of the king of Bohemia. Up to this point, his career and his work resembled those of other composers of the later Netherlands school among whom he may be numbered.

It was his appointment as director of music at St. Mark's, Venice, that marked a turning point in his career and led to his being considered the founder of the Venetian school.

The architecture of St. Mark's had a profound influence on the type of music that developed there. The building was in the shape of a Greek cross, the transepts opening from the middle of the nave, which was thus divided into two parts of equal length. The choir, instead of being placed conventionally at one end of the nave, was divided, one half being placed in a low balcony at the end of each transept. Separate organs were provided for each choir.

This arrangement, which had been in existence for over two hundred years before Willaert arrived upon the scene, must have been an awkward one. The two organs could not be brought under the control of one performer as they could be today, and two widely separated choirs would pose a problem for a conductor. Nevertheless, Willaert's predecessors had managed to win an enviable reputation for the cathedral, perhaps by clever and judicious use of antiphonal singing.

It remained for Master Adrian, as Willaert was called, to make capital of the unusual deployment of choral forces. This he did by making extensive use of music for a double choir. His bold harmonies and rich polyphony created effects in antiphonal singing of a magnificence that had never been approached until that time. Musicians from all Europe came to study with Willaert. Flanders, which had hitherto furnished masters and teachers to Italy, now sent students to their famous expatriate in Venice.

That Willaert made considerable progress towards the principle of key tonality is indicated by his strong advocacy of a system of tuning something like our modern equal temperament, which permits easy modulation from one tonal center to another. We often forget that the progressiveness of men like Willaert led to developments which made possible Bach's *Well-Tempered Clavier* over a century and a half later.

Cipriano de Rore (1516–1565), born in Flanders, followed Willaert to Venice and became his pupil. He worked with his teacher for a number of years and also spent periods in Ferrara and Parma where, no doubt, he served as a sort of missionary for the new Venetian school. From the ranks of many famous pupils of Willaert, de Rore was chosen to succeed to the directorship of St. Mark's when Master Adrian died.

Gioseffo Zarlino (1517–1590), born at Chioggia, became a Franciscan monk and a pupil of Willaert. After a brilliant career elsewhere in Italy, he returned to St. Mark's, Venice, in 1565 to succeed de Rore as director of music. For the first time, leadership of the Venetian school passed to a native Italian.

Zarlino probably wrote a great deal of music, although little has survived. His most important contribution to music was his theoretical writing. His works served as a summary and clarification of the methods and successful experiments of the great composers to that time and were used as textbooks for many years.

Andrea Gabrieli (1510–1586), another pupil of Willaert, composed extensively but was more prominent as an organist at St. Mark's than as a composer. He was the teacher of the great Dutch organist Sweelinck.

Giovanni Gabrieli (1557–1612), a nephew of Andrea, was also an organist at St. Mark's and a composer. His most distinctive work was the development of the orchestral accompaniment. The German composer Schütz was his pupil.

There were, of course, many other musicians who kept alive the style and traditions established by Willaert until, in the early seventeenth century, the Venetian school lost its identity and merged with larger movements.

✣ THE LATER TUDOR SCHOOL

In England, after a somewhat drab half century following the death of Dunstable, a new and significant generation of musicians arose. None of them quite equalled Josquin des Prés, Willaert, and other continental composers either in fame or accomplishment, but they wrote much fine music which, perhaps more than that of any other of the period, has influenced Protestant church music in the west.

Since their activities were largely affected by the Reformation, which will be considered in the next chapter, we shall mention here only their general accomplishments.

John Taverner (c. 1495–1545) as a young man held an obscure place as lay clerk in a parish church in Lincolnshire. When he was thirty, his bishop recommended him to Cardinal Wolsey, who appointed the young man as master of the children at his recently established Cardinal College (now Christ Church) at Oxford. He held that post for only three or four years when he was accused of heresy and thrown into prison by Wolsey. What happened to his accomplices is not known, but Taverner was released because he was "merely a musician." Perhaps because of the danger of association with a prelate who was at odds with the civil authority or possibly piqued by the low esteem to which he owed his pardon, he gave up music altogether.

In his short, active career, however, he wrote much music which shows a strong Flemish influence. His most famous work was his mass called *The Western Wind,* based on a folk song of that name. While most composers took pains to disguise secular melodies used as canti firmi for church music, Taverner used every device to make this particular one conspicuous. The tune moves along at a tempo which makes it easily recognized, is allotted generally to the sopranos, and even when in the tenor or bass the other parts are written so as not to obscure it.

Christopher Tye (c. 1497–1572) did not achieve prominence until he was forty, when he became organist and choirmaster at Ely Cathedral. Later, he was a gentleman of the Chapel Royal during the reign of Edward VI and part of that of Elizabeth I. In 1560 he became a clergyman and served in a parish near Ely.

He is called "the father of the English anthem," having begun the development of a form of choral writing which has never been wholly neglected by succeeding generations.

Thomas Tallis (1505–1585) acquired musical stature far greater than any of his contemporaries. Some place his work very close to that of Palestrina.

Nothing is known of his early training. He was organist at Waltham Abbey when it, along with other monasteries, was closed in the 1540's; and from that time he served as a gentleman of the Chapel Royal.

With Byrd he shared the position of organist of the Chapel, and also a monopoly of printing music and music paper, granted to them by Elizabeth I. In 1575, Tallis and Byrd published a collection of their own motets.

The music of Tallis is still sung: his anthems and motets in cathedrals and churches with capable choirs, his adaptation of plainsong to the English rite in hundreds of parish churches.

The Reformation brought about no great change in the style of Tallis. His anthems became rather simpler and written to English texts, but he continued to write elaborate motets for secular use.

William Byrd (c. 1542–1623) was a pupil of Tallis, with whom he was long associated. As a very young man, he was appointed organist at Lincoln Cathedral. In 1569 he came to the Chapel Royal, sharing the duties of organist with Tallis, although he also retained his post at Lincoln for a few years.

There are many evidences of the high esteem in which Byrd was held by Queen Elizabeth I. In addition to his appointment to the Chapel Royal, in itself a mark of royal favor, he shared the monopoly of printing music with Tallis, and was permitted to serve a Protestant church and a Protestant queen even though he remained a Roman Catholic.

Byrd, who has been called "the English Palestrina," was more versatile than other English composers, being equally at ease with the Roman mass, the elaborate motet, the Anglican anthem, the solo song, and music for strings and virginal. An analysis of his work reveals a great deal of similarity to the compositions of his immediate predecessors and his contemporaries, yet there are certain qualities that are hallmarks of Byrd. There is a virility, an incisiveness about his music, even that for the Roman church which was seldom strongly rhythmic. His un-questioned technical mastery was never used as an end in itself, but to heighten the aesthetic effects which he successfully sought.

✤ THE PERFECTION OF POLYPHONY

Polyphony reached its highest point in the works of Lasso, Vittoria, and Palestrina. Some would include Byrd in this small, select group; but, excellent though his work was, the English school was somewhat insular, whereas the three composers mentioned were cosmopolitan in their style and use of material, transcending all the limitations of "schools."

Orlando Lasso (1530–1594), known variously as Orlandus Lassus and Roland de Lattre, was the natural successor of the Netherlands school. A native of Mons, he began his career as a choir boy in the cathedral there at a period when the great works of Josquin des Prés and his contemporaries would be part of the choir's repertoire. He must have had an exceptionally fine voice, for at least twice he was impressed for service in the royal chapel. With or without the consent of the chapel authorities, he returned each time to Mons.

Lasso was only fourteen when he went to Italy, possibly as a singer, certainly as a gifted student. He studied chiefly at Milan and Rome, and at twenty-two was for a time chapel master at St. John Lateran, Rome.

He returned to Antwerp for a short time, and in 1556 went to Munich as musical director at the court of the Duke of Bavaria, where he re-mained until his death.

Lasso was a prolific and versatile composer, known to have written some two thousand works which included every musical form known up to that time. While his compositions show a complete mastery of all the latest accepted musical devices, the bulk of his work tended towards the conservative. The masses, motets, penitential psalms which mark his ma-ture period are among the finest examples of polyphonic writing.

Although much of his music is so like Palestrina's that it might have been written by either master, Lasso was more versatile and, at times, dis-played a greater sense of the dramatic than Palestrina.

Tomás Luis da Vittoria, or Victoria (c. 1540–1611), is called "the priest who happened to be a musician." Perhaps it would be more ac-curate to call him a musician who decided to become a priest. He did not leave his native Spain for a Roman seminary until he was twenty-five, by which time, judging from his accomplishments in the next few years, he must have been a competent musician.

He succeeded Palestrina, who may have been his teacher, as music master at the *Collegium Romanum* in 1571, and later held two or three other important musical posts.

After thirty years in Rome, Vittoria returned to Spain as chaplain and chapel master to the empress.

Vittoria wrote only for the church. This is not surprising, considering his vocation; but he proved himself to be something of an extremist in his declaration that music should not be used for secular and profane purposes.

The music of Vittoria, Lasso, and Palestrina had much in common. All three were masters of polyphonic technic and possessed the art of diverting attention from their technical mastery by subordinating it to the broad, flowing lines of their music. Their distinguishing features—which were not invariably present—lay not in differences of approach or of technic, but in inherent qualities which sometimes revealed themselves in their music. Lasso was more versatile, sometimes gayer and more dramatic than his great contemporaries; Palestrina was ever serene, often austere; Vittoria displayed the warmth of feeling and passionate mysticism that one would expect from a native of Spain. More than the others, Vittoria made use of the chordal style of writing and made frequent use of double choirs.

Giovanni Pierluigi da Palestrina (c. 1525–1594) takes his name from his native city in central Italy. He served as a choir boy at the cathedral in Palestrina, and at the age of twelve was in the choir of the Church of Santa Maria Maggiore in Rome. After his voice changed, he continued to study in Rome, and at the age of eighteen or nineteen became organist and choirmaster at the cathedral in Palestrina.

A young man of such outstanding ability would no doubt have achieved fame in any case, but Palestrina's career was given early impetus as the result of his bishop's election to the papacy. In 1551, Pope Julius III appointed Palestrina choirmaster of the Julian Chapel at the Vatican. Palestrina served successively in the choir of the Sistine Chapel, at the Church of St. John Lateran, at Santa Maria Maggiore, and returned in 1571 to the Julian Chapel, where he remained until his death.

It is said that when the Council of Trent got around to a consideration of liturgical music, many drastic reforms were proposed, including the banning of music by contemporary composers. It was Pope Pius IV who, in 1564, championed the cause of contemporary music, using Palestrina's *Missa Papae Marcelli* as a model. The council, while decreeing certain restrictions and reforms, sensibly decided that the Church could not afford to lose such music.

In 1576, Pope Gregory XII commissioned Palestrina to make a complete revision of plainsong, an indication of the high esteem in which Palestrina was held by the Church.

The accomplishments of Palestrina may be summed up by saying that, in his work, the struggles and aspirations of generations of musicians found their culmination.

Doubtless, composers continued to write good modal music in the polyphonic style for some time to come, but there existed such a wealth of composition that their efforts were pointless and unnecessary. Progressive composers had to find new modes of expression, not because they belittled the old or because people were tired of the polyphonic modal style, but because the field had been so thoroughly covered that nothing remained to be done.

The pinnacle had been reached: there were no more ascents to be made.

✣ MUSIC PRINTING

The art of printing as applied to music was of inestimable value in the spread of musical knowledge and the performance of compositions over a wide area.

As long as copying by hand was the only method of duplicating the composer's original manuscript, opportunities for the study and performance of any particular composition were few. In order to study the work of a composer, it was necessary to journey to some center where copies of his work were available. Because copies were scarce, they were costly, and it was thus beyond the hopes of individual musicians to possess them. Only those who had access to the libraries of royal chapels, monasteries or cathedrals, or personal acquaintance with the composer himself could enjoy the pleasure and profit of examining either the original manuscripts or copies of them.

One of the reasons that our knowledge of early church music far exceeds our knowledge of secular songs and instrumental music is that the Church could appoint men with the time, skill, and materials to make copies of such music as was considered worthy of preservation.

Copies were not always reliable. A copyist, unable to read or interpret a composer's peculiar method of writing or notation, might jump to conclusions, writing what he thought was intended. Copyists sometimes made what they believed to be improvements on their own account; and there was, of course, the danger of inaccuracy.

The reproduction of manuscripts by printing insured uniform copies (even errors appeared uniformly) and the provision of copies in greater quantities and at lower cost than had been possible when handwriting was the only method. It must not be inferred that printed music was cheap, but only that it was made available to more people.

Printing in a practical form was introduced into Europe early in the fifteenth century and was applied to music during the latter half of the same century.

There was still some confusion regarding notation. The staff might be made up of four, five, six, or even more lines. The notes were not always the same shapes; and even when they were, their values were not always the same. (It will be recalled that a note might be one half or one third the time value of the note of the next highest denomination.)

During the sixteenth century, however, there was a strong trend towards the adoption of the duple system — the *modus imperfectus* of the ars nova period—to the exclusion of all others. The longa was equal to two breves, the breve equal to two semibreves, for instance.

When triple time was desired, a dot called the prick of perfection was placed after a note to signify that it was equal in value to three notes of the next smallest denomination, a practice followed in modern notation.

Probably music printing as much as anything else contributed towards standardization, since there would be no point in publishing a composer's private system of notation if it could not be read by others.

The process of printing music varied. Many obstacles and difficulties had to be overcome; but the important fact is that it was begun in time to circulate and preserve the great works of the polyphonic masters.

✤ THE ORGAN

It was during the fifteenth and sixteenth centuries that the organ ceased to be an instrument solely for the accompaniment of voices. True, that ancient function continued to be its principal one, but it began to come into its own as an independent means of producing music.

The organ's long servitude led to its freedom. The many changes that crept into choral writing made it imperative that the organ be improved and adapted sufficiently to provide the wider variety of sounds necessary for accompaniment.

The most significant addition was that of keys which made possible the use of chromatics, corresponding to the black keys on a modern organ or piano. These were placed over and between the naturals which, on large instruments, were three or four inches wide. Because of their cumbersome mechanisms, large organs had still to be played with the fists.

Smaller organs were used in chapels and in the homes of the few wealthy musical people able to afford them. Those of fixed position were called *positives;* but there was a wide use of *portative* organs, small enough to be carried about in processions. These smaller organs contained fewer ranks of pipes—only one rank in many cases—and the pipes themselves were smaller.

Because the force required to play the organ was in direct proportion to the number and sizes of the pipes, the smaller instruments required much less pressure than larger ones. No doubt the facility which their smaller keys offered the performer emphasized the desirability of smaller keys and lighter action that would enable organists to play large organs with the fingers rather than the whole hand. This change was slow in coming, however, and it is probable that much of the early purely organ music, especially that containing rapid passages, was intended for the more easily manipulated manuals of comparatively small organs.

Until about the fifteenth century, the depressing of a key brought into play all the pipes controlled by that key—generally several pipes tuned to the fundamental pitch or its octave, and some tuned a fifth higher. These were of diapason tone, the quality peculiarly associated with the organ, and, since there was no mechanism for controlling the volume, the music was loud and expressionless.

A method of "stopping" the flow of air into certain ranks of pipes was discovered about this time, enabling the performer to reduce the volume by reducing the number of pipes that would speak when a key was depressed. Such a contrivance was aptly called a *stop*.

New timbres were introduced by the addition of flute and reed pipes which, by means of stops, could be played alone or in combination with other ranks of pipes.

Many church organs had two manual keyboards. As early as 1381 the organ in Halberstadt Cathedral had three manual keyboards and pedal keys. The development of the instrument was largely the work of German builders, who early and almost exclusively included pedal keyboards. The pedals were short and clumsy and probably few in number, although the number varied.

Competent organists, in addition to playing music written for voices and, occasionally, trying their hands at pieces written for the virginal and clavichord, indulged in some extemporization that would make them familiar with the possibilities as well as the limitations of their instruments. As builders gradually removed certain limitations and extended others, composers were not slow to take advantage of the improvements.

It was in Germany, during the fifteenth century, that a significant school of organists, teachers, and composers arose. Conrad Paumann and Paulus Hofhaimer were its chief exponents.

In 1452 Paumann prepared an instruction book on the application of counterpoint to the organ, often using popular airs as canti firmi. He also made arrangements of some of the compositions of early polyphonic writers.

Early in the sixteenth century, in addition to instruction books, collections of pieces written for the organ, notably those of Sebastian Virdung in 1511 and Arnolt Schlick in 1512, were published and enjoyed wide circulation in western Europe.

Perhaps the greatest contributors to the organ literature of the time were three members of the Venetian school: Andrea and Giovanni Gabrieli, uncle and nephew, and Claudio Merulo (1533–1604). They did much to develop the possibilities of the organ, especially in the *ricercare* and *toccata* forms which were to be further developed later in the toccata and fugue. These three men not only provided a foundation for the work of the succeeding generation of organists: they may be said to have provided the organists themselves, for the great Germans who were soon to inaugurate a new and splendid era of organ playing were pupils of the Venetians.

✤ REFERENCES

The following works are representative of the period covered by this chapter. The list could have been made much longer had it not been restricted to publications easily obtainable in the United States and Canada. The reader may, if he so desires, supplement it by reference to catalogues of music publishers.

The letters in brackets refer to the publishers or publishers' American agents from whose catalogues the list was compiled: [B] The Boston Music Company, Boston; [F] Carl Fischer, Inc., New York; [N] Novello and Company, Ltd., London; [S] G. Schirmer, Inc., New York.

Asterisks denote complete masses or other extended works.

While these compositions are recommended chiefly for study purposes, they are in current use by choirs whose taste and ability make their use practicable. Many of them are not beyond the capabilities of average volunteer choirs whose members are not afraid of a little work.

The Latin titles need not serve as a bar to their use in Protestant churches where everything is sung in the vernacular. In nearly all cases suitable English translations are provided.

> Allegri, G.—
>> *Misere mei, Deus* [S]
>
> Anerio, F.—
>> *Alleluia, Christ is risen* [N]
>> *Christus factus est* [N]
>
> Arcadelt, J.—
>> *Ave Maria* [N]

Bateson, T.—
Holy Lord God Almighty [N]

Bernardi, S.—
Benedixisti Domine [S]
Laudate Dominum [S]

Bruck, Arnold von—
Know'st thou then, poor Judas [S]

Byrd, William—
Ave Verum Corpus [F]
Christe qui Lux es et Dies [F]
Exsurge Domine [F]
Justorum Animae [N]
Laetentur Coeli [F]
Vigilate [F]

Causton, T.—
O sacred and holy Banquet [N]

des Prés, Josquin—
Ave Verum Corpus [S]
Tu pauperum refugium [S]

Farrant, John—
Magnificat and Nunc Dimittis [F]
Te Deum and Jubilate Deo [F]

Farrant, Richard—
Call to remembrance [S]
Hide not Thy face from us, O Lord [F]
Lord, for Thy tender mercies' sake [S]

Gabrieli, G.—
Benedixisti [S]
In ecclesiis [S]
Jubilate Deo [S]

Goudimel, C.—
Bread of the world [F]
Psalm XXXIX [S]

Handl, Jacobus (also known as J. Galus) —
Behold how the Righteous dieth [F]
Diffusa est gratia [S]
Lord in Thy resurrection [S]
Mirabile mysterium [S]

Hilton, John—
Call to remembrance [F]

Lasso, O. (also known as Lassus) —
Adoremus Te [S]
In hora ultima [S]
Liberate me [F]
Surrexit pastor bonus [S]

Morales, C.—
Me ye have bereaved [N]

Morley, Thomas—
    Hark! Alleluia [F]
    Nolo Mortem Peccatoris [F]
Mundy, John—
    Hear my prayer, O Lord [F]
    Sing ye unto the Lord [F]
Palestrina, Giovanni P., da—
    Come, Thou Holy Spirit, come [F]
    Confitebor Tibi, Domine [F]
    Exaltabo Te, Domine [S]
    Let us praise Thee, O Christ (Adoremus Te) [F]
    Like as the hart [S]
    Missa Brevis [S]
    Missa Papae Marcelli [S]
    O bone Jesu [S]
    O che splendor [B]
    Popule meus [S]
    Tollite jugem meum [S]
Power, Lionel—
    Sanctus [S]
Tallis, Thomas—
    Blessed are those [S]
    Blessed be Thy Name [F]
    If ye love Me [S]
    O God, be merciful [F]
    Purge me, O Lord [F]
    Rise, God, judge Thou the earth [S]
Taverner, John—
    Christe Jesu, Pastor Bone [F]
    Hear my prayer, O Lord [F]
Tye, Christopher—
    Give alms of thy goods [F]
    I will exalt Thee [F]
    Laudate Nomen Domini [N]
    Sing to the Lord [N]
Vittoria, T. L. da (also known as Victoria) —
    Deliver us, O Lord [F]
    Estote fortes in bello [S]
    Jesu, dulcis memoria [S]
    Ne timeas Maria [F]
    O magnum mysterium [S]
    O Quam Gloriosum [N]
    Tantum ergo [S]
Whyte, Robert—
    Christe qui Lux et Dies [F]
    O praise God in His holiness [F]

10

THE REFORMATION

❖ PRECURSORS OF THE REFORMATION

In following the main road of polyphonic choral music to its culmination at the end of the sixteenth century, we have purposely avoided certain bypaths that were to lead to newer types of church music through the reform movement. It becomes necessary now to retrace our steps a little and to explore these deviations from the main trend of composition.

The weakening of the authority and prestige of the Church, which has been mentioned in earlier chapters, was not wholly the result of dissatisfaction on the part of civil rulers and governments. It was the revolt against its spiritual authority that weakened the Church's influence. Attacks at the very root of its power came not from princely rivals for wealth and power, but from within its own ranks—from clerics and laymen who, appalled by the ever-increasing worldliness of the Church, sought its reform.

From the eleventh century on, the Church was plagued by heresies —the Cathari in the eleventh and twelfth centuries, the Waldensians in the twelfth, the Lollards and the Hussites in the fourteenth. Although sometimes driven under cover by rigorous persecution, these movements, heretical or reform, according to the point of view, persisted.

The bulk of the people, although far removed from theological and doctrinal discussions, and perhaps only vaguely aware of the bitter struggle between rival popes and emperors, were fertile soil for the seed of the reformers. Oppressive rule, poverty, and hunger, all countenanced by a wealthy, worldly, demanding, and neglectful hierarchy, bred discontent. It required very little persuasion to turn their discontent to contempt.[1]

The spirit of religious unrest that was abroad resulted in no sudden or drastic changes in the traditional services of the Church. Nevertheless, the weakening of ecclesiastical authority robbed its disapproval of much of its meaning. Innovations pressed by small groups of reformers were not always stoutly opposed by local clergy, especially in rural districts where priests were sometimes absent from their parishes for long periods.

That official edicts against innovations in liturgical music were considered necessary is evidence of dissatisfaction with the old, traditional restrictions.

In villages and rural areas, where music of contemporary composers was not heard anyway (and perhaps no music written within the past century), papal edicts did not apply. Here, innovations of an entirely different kind were creeping in. Perhaps, in the presence of the priest, there was no departure from the few ancient, austere plainsong chants that constituted their complete liturgical music. Left to themselves, however, the people often showed a preference for the type of music to which they sang their secular songs.

When men were moved to private prayer or thanksgiving, they resorted to their native tongue, since they were not well enough acquainted with Latin to express themselves in that language. Likewise, when moved to praise, they were apt to voice their pious thoughts to worldly music. They were in no sense composers. They simply adapted familiar airs to accommodate the words they wished to sing, thus unconsciously following the example of some of the learned musicians of the day.

This practice was probably more common than existing evidence would seem to indicate. Certainly it would be encouraged by the reformers, who opposed formalism and advocated worship in the vernacular. John Huss is known to have written hymns; and so, no doubt, did other literate members of the reform movement. What music they used, we

---

1 Excellent pictures of fourteenth-century England, emphasizing the strong influence of the clergy upon the daily lives of the common people and the lack of real respect towards the clergy, are contained in *The Golden Hand* by Edith Simon (London: Cassell & Company, Ltd., 1952) and *The Corner That Held Them* by Sylvia Townsend Warner (London: Chatto and Windus, 1948).

cannot tell. There may have been some new tunes composed, but it is more likely that the words were sung to airs with which the people were already familiar.

The first known published hymn book was that of the Hussites, later known as the Moravians, in 1501, eighty-six years after the death of Huss. By this time, many tunes formerly associated with secular words had become identified with hymns, and many new tunes had been written. Although the Latin liturgy had been abandoned, depriving the sect of the great polyphonic music that was being written at the time, the tunes were necessarily modal and irregular in rhythm. Modern harmonizations of early hymn tunes can give us only a vague notion of the original forms. The Hussites were very fond of unaccompanied congregational singing, and many of their tunes were of a style later developed as the choral. A second hymnal was published in 1505.

The Hussite hymnals, and one published in German by Michael Weiss in 1531, were to influence strongly the music of the Lutheran church. Possibly some of the tunes survive improperly identified or attributed to Lutheran writers. The twelfth century German tune *Christ Ist Erstanden,* contained in some modern hymnals, may have appeared in the book of Michael Weiss; for it has long been associated with his hymn beginning with the same words ("Christ the Lord is risen again" as translated by Catherine Winkworth). This is one tune that retains its modal form, especially if sung in free rhythm with a disregard for bar lines.

Although the Reformation is considered to have begun in the sixteenth century, it could not have won popular support had it been conceived suddenly, even by such a man as Luther. It was the climax of a movement which had been in the building for four hundred years. Its doctrines and practices and music had to grow and take shape through generations in order that they might finally gain acceptance.

✣ THE GERMAN REFORMATION

Martin Luther (1483–1546) is the only leader of a strong, organized Protestant movement who has considered music of sufficient importance in worship to warrant his personal attention and direction.

Among Luther's several objectives for reform was the active participation of the people in public worship, an ancient privilege that had been gradually whittled away through the centuries until little remained. A prerequisite was the translation of the liturgy from Latin to the vernacular: a stimulus would be the introduction of hymns with familiar tunes which the people would join in singing.

The idea of reviving congregational singing was not new with Luther. He was aware of its unifying and inspirational effect among the Hussites, and he was acquainted with their hymnals and that of Michael Weiss. It was their example that he followed, in part, in developing congregational music of the German Evangelical (Lutheran) Church.

Germany was a promising field for such an experiment. Secular choral music, simple enough to be sung in unison or in parts, had been growing in popularity for nearly a century. Early examples may have been insignificant, but as competent musicians began to compose new melodies and arrange the existing ones, these choral songs gained in character without loss of simplicity. Among the chief contributors to the famous Nuremburg song collection (published 1539–1556) were Heinrich Isaac (who was at the height of his career when Luther was a young man), Isaac's pupil, Ludwig Senfl (1492–1553), and Georg Forster (1514–1568).

From these familiar songs Luther drew freely, but not indiscriminately. There must have been many trivial airs in current use, yet not one of those chosen bears any mark of triviality. One of the tunes thus elevated from secular to sacred use was that known to us as *Innsbrück:* "The duteous day now closeth."

Some new tunes were composed, a few, including *Ein' Feste Burg:* "A mighty fortress is our God," by Luther himself.

Unlike some other reformers, Luther had no desire to break completely with the past. On the contrary, he would have preferred carrying out his reform methods within the framework of the Roman Catholic Church to setting up a new church. Certainly he did not intend to abandon the best features of liturgical worship simply because they were shared by the adherents to the old order. Some Latin hymns, with which the people had been long familiar, he translated into German, adapting the plainsong melodies to accommodate the translation where necessary, and adding harmonies.

From these three sources—secular songs, inspiration, and plainsong—came the type of hymn tune known as the *choral,* a term formerly used for certain parts of the Latin liturgy sung by the choir.

The even, measured rhythm with which we associate chorals today was not always present in the early versions. In many cases, there was a mixture of duple and triple rhythm and, especially in those chorals borrowed from the Latin liturgy, a great deal of the free rhythm of plainsong. The harmonies, too, were chiefly modal and would sound quaint to our ears. When reading chorals from modern hymnals it must be remembered that, much as they have gained from the attention of later writers, they differ considerably from the originals.

The melody was, for a long time, allotted to the tenor, following the custom of the day. Chorals were generally sung in unison by the congregation. They were, and still are, sung very slowly, almost ponderously, perhaps to lend dignity to tunes that had been associated with less serious words.

In a country which had contributed so much to the development of the organ, and among musicians who had raised that instrument to a position of dignity and importance, it was natural that chorals should early be sung with organ accompaniment. Elsewhere, musical instruments were associated with profane uses and generally considered unfit for worship: it was in Germany that the organ became almost inseparable from public worship.

Luther's methods of stimulating congregational singing might well serve as an example to modern compilers of hymnals. He brought to his task sound musicianship (for he was a musician, although not a professional one) and gave the people tunes they would enjoy singing without loss of dignity to worship music. He sanctified good secular airs and the use of the organ when others feared that such devices would profane church services, and he sought assistance from those who could combine ability with willingness.

Luther's first hymnal, *Etlich cristlich lider Lobgesang,* containing eight hymns and five tunes, appeared in 1524. At about the same time were published two other books, *Enchiridion* by Jonas and Lange (twenty-five hymns, sixteen tunes); and *Geistliche gesangk Buchleyn* (thirty-two hymns, thirty-five tunes) edited by Johann Walther, who was Luther's friend and collaborator. In 1545, *Geystliche Lieder mit einer newen Vorrhede,* containing 101 hymns, including all Luther had written, was published. The popularity of choral singing may be judged by the large number of hymnals that came into existence within a period of some seventy years. It may be noted that the first harmonized tunes with the melody in the treble, instead of in the tenor as previously, made up a collection, *50 Geistliche Lieder,* published at Nuremburg in 1586.

Many German composers contributed hymns, tunes, or chorals as the demand for them increased. Only the best survived, including a number by Johann Crüger (1598–1662). Even secular part songs were composed in the manner of chorals, and some of them were early adapted to words of hymns with which they are still associated. A secular choral song of Hans Hassler is known to us as *Passion Chorale:* "O sacred head, surrounded."

Luther's enthusiasm for congregational singing did not lead him to abandon or even neglect music that could be sung only by trained choirs. The retention of the choral parts of the mass (some in translation, some still in Latin) required the services of choirs. There seems to have been no objection, then or later, to the use of polyphonic choruses, the best of which were composed for Latin words. Nor was there any interruption in the experimental, forward movement of church music.

Whereas music, apart from simple hymn and psalm tunes, ceased to exist among the stricter reforming sects, musicians of the Lutheran church continued to extend and enrich worship music, using either German or Latin words as it pleased them. Some of them continued to write in the polyphonic modal style; others, when it became evident that the resources of modal composition had been pretty well worked out, did valuable service in bridging the transition period between modal harmony and the newer school of the late seventeenth century.

Especially in the field of organ music was the Lutheran practice influential. If it had done no more than to lend respectability to the instrument at a time when strong prejudice against the organ survived in many quarters, the contribution of Lutheranism would have been considerable. But the employment of organists in Lutheran churches, both as performers and choirmasters, and the high standard expected in worship music, served as encouragement and incentive seldom enjoyed by musicians of the past.

Lutheranism spread through the German principalities to the Scandinavian countries, notably Sweden. Thus, composers and organists of a fairly large and thickly populated area enjoyed the opportunities offered by Lutheran trends. Even in Holland, where there was a strong leaning towards Calvinism, organ music flourished. The organ was there rarely used in public worship, but people flocked to churches to hear it at other times.

A distinct style of organ music developed in northwestern Europe. In addition to other forms which have come to be considered as classic, there came into existence the *choral-prelude.*

It early became the custom for the organist to play interludes between verses of the chorals, sometimes between portions of verses. These interludes might be very simple or very elaborate, depending upon the skill and ingenuity of the organist. The tunes were so popular and offered such an admirable basis for improvisation that organists began to use them as themes for their preludes. Often the whole tune was used, overlaid with more or less elaborate contrapuntal harmony, and divided into sections between which counter themes were given free rein. Sometimes the tune was only suggested or approximated, serving as a sort of text for the musical discourse that followed. The skill of what we may call the Lutheran school of organists in the writing of choral-preludes has never been surpassed.

Before mentioning briefly the most important musicians who influenced and were influenced by Lutheranism, it might be well to remind the reader that they were not widely famous in their generation or for some generations to come. Whereas earlier composers, writing for the Roman liturgy, could count on their works being favorably received anywhere in Europe, the music of Germanic composers was excluded from the greater part of Europe that remained Catholic, and from large areas of Calvinism where church music was generally frowned upon. They worked on a religious island—a large island, it is true, but, as far as church music was concerned, cut off from the rest of the world.

Johann Eccard (1553–1611) studied at Munich with Lasso. He wrote a great deal of fine church music and contributed much to the development of the choral.

Jan Sweelinck (1562–1621) was born in Amsterdam where, except for his period of study with Zarlino and Gabrieli in Venice, he spent all his life. He ranks among the foremost organists and composers of organ music of any age. The Old Church of Amsterdam was frequently crowded with people who came to hear him play.

Something of his skill as an organist is reflected in Sweelinck's composition. He was among the first to write an independent part for the pedals. The ricercare and fantasia, forms which had tended towards the fugue, became very definitely fugues in his hands, although not as fully developed as they became later. The toccata and prelude, designed to display the performer's virtuosity, gained much from an organist of Sweelinck's ability. He, perhaps more than anyone else of his time, envisioned the possibilities of the choral-prelude. It is interesting to note that his compositions were written on a six-lined staff.

The foundation of sound organ playing and composition, that reached a high point with Bach, was laid by Sweelinck and built upon by his pupils, who came from all northern Europe. It might be said that without Sweelinck there could have been no Bach.

Important though Sweelinck's contributions to organ literature are, they scarcely exceed the value of his vocal compositions. Here, the influence of his teacher Lasso remains strong; yet Sweelinck was no mere imitator. Originality is evident in his abandonment of the traditional cantus firmus and definite though cautious steps towards newer harmonies. Perhaps his advance may be best summed up for a layman by saying that his compositions sound less strange to modern ears than the polyphonic writings of half a century earlier. As a matter of fact, Sweelinck's works (republished in modern times) are frequently performed by choirs who aim for the best in church music.

Hans Hassler (1564–1612), born in Nuremburg, was one of the first German organists and composers to study in Italy. He was a pupil of Andrea Gabrieli, perhaps at the same time as Sweelinck, and carried the traditions of the Venetian school to Germany. His compositions and harmonizations of chorals, many still in use, added much of value to the repertoire of Lutheran church music.

Heinrich Schütz (1585–1672), a native of Saxony, was a law student at Marburg University when, at the age of twenty-four, he decided to make music his career. He must have been an exceptionally accomplished amateur for, after only three years of study with Giovanni Gabrieli in Venice, he returned to Cassel as a concert organist. In 1615, he became the musical director at the court of the Elector of Saxony, a post which he held for well over half a century until his death.

Schütz was a fine organist and an excellent and prolific composer. (A complete edition of his works, published in modern times, comprises sixteen volumes.) A master of polyphony, he combined it with the changing trend of musical thought and, like Sweelinck, served as an important link between the modal period and that of Handel and Bach. His music displays a dramatic sense and a vitality surpassing the Germanic composers of his time. His use of the recitative style suggests a familiarity with the music of Monteverde, who was developing opera.

Several trips to Italy broadened Schütz's outlook and resulted in a certain fusion of German and Italian styles of composing that distinguished his own work and influenced that of his successors.

His cantatas, the *Seven Words of Jesus Christ,* the *Story of the Resurrection,* and the *Passion According to St. Matthew,* are masterly enough to stand on their own merits without their added significance as precursors of the great Passion music of Bach.

Johann Schein (1586–1630), another native of Saxony, contributed much to the development of German music in the way of motets, madrigals, instrumental music, and chorals. He, too, brought to his composition an understanding and feeling for Italian forms then current. Schein was one of Bach's predecessors as cantor at St. Thomas' Church, Leipzig.

Samuel Scheidt (1587–1654), a pupil of Sweelinck, was a famous organist, and a composer of organ music and chorals. His organ pieces transferred the emphasis from mere virtuosity to a more serious, purposeful type of music than had previously been found in the literature for that instrument.

✤ CALVINISM

Calvinism might be called Protestantism in exile, since it was developed in Geneva by men who had fled their own lands—at least temporarily—to escape the persecutions suffered by dissenters. It lacked the national characteristics and the strong organization of Lutheranism. No rulers of principalities supported Calvin as they supported Luther. Except in parts of Switzerland, Calvinism was subject to effective opposition from the Catholic church, which held sway in most countries where the Calvinists sought to establish their reform.

Unlike Luther, who retained many of the traditional forms and adapted much of the Latin liturgy, the Calvinists made a clean break with the past, eschewing all ceremonies and customs that could be identified with the Roman church.

Among the babies thrown out with the bath water was worship music. All the slow, painful advances of centuries which have so far been described in this book, all the flower of church music that had blossomed in their own time, became as if they had never existed as far as the Calvinists were concerned.

Church musicians are apt to deplore the brake applied to church music by Calvinistic influence. The tradition that none but the very simplest of music has a place in public worship remains strong to this day among large groups of people and has, to some extent, thwarted the efforts of those who would dedicate the very finest of music to the service of Him by whom it was inspired.

In fairness to Calvin and his early followers, it must be admitted that there was some justification for their drastic action. Traditional forms had lost much of their original meanings. Intended as aids to worship, they had been invested with such importance in themselves that they had become distractions. Music was no exception. The elaborate motets and masses of the time, requiring all the skill of trained choirs, often missed their real purpose. The situation described in Chapter I existed then as now: worship ceased while the attention of singers and congregation was diverted to a musical performance. Even the ecclesiastical authorities, who countenanced a great deal of formalism for its own sake, were moved to protest the elaborations of the music from time to time.

Where Luther sought to restore to music its proper function as an aid to worship, the Calvinists threw it out almost completely.

There were practical reasons for abolishing all but the simplest of music, although how far they were taken into account at the time we cannot know.

Although inspiration for the movement stemmed from Geneva, there was nothing like a central governing body, nor would the Calvinists have wished one. A great deal of freedom for individual congregations was advocated; and it may have been feared that the retention of music would lead not only to the continuance of some Latin forms but also to the introduction of frivolous, worldly airs.

There were probably few musicians among the Calvinists. The reform movement had not the support of kings and nobles, except in some Germanic principalities, and most musicians were dependent upon royal, noble, or ecclesiastical patronage for their livelihood. Nor did the Calvinists inherit large churches with organs, trained choirs, and a tradition of music as the Lutherans did.

Without competent musicians to give it direction, and lacking facilities for worthwhile performance, perhaps it is as well that music was dropped from Calvinistic worship.

There seems to have been no objection to music as such. We have seen that, in Calvinistic Holland, Sweelinck and others entertained audiences in churches at times other than those of public worship, and editions of psalm tunes in four parts argue that people were able to sing those parts.

But in public worship, organs were silenced; and the singing was confined to rhymed paraphrases of the psalms, sung in unison. These *metrical psalms,* as they are called, followed closely the original prose settings in the Bible.

Following is Psalm 100 in its biblical and metrical forms.[2]

O be joyful in the Lord, all ye lands: serve the Lord with gladness, and come before his presence with a song.

Be ye sure that the Lord he is God: it is he that hath made us, and not we ourselves; we are his people, and the sheep of his pasture.

O go your way into his gates with thanksgiving, and into his courts with praise: be thankful unto him, and speak good of his Name.

For the Lord is gracious, his mercy is everlasting: and his truth endureth from generation to generation.

> All people that on earth do dwell,
> Sing to the Lord with cheerful voice;
> Him serve with fear, His praise forth tell,
> Come ye before Him, and rejoice.
>
> The Lord, ye know, is God indeed;
> Without our aid He did us make;
> We are His flock, He doth us feed,
> And for His sheep He doth us take.
>
> O enter then His gates with praise,
> Approach with joy His courts unto;
> Praise, laud, and bless His name always,
> For it is seemly so to do.
>
> For why? the Lord our God is good;
> His mercy is for ever sure;
> His truth at all times firmly stood,
> And shall from age to age endure.

> Wm. Kethe, 1561.

[2] The prose version is that of the Great Bible of 1539, translated from the Vulgate by Coverdale. The Authorized, or King James, Version was not yet in existence when the metrical paraphrases were made.

All paraphrases were not as well done as this one. Some of the early ones were crude: even some that have survived until the present day would make a poet squirm.

The Calvinists' insistence on the use of metrical psalms to the exclusion of all other types of hymns had a twofold purpose: first, to avoid the Latin hymn which, in addition to its association with the Roman church, sometimes expressed doctrines contrary to the reformers' beliefs; second, to discourage a crude hymnody in the vernacular which might go quite as far afield in the matter of doctrine.

The objection to "human" hymns did not extend to the psalms for, while the paraphrases were certainly the work of men, the subject matter was clearly defined in the prose version. A passion for purity could have been more completely satisfied by retaining the prose psalms; but that would have meant the retention of the plainsong chant which bore the stamp of Rome, while the trend was towards measured music to tunes more readily sung by the people.

Metrical versions of the psalms were many. Two of Calvin's countrymen, Clément Marot and Théodore de Bèze, prepared paraphrases in French between 1539 and 1562, and these were translated for the use of the German Reformed Church by Ambrosius Lobwasser. The tunes were largely the work of Loys Bourgeois (c. 1523–1600), Claude Goudimel (c. 1505–1572), Guillaume Franc (d. 1570), and Claude Le Jeune (1528–1601) who, besides their compositions in other fields, identified themselves with the French Huguenot movement. Both Bourgeois and Franc spent some years in Switzerland as a result of their Protestant activities in France.

In 1540, *Souter Liedekens,* perhaps the first complete metrical psalter, was published in Antwerp. The tunes were borrowed from Dutch folk songs; and many of them were, in turn, borrowed by the Genevan compilers of psalters.

The English and Scotch, too, had paraphrases to some of the psalms, although it is not known where they got their earlier tunes. A curious collection was that of Robert Crowley, whose complete book of metrical psalms (1549) was provided with only one tune—a plainsong chant in the tenor, harmonized for four voices. The melody note was unchanged in the first and third lines (the harmonizing voices changed only once), and the only variety was provided by the inflections of the chant which appeared in the second and fourth lines. The British carried these psalms, and those of Sternhold and Hopkins, without tunes, to Geneva, where they were placed in the melting pot of psalmody.

The first Anglo-Genevan psalter, based on Sternhold and Hopkins and containing tunes, appeared in 1556. John Day published editions of Sternhold and Hopkins in 1561 and 1562, the first prefaced with instruc-

tions for learning to sing—thus setting a fashion—the second containing
the whole psalter and sixty-five tunes.   Thereafter, new collections of
metrical psalms were numerous and frequent.

It was the incomplete psalter of 1561 that the Scottish reformers took
home from Geneva.   It was completed and published in 1564 and was
in use in the Presbyterian Church for many years.

At first, only the melodies of the tunes appeared in the psalters and,
since congregational singing was in unison and there were no organs, the
melodies were sufficient to meet all needs.   Later on, first on the continent then in Scotland, harmonized tunes appeared with the melodies in
the tenor, although they were by no means generally used in public worship. With parts provided, the people were enabled to indulge their love
of music in seemly fashion and to practice the art of part-singing—but
principally in their own homes.

In the Presbyterian Church in Scotland, particularly, where the tradition of austerity in public worship persisted until late in the nineteenth
century, and still persists in some localities, many interesting and quaint
practices became themselves traditional.   Some were begun quite early;
others came later.   Few of them were adopted by all congregations, but
the use of most of these practices spread to England and, later, to America.

On the precentor, or "uptaker of the psalms," rested the responsibility of leading the singing.   Some precentors sounded the opening note on
a pitch pipe, a graduated wooden tube whose length, and therefore pitch,
could be adjusted by a stopper.   But even such an innocent instrument as
a pitch pipe was considered unseemly by many congregations, and the
precentor had to find the note unaided.   The mark of a good precentor
was the ability to set a pitch that would be within comfortable range of
all the congregation.   He did not always find the desired note on his first
attempt and would allow his voice to rise and fall, something in the manner of an intonation, until he felt that he had achieved the right pitch.
Possibly because of his unwillingness to admit his inability to give out
the correct note at once or because he thought he was adding something
desirable to his performance, he might add some ornamental notes to
the principal one whether he needed to or not.

The pitch having been decided upon, the congregation was still not
ready to sing the psalm.   In the early days of the reform movement,
books were not always available; and even when they were, many people
could not read them.   That the congregation might know and sing the
words, the minister or the precentor read out the psalm a line at a time,
the people singing each line after it was read.   This practice, besides in-
terfering with the sense of the words, frequently led to confusion in singing the tune.   Intent upon listening to the words, the congregation—and
often the precentor—forgot the pitch and might begin the second line

higher or lower than the first.   Precentors sometimes actually forgot the tune to which the first part of a psalm had been sung and wandered to another one.   Canny precentors who were "lining out" the psalms avoided such confusion by monotoning the line on the first note that was to be sung.   In the Scottish highlands, later on, precentors lined out psalms in a sort of improvised melody which centered around the dominant and led into the proper tune which the congregation was to sing.

Lining out or "deaconing," as it was later called in America, was intended only as a temporary measure to be used until the people could read the psalms from their books.   Unfortunately, the custom became so firmly established that it was continued long after its usefulness was past. As late as the middle of the nineteenth century it was abandoned by some religious bodies only in the face of bitter opposition from some of their members.

The pitch set and the first line announced (in far less time than it has taken to read about it) , the precentor began the psalm, lengthening the first note to give everyone a chance to join him.   The line was sung very slowly, becoming even slower as the end was approached, and the second line was announced.   The lengthened first note of each line, called the *gathering note,* came to be recognized by publishers of psalm tunes; and even some modern hymnals use it, together with a lengthened last note to balance it off.

Even if nothing had been added to the precentor's giving out of the note and the lining out of the psalm, the intention of the leaders of the reform to have the psalter sung in a dignified, straightforward manner would have been defeated to some extent.   But, human nature being what it is, the people could not resist adding something of their own to the simple tunes.   As the austere plainsong chant had been made the subject of elaboration and variation centuries before, so the English and Scottish Calvinists sought to ornament the psalm tunes, generally with less happy results.

The more musically gifted of the reformers did make a worthwhile contribution by a type of composition known as *reports,* motet-like versions of the psalms, such as those by Goudimel.   Those which appeared in the Scottish psalter of 1635 generally allotted the psalm tune to the tenor, with long gaps between the lines which were filled by imitations and elaborations by the other voices.   (This is reminiscent of the more skilled treatment of the German choral in the choral-prelude form.)

Amateur attempts to brighten up the psalm tunes were, however, cheapening and disastrous.   The long, sustained notes were replaced by trills or any other ornaments that suited the fancy—and the fancies of all members of the congregation did not always agree.   Skips of intervals beyond a second were often filled in with improvised notes "to avoid the roughness of a leap," as one later writer put it. In fact, the number of added notes often far exceeded the original, and some of the tunes in their "ornamented" state defy recognition.

The metrical psalms laid the foundation for the modern hymn— indeed, the transition from psalter to hymnary was easy and natural once the prejudice against "human hymns" was overcome. That their greatest possibilities were seldom realized by early congregations does not lessen their value to later generations.

Their popularity led to a widespread interest in part singing, even where harmonized versions were not in use in public worship. It became customary to preface the tune book proper with instructions for singing in parts, and those capable of teaching the art had no lack of pupils. There were far more people capable of singing four-part harmony than there are now.

Again we must caution the reader who uses the list of references at the end of this chapter that modal harmony and irregular rhythm, which marked the original versions of many metrical psalms, are not reflected in modern versions.

✣ THE REFORMATION IN ENGLAND

More than a century was required for the consummation of the Reformation in England. Although its date is often given as 1534, there was no actual reformation at that time, but only a separation from the church of Rome.

Whereas the reform movement, which had been gaining force for two hundred years or more, was concerned with faith and doctrine, the events leading to the separation were on a less idealistic plane. The king and the nobles had long been as resentful towards the Church as had the reformers, but for different reasons. They found irksome the Church's interference in affairs of state, and they were envious of the wealth of the Church, whose revenues never failed even when the civil government was hard pressed for money.

It is doubtful that the most loyal subjects of Henry VIII approved of his six marriages, two divorces, and the beheading of two wives, all in the space of thirty-four years. His marital adventures were condoned simply because, as a result of them, he became an ally of the nobility and commonalty against ecclesiastical power and authority.

Henry, who is often regarded as a foe of Catholicism, was one of its strongest supporters. It was he who, in 1521, replied to Luther's ninety-five theses with the Assertion of the Seven Sacraments, and was rewarded by Pope Leo X with the title of "Defender of the Faith." Eighteen years later (and five years after the Act of Supremacy had made the king and his successors supreme heads of the Church of England), there was published the Statute of the Six Articles, defining heresy and upholding Catholic dogma. Apart from acknowledging papal authority, Henry remained Defender of the Faith. The more zealous reformers received short shrift from him; and when he meted out punishment to Catholics, it was not for practicing their religion, but for trying to restore papal authority.

The services and music of the church changed little, if at all. There was no new, distinctive liturgy, as was the case with the Lutherans; and composers continued to write in the polyphonic style then current.

Musicians fared rather well under Henry, who was something of a musician himself. The staff of the Chapel Royal was increased to seventy-nine. A small choir accompanied the king on his travels, to sing the daily mass. In 1520, the entire Chapel Royal choir was taken to France, where it combined with the Chapelle de Musique du Roi to sing for the kings of England and France.

The suppression of the monasteries (c. 1536–1540) was not, from the point of view of musicians, as great a tragedy as some historians would have us believe. True, some valuable manuscripts were probably lost or destroyed, but the continuity of liturgical music was maintained in the Chapel Royal and the cathedrals.

Unfortunately, musicians in the service of abbeys and monasteries shared the wrath visited upon their superiors. Pygott, Dygon, and Tallis lost their positions and their property was confiscated: Merbecke, who was to perform a signal service for the Church of England later on, was condemned to death for heresy. But the crown relented and dealt leniently with musicians. Most of those who forfeited their property received pensions in return: Merbecke not only escaped execution but was restored to his position as organist of St. George's, Windsor.

The difficulty lay in the fact that no one quite knew from one day to the next what might constitute heresy. The Calvinists, quick to take advantage of the quarrel between king and Pope, pressed their doctrines and, at times, succeeded in influencing the doctrines of the Church of England to some small degree. Without warning, some move of the king (such as the Statute of the Six Articles) would make illegal today something that had been tolerated yesterday. We may be thankful that musicians were permitted opportunities to repent and turn their coats. Many other people were less fortunate.

The Reformation began to make some headway in 1547, after death removed Henry VIII from the scene.

Thomas Cranmer, Archbishop of Canterbury, was one of the prime movers towards a compromise between Romanism and Calvinism. He had opposed Henry's Six Articles, but not very strenuously, since discretion was a condition of survival under that temperamental monarch.

The accession of Edward VI, a mere boy of ten, put a different complexion on the situation. No opposition could be expected from him; and his protector, the Duke of Somerset, was of the same mind as Cranmer regarding the desirability of devising a doctrine and liturgy that would bring Calvinist and Catholic at least a little closer together.

The Statute of the Six Articles, upholding the Roman dogma, was immediately repealed. In its place were formulated and published, in 1553, the Forty-Two Articles of Religion, later revised and reduced to thirty-nine, setting forth the doctrines of the Church of England as distinct from those of Rome.

In 1549 appeared the first Book of Common Prayer, designed to bring uniformity to the services, which were to be in English. (It was replaced by a second, revised book in 1553.)

There was ample provision for music in the new Anglican liturgy, but no music except for that of the Latin offices existed. It was John Merbecke (d. 1585), who had narrowly escaped a heretic's death under Henry, who made good the deficiency. Since a great deal of the new liturgy was a translation of the old, Merbecke retained much of the traditional plainsong setting, adapting it to the English words.

As noted earlier, it is no easy task to adapt music written for a text in one language to the needs of a translation into another. Accents and inflections which admirably suit the original may all fall in the wrong places in the translation. Moreover, the vernacular may contain fewer syllables than the original, which leaves one wondering what to do with the extra notes; or it may contain more, which raises the problem of where notes to accommodate the extra syllables are to come from.

In *The Booke of Common Praier Noted,* Merbecke succeeded, both by adaptation and by the use of some original music in the plainsong style, in wedding the Anglican liturgy to the plainsong idiom in a manner that has compelled the admiration of succeeding generations.

Cranmer deplored contrapuntal motets on the ground that they obscured the words and urged composers to write syllabically—that is, one note to each syllable. Most of the polyphonic music was written for Latin words and, while some attempts were made at translation, Cranmer's objection remained valid. Church musicians began to write more and more in the chordal style, using English words and inaugurating the now familiar anthem form. Both Tallis and Tye proved themselves as skilled in this form as in the contrapuntal style, which marked their earlier works.

The anthems and motets, and even *The Booke of Common Praier*

Noted, were used only in the cathedrals and the comparatively few large city parish churches that had trained choirs. No provision was made for congregational singing. It is true that Merbecke's setting of the liturgy contained much that was sung by the laity, but such parts were intended for the choir rather than for congregational use. In small parish and rural churches which lacked choirs, the laymen's parts of the service were generally sung by clerks, if they were sung at all. The Merbecke setting was probably unknown in most small churches or, if known, ignored. It would be far easier to continue the traditional liturgy or, if discretion dictated the use of the liturgy in the vernacular, to say the service.

As was to be expected, since the liturgy provided no opportunities for congregational singing, the people created their own opportunities.

The amazing popularity of metrical psalms antedated the publication of the Genevan collections by many years. Crude paraphrases probably existed from the early days of the reform movement, and their use was tolerated even by the Roman church until they became closely identified with Protestantism. They were not supposed to be sung in churches, but they were probably sung sometimes.

In 1539, Coverdale, encouraged by the royal acceptance of his English Bible, had published a translation of German hymns with tunes, *Goostly Psalms,* which was promptly suppressed by Henry VIII.

But the toleration which marked the Reformation proper in England gave impetus to the use of metrical psalms. In 1549, coincident with the issuing of the first Prayer Book, there were published three collections of psalms, although there was no official connection between the Prayer Book and the psalm books.

Robert Crowley's psalter containing one tune (based on a plainsong chant) has already been mentioned.

A collection of nineteen psalms by Thomas Sternhold and another of forty-four psalms by Sternhold and John Hopkins had no tunes. The printing of tunes was perhaps considered unnecessary, as they were few in number and so well known that they could be sung without notes.

The singing of metrical psalms in public worship was not authorized. The prose version from Coverdale's English Bible was provided for church use (and is still contained in the Prayer Book) to be chanted to plainsong adapted to the English words. The paraphrases were intended for services in domestic chapels and for family or social use. It was not unusual for groups to sing metrical psalms for pleasure and not particularly as an act of devotion.

There is little doubt that there was much unauthorized singing of metrical psalms, especially in churches far removed from central authority. The uniformity aimed at by the publication of the Prayer Book was far from realized. Congregations with strong Calvinistic leanings were apt to introduce Calvinistic customs: those who resented the break with Rome retained much or all of the Latin liturgy.

An attempt at metrical paraphrases of portions of the Bible other than the psalms was made by Tallis in 1553, when he wrote *The Acts of the Apostles*. This, too, was intended only for domestic use.

It must be remembered that music was widely cultivated among the nobility. The fact that the royal family had for many years shown an interest in the art guaranteed a like interest on the part of the courtiers. All had their private chapels and music rooms. If there were not enough musical members of the family to provide all the parts, servants with some musical ability were often employed to round out the little domestic choir or orchestra. Those who could afford to do so engaged professional musicians, either permanently or for special occasions. However, the practice of patronage was less in evidence in England than on the continent.

The new order of things was short-lived. Only four years after the publication of the first Prayer Book, the young King Edward died. Those who had guided the nation's affairs during his reign were deposed.

Queen Mary, who succeeded him, was an ardent Catholic. She and her advisers had no intention of merely halting the progress of the Protestant movement. They were firmly resolved to stamp it out completely, once and for all. The persecution of the Protestants was savage. Archbishop Cranmer and several bishops were executed and replaced by clerics of the Roman church. Thousands were punished by execution, imprisonment, or confiscation of property. There were no more services in English, no more Prayer Book, no more psalm singing. In a very short time, the country was as Catholic as it had been at any period of its history—as far as outward appearances went, at any rate.

One is lost in admiration at the talent for survival displayed by church musicians. They seemed able to adapt their writings to whatever style of liturgy was in favor at the time and to escape the penalties suffered by others. Tallis for instance, composed in the contrapuntal style of the Latin services under Henry VIII, contributed much to the English service as prescribed by the Prayer Book and chordal writing as enjoined by Cranmer, and received special favors under both the Catholic Queen Mary and the Protestant Queen Elizabeth. Even Merbecke, closely identified with the Prayer Book, managed to survive unscathed, although there is no record of his being very active in Mary's reign. Indeed, there was little composition of church music during the period of Catholicism.

After five years, the pendulum swung again to Protestantism with the accession of Elizabeth I in 1558. The papists were turned out of office. In a very short time, the Act of Supremacy was restored, an Act of Uniformity passed, the Prayer Book and the Articles of Religion revised.

There was little activity among composers of church music during the early years of Elizabeth's reign. The sudden and drastic changes that had taken place in eleven years made musicians cautious of spending their efforts on compositions that might be discarded should another upheaval take place. Moreover, the queen was known to be capricious, and it seemed wise to wait until her policies became definite.

Perhaps the greatest activity was in the field of metrical psalms. The *Anglo-Genevan Psalter* of 1556, and the *Scottish Psalter* of 1564, were followed by several collections published in England. There were, of course, a great many people in England of such strong Calvinistic leanings that they preferred to restrict the use of music to the psalms. Even the liturgy of the reformed Church of England in the vernacular was too elaborate and too reminiscent of Romanism for their taste. Encouraged by the Reformation in Scotland, which in 1560 had rejected Catholicism for the opposite extreme, Calvinism, or Presbyterianism, they strove mightily for separation from the state church.

But the separatists were not alone in their demand for metrical psalms. Although this form of congregational singing had no authorized place in the liturgy, and certainly was not to be heard in cathedrals and collegiate churches, many congregations began the practice of singing a metrical psalm now and then, generally before or after the service proper.

In many places where the paraphrases were not sung within the church, the people would gather in some convenient place, often outside the church, to sing them.

Unless the separatists or Calvinists were of greater number than evidence seems to indicate, there must have been very many Church of England people among whom psalm singing was popular. The number of metrical psalters published in England was not exceeded even in countries where the Calvinistic mode of worship was the only one.

Later in Elizabeth's reign, there began the development of the English style of church music whose influence remains today in all English-speaking countries. While it may not be considered great music as compared with that of Bach, Mozart, Beethoven, and others, it has distinctive qualities which we have come to associate with worship music —a quality which, indeed, is often described as "churchy" for want of a better term.

It was inevitable that English church music should be distinctive, since it was subject to no outside influences. Lutheran music was adapted to another language, generally German, but sometimes Latin; and the choral was distinctly German as regards both words and the sources of the music. Moreover, the development of the choral to the point where the organ interludes played a great part was not practical in England, where organs did not possess the capabilities of German organs.

Latin liturgical music was unsuitable, not only because of language difficulties but also because its elaborate, contrapuntal style was foreign to the intelligible syllabic form of writing that was being encouraged at the time.

The Huguenots and Presbyterians had no worship music to offer except the metrical psalm, and that was developed independent of the state church.

Very soon after Elizabeth's accession, service books began to appear. That published by John Day in 1560, containing the liturgy set to music by several composers, was among the first. Tallis, at about this time, adapted and harmonized parts of the service from Merbecke's setting.

These service books may not in themselves be important to Protestants who use nonliturgical forms of worship. Nevertheless, they did much towards establishing the type of church music that was to follow. Plainsong, which was all that Merbecke had to adapt for his *The Booke of Common Praier Noted,* was gradually dying out—slowly in purely liturgical music, less slowly in the English anthem.

Tye contributed to Day's psalter of 1563, and nine tunes by Tallis were contained in Parker's psalter of 1567. Both of these composers resumed their composition in the anthem style when it became apparent that the Protestant order of things was likely to continue.

William Byrd, despite his avowed Catholicism, was made organist of Lincoln Cathedral at the age of twenty-one and transferred to the Chapel Royal eight years later. Although Byrd's accomplishments were mentioned in the last chapter, we must here recall his significant contribution to Protestant church music while continuing his composition of Latin masses and motets.

After the death of Tallis in 1585, Byrd was the only outstanding composer of church music, and even he divided his talents between the sacred and the secular. There was no lack of musical activity, but interest lay chiefly in songs, madrigals, virginal music, and other forms designed for entertainment rather than worship. While church music from the pens of other composers of this period survives, no new ground was broken. The style was generally that of Tye and Tallis without quite reaching the standard of those composers.

During the reigns of James I and Charles I, the Stuarts who followed Elizabeth, the Calvinists and other separatists became a political as well as a religious group, under the general name of Puritans. James I had been brought up in the Calvinistic faith and nearly all of his Scottish subjects were of like persuasion. He and his son were constantly harassed by religious extremists who managed to wind their cause inextricably with political and constitutional issues. The violence which had marked the early days of the reform movement in other lands was not lessened in England by the fact that it had been averted for a hundred years. Bitterness increased steadily during the first Stuart regime (1603–1649).

Only one name stands out among the church musicians of this period —that of *Orlando Gibbons* (1583–1625). Educated as a chorister at King's College, Cambridge, Gibbons became organist of the Chapel Royal under James I and, later, of Westminster Abbey. He wrote much fine music for the English liturgy and many anthems, all marked by the dignity and inspiration of the Latin school. He had the knack, in polyphonic writing, of providing melodious parts for all the voices without permitting them to overlap in such a way as to obscure the words. He sometimes wrote parts for instruments to accompany the choir and, a new departure at that time, as accompaniment for a solo voice. The influence of the Italian operatic composers is seen in his work.

The low point, as far as worship music was concerned, was reached when civil war resulted in victory for the Puritans and the establishment of the Commonwealth in 1649, with Oliver Cromwell as the Protector. The liturgy and the Prayer Book were abolished, choirs dispersed, all organs silenced, and many destroyed. The only singing permitted in churches was that of the metrical psalms, and even they were allowed only in their simplest forms.

Not until this time may the Reformation in England be said to have been consummated. The decline of worship music after Elizabeth, and its disuse during the Commonwealth, constituted a misfortune that broke completely the continuity of English church music. The fine repertory of Tudor days was lost, not to be rediscovered for many years. When music was heard again in churches, it was not built upon what had gone before, but was the product of a new age.

✤ REFERENCES

Psalm and Hymn Tunes, Chorals

Near the back of the music edition of most hymnals is an Index of Composers, Arrangers, and Sources of Tunes. From such indexes of several hymnals, the following list relating to tunes of the Reformation period is compiled.

It is unlikely that any one hymn book will contain all the references, but it will contain many; and the entries, together with the hymn numbers, will enable the interested reader to examine a number of tunes in the particular book he happens to be consulting. The field may be widened by borrowing the tune books of several denominations.

The list is not selective, but has been compiled from sources available to most readers. The dates given are those generally accepted; and when two or more dates follow the name of a psalter or hymnal, they refer to its various editions.

Where melodies have been altered, that fact will generally be noted above the hymn tunes. Harmonies in modern hymnals are seldom the original ones.

Ahle, Johann Rudolph, 1625–1673.
Albert, H., 1604–1651.
Andernach Gesangbuch, 1608.
Anglo-Genevan Psalter, 1556.
As Hymnodus Sacer, Leipzig, 1625.
Ave Hierarchia, 1531.

Bohemian Brethren's *Gesangbuch,* 1539, 1566.
Bourgeois, Loys (or Louis), c. 1523–1600.

Campion, Thomas, 1567–1620.
Catholische Kirchen-Gesäng, Cologne, 1619.
Cölner *Gesangbuch,* 1623.
Cologne *Gesangbuch,* 1619.
Corner's *Gesangbuch,* 1625, 1631.
Corner's *Geistliche Nachtigall,* 1649, 1658.
Crüger, Johann, 1598–1662.

Damon's *Booke of Musicke,* 1591.
Damon's *Psalter* (or *Psalmes*), 1579.
Day's *Psalter* (or *Psalmes*), 1562, 1563, 1564, 1565.
Dowland, John, 1563–1626.
Drei schöne neue geistliche Lieder, Munchen, 1637.
Dresden *Gesangbuch,* 1593.

Ebeling, Johann Georg, c. 1620–1676.
Este's *Psalter* (or *Psalmes*), 1592.

Geistliche Kirchengesäng, Cologne, 1623.

Genevan Psalter, 1542, 1543, 1549, 1551, 1562.
Gesius, Bartholomaus, 1555–1613.
Gibbons, Orlando, 1583–1625.
Görlitz Gesangbuch, 1599.
Goudimel, Claude, c. 1505–1572.
Greiter, M., 1500–1552.
Guidetti's *Directorium Chori,* 1582.

Hassler, Hans Leo, 1564–1612.
Heinlein, Paul, 1626–1686.
Helder, B., 1585–1635.
Hemmets Koral Bok, c. 1539.
Herbst, Martin, 1654–1681.
Hermann, N., 1485–1561.
Hintze, Jakob, 1622–1702.

Katholische Kirchengesänge, 1616.
Kirbye, George, d. 1634.
Knorr's *Neuer Helicon,* Nürnberg, 1684.

Lawes, Henry, 1596–1662.
Leighton, William, c. 1614.
Leisentritt's *Gesangbuch,* 1584.
Llyfr y Psalmau, 1621.
Löwenstern, M. A., von, 1594–1648.

Neumark, G., 1621–1681.
Nicolai, P., 1556–1608.
Nigidius, P., 16th cent.

Peters, C., 1626–1669.
Piae Cantiones, 1582.

Praetorius, Michael, 1571–1621.
Prys's *Llyfr y Psalmau*, 1621.
Psalmes, Edinburgh, 1635.
Psalmes, The cl, Edinburgh, 1615.
Psalteriolum Harmonicum, 1642.
Psalterium Chorale, c. 1500.

Ravenscroft's *Psalter* (or *Psalmes*),
1621.
Regnart, Jacob, 16th cent.

Schein, Johann Hermann, 1586–1630.
Schop, J., d. 1664.
Schumann's *Gesangbuch,* 1539.
Scottish Psalter, 1615, 1635.
Selnecker's *Christliche Psalmen,* 1587.

Seven Sobs of a Sorrowful Soul, 1583,
1585.
Strassburger Kirchengesang-Buch, 1616.

Tallis, Thomas, 1505–1585.
Teschner, Melchior, early 17th cent.
Trutz-Nachtigall, 1649.
Tye, Christopher, c. 1497–1572.

Unitas Fratrum, 1566.

Vollständige Psalmen, 1639.
Vulpius, Melchior, 1560–1616.
Vulpius's *Gesangbuch,* Jena, 1609.

Wolder's *Catechismus Gesangbüch-
lein,* 1598.

Anthems, Motets, etc.

The following choral works are fairly representative of the types of church music composed by musicians who were influenced by the German and English Reformation movements. The references at the end of Chapter IX (intended to illustrate the development of choral writing rather than the influence of any particular religious trend) also list German and English composers who wrote for the reformed churches.

Due to the scarcity of choirs in parish churches, these works were not as widely known during the Reformation period as they are now. They were sung only in large, well-equipped churches, cathedrals, and private chapels.

Asterisks denote extended choral works.

Amner, John—
  He that descended man to be [N]
Batten, Adrian—
  Deliver us, O Lord [F]
  Haste Thee, O God [F]
  ✱*Hear my prayer* [N]
  O praise the Lord [F]
  Sing we merrily unto God [N]
Bull, John—
  *Almighty God, Who by the leading
  of a star* [F]
  In the departure of the Lord [N]
  O Lord, my God [N]
Child, William—
  If the Lord Himself [N]

O pray for the peace of Jerusalem
  [N]
Praise the Lord, O my soul [N]
Sing we merrily [N]
Eccard, Johann—
  From heaven's heights I come to you
  [F]
  Presentation of Christ [S]
  See what affliction [S]
  Sweet Mary to the Temple fares
  [F]
Gesius, Bartholomaus—
  The day is past and over [F]
Gibbons, Orlando—
  Almighty and everlasting God [B]

Almighty God, Who by Thy Son
[F]
Hosanna to the Son of David [B]
*O clap your hands [F]
O God, the King of glory [F]
This is the record of John [F]
Ye that do your Master's will [F]
(An extensive list of Gibbons' works
is to be found in the Novello cat-
alogue.)
Hassler, Hans Leo—
Blessed Savior, our Lord Jesus [S]
Gabriel said unto the shepherds [S]
O God, beneath Thy guiding hand
[S]
King, William—
The Lord is King [N]
Kirbye, George—
O Jesu, look [F]
Le Jeune, Claude—
Dear God, O bless us [S]
Lock (or Locke), Matthew—
In the beginning, O Lord [N]
Lord, let me know mine end [N]
Sing unto the Lord a new song [N]
When the Son of Man shall come
[F]
Parsley, Osbert—
*Morning and Evening Service in G
minor* [F]
Philips, Peter—
The Lord ascendeth [F]
Pilkington, Francis—
High Mighty God [N]
Praetorius, Michael—
Be not dismayed [F]
From heaven on high [S]
Lo, how a rose e'er blooming [S]
Praise God, ye Christians [S]
Sing we now with one accord [S]
*While shepherds watched their
flocks* [S]
Redford, John—
Rejoice in the Lord alway [F]

Rogers, Benjamin—
Behold now, praise the Lord [N]
Lord, who shall dwell [N]
O pray for the peace of Jerusalem
[N]
Teach me, O Lord [N]
Scheidemann, Heinrich—
Awake and sing full gladly [F]
Schütz, Heinrich—
Blessed are the faithful [S]
Christ, be Thine glory [S]
*Christmas Story, The [S]
*German Requiem [S]
He who with weeping soweth [S]
I will praise the Lord [S]
Jesus, our Lord and Master [S]
*Lo, I am the voice of one crying in
the wilderness* [S]
Pharisee and the Publican, The [S]
**Seven Last Words of our dear Re-
deemer and Savior, The* [S]
Song of praise [S]
Sweelinck, J. P.—
*Arise, O ye servants of God (Psalm
139)* [S]
*O Lord God, to Thee be praise
(Psalm 75)* [S]
Tomkins, Thomas—
Great and marvellous [F]
I heard a voice from heaven [N]
O God, wonderful art Thou [F]
O pray for the peace of Jerusalem
[F]
Praise the Lord, O my soul [F]
Weelkes, Thomas—
Alleluia! [F]
Let Thy merciful ears, O Lord [F]
O how amiable [F]
Sing, my soul, to God [F]
Wilbye, John—
*O God, the Rock of my whole
strength* [N]
O Lord, turn not Thy face from me
[N]

II

WORSHIP MUSIC IN
THE AMERICAN COLONIES

✤ LINKS WITH THE OLD COUNTRIES

Lest, on noting the heading of this chapter, the reader is led to say: "Ah! At last we come to something of interest and concern to Americans!" he is reminded that the music of this continent had its beginnings in the same remote past as that of Europe.

We forget, sometimes, that the early colonists were transplanted Europeans, and that their ancestors and ours were also progenitors of present-day Europeans. While we have, in some respects, developed along quite different lines, our basic characteristics and culture have been inherited from the same sources as those of the people of western Europe.

The people who sang plainsong, organum, and conductus were not a race as strange and remote as mythical Martians. The composers and singers of the great polyphonic music, of motets and masses, of madrigals and glees, were not foreigners. They could all be found in our own family trees were we able to trace our ancestry back that far.

An American in New York, a Canadian in Toronto, and an Englishman in London listening to a motet of Byrd, might all say, with equal truth: "This is the music bequeathed to me by my forefathers." Congregations singing a grand old German choral in Cincinnati, Kitchener, or Cologne are all justified in saying: "This is the music of *our* forefathers."

The development of worship music as outlined in the earlier chapters of this book is, therefore, pertinent to a consideration of music on this continent. Much that remains to be said about the development of music in Europe is equally pertinent, for Americans were long dependent upon Europeans for their music.

It is not to be inferred that early settlers were less musical than the cousins they left behind in the old land. What evidence we have is to the contrary. But art develops slowly in a new country. There are more pressing matters to occupy the attention of the people. Land must be cleared, crops sown and harvested, homes and factories built, trade and commerce developed. While people engaged in these strenuous pursuits enjoyed the relaxation of music, they were not prepared to nurture the art. Few of them had enjoyed the amenities of life in Europe, and their taste in music was simple.

It is not likely that many, if any, professional musicians were to be found among the earliest settlers. Life in the colonies was not such as would attract artists. Nor would their presence be tolerated. Hard work was the order of the day, and those engaged in wresting a livelihood from virgin fields and forests would accord no place to livers of soft lives. Amateur musicians were welcomed at social gatherings, but they were obliged to earn their living in the workaday world.

While the position of the musician improved somewhat in succeeding generations, there was still no place for the composer who would make a significant contribution to the development of music. Composers, like other mortals, must live; and, in order to do so, they must have a public willing to support them. Even in Europe, the percentage of people able to appreciate and willing to encourage advanced music was small. The percentage in America was even smaller, since its population was drawn largely from the less cultured segment of European society. There were no patrons in America to support and encourage artists, no wealthy church to maintain institutions of art and learning. This "land of opportunity" offered no opportunity for a potential native Beethoven or Wagner. Nearly three centuries elapsed before Americans awoke to the presence of musical genius within their gates.

In the next few chapters, then, our comments on music in North America must be concerned not with any major developments made here, but with the uses made of developments that were taking place in Europe, and which were to determine the trend of American music.

✤ ROMAN CATHOLIC SETTLEMENTS

The Spaniards who, as early as the 1520's, attempted to form settlements in what we know as Florida and the southwestern United States, were, of course, Catholics. Priests always accompanied explorers and conquerors on their expeditions, and it is reasonable to suppose that the daily masses were sung whenever feasible.

The music would be simple. The celebrant would sing his part well enough (for most of the clergy who volunteered for colonial service were capable men), and the responses would be sung in simple plainsong when they were sung at all. Perhaps some of the more musical of the congregation might attempt organum or some other form of part singing, but that was probably unusual. Some Latin hymns might also be sung in unison at times.

Although Spanish occupation of parts of this continent continued for nearly three centuries (Florida remained Spanish until 1819), little remains of their culture. No waves of immigration came from Spain as from other European countries. There were no communities of Spaniards left here to be assimilated with other racial groups into the American body politic.

The French who, after nearly three quarters of a century of exploration, founded settlements in Quebec and Acadia (Nova Scotia) in the first decade of the seventeenth century, established the Catholic church in those regions. Like the Spaniards in the south, they were accompanied by capable priests who celebrated sung masses as well as conditions permitted. Simple plainsong and Latin hymns sung in unison constituted their worship music for a long time.

Unlike the Spaniards, however, the French were settlers in the true sense of the word. Large numbers were to emigrate to New France with the intention of making a permanent home there. As the colony grew and flourished, churches were built; and, in time, those of Quebec and Montreal (the chief centers) compared favorably with those in the homeland. At one time the French occupied all eastern Canada, and that part of what is now the United States from Lake Superior to the Gulf of Mexico. Strong traces of their culture remain in Louisiana, and the province of Quebec is predominantly French. Because their religion, language, and culture have made them a people apart, they have had little influence upon the cultural life of their fellow-Canadians, and none at all on that of Americans.

One other Catholic settlement must be mentioned: that established by Lord Baltimore in Maryland in 1634, as a refuge for Catholics who were undergoing persecution in England. It remained a purely Catholic colony for only a very brief period, although most of the original colonists remained. An influx of Protestants led to strife hardly less bitter and violent than had been experienced in the old country. In spite of early hostility, it was in Maryland that Catholics and Protestants first learned to live and work peaceably together for the common good.

❖ PROTESTANT COMMUNITIES

The Protestant groups, to whom our minds first turn when we are thinking of our early American forebears, came chiefly from England.

Transient settlers were the French Huguenots who, in the 1560's, sought to establish colonies in parts of Florida and South Carolina in rivalry with the Spanish. Their stay was too brief to have made any impression.

The first permanent English settlement was that of Jamestown, Virginia, in 1607. The leaders of the colonists were all loyal subjects of the king, as they had been of Queen Elizabeth, and their religion was that of the established Church of England. Apparently not all settlers were enthusiastic churchgoers, for, in 1610, it was considered necessary to pass a law making attendance at church services compulsory. (The law was not strictly enforced for long.)

It is regrettable that records are concerned with the all-important problem of making a living to the exclusion of such things as religion and music. There would almost certainly be some in the community who possessed and could play musical instruments. These amateurs would be centers of social gatherings where people would sing songs learned in the homeland and dance to whatever tunes the memory and skill of the musicians made possible.

The church services, however, would be almost entirely unmusical. The Prayer Book and the Anglican liturgy were less than sixty years old, too new to have acquired the tradition that made the Latin liturgy familiar to Catholics from early childhood. Many, if not most, of the colonists came from parishes that did not boast choirs, and where little attempt was made to follow the services exactly as the Act of Uniformity directed. Probably few in the Virginia settlement had heard the liturgy sung properly by the choir of a cathedral or fashionable parish church. Prescribed forms of worship distinguished the services from those of the Nonconformists, but there were no facilities for taking advantage of the possibilities for music that the liturgy provided.

Singing at church services was confined to the metrical psalm which, although not officially prescribed by the Church of England, had achieved respectability through popular acceptance. The paraphrases were those of Sternhold and Hopkins. The tunes used would be those familiar to the largest numbers of settlers. Perhaps the tunes from Day's psalters of

1561 and 1562 were most popular; but some of the community might have known and introduced tunes from the newer books of Este (1592) and Alison (1599).

At about the same time that the Jamestown settlement was being established, a number of separatists from the Church of England formed a congregation at Scrooby, Nottinghamshire, England. The lot of Nonconformists in England was not pleasant; and in 1608 the Scrooby group decided to emigrate to Holland. They little thought that they were taking the first step of a journey that would eventually lead them to the New World.

During their eight years in Holland, they produced (through the efforts of their minister, Henry Ainsworth) a new psalter: the *Book of Psalms englished both in prose and metre.* This collection differed from its English predecessors chiefly in the variety of meters. Most paraphrases had been in Long Meter (8.8.8.8., or eight syllables to each line) or Common Meter (8.6.8.6.). Consequently, most tunes had been devised to fit these meters. To provide thirty-nine tunes that could be sung to his paraphrases in other than the conventional forms, Ainsworth supplemented English melodies with others drawn chiefly from Dutch and French sources.

When the group from Holland, together with Pilgrims from the south of England, sailed on the *Mayflower* to America in 1620, it was Ainsworth's book they took with them, and it served them in their new home for twenty years.

The group headed by John Endicott, which settled at Salem in 1628 (to be known as the Massachusetts Bay Colony), were Puritans in the sense that they disapproved of the doctrines, liturgy, and ritual of the Church of England; yet they considered themselves dissenters rather than separatists, reluctant to surrender completely their membership and rights in the established church. Nevertheless, their lack of recognition by and connection with the Church of England soon resulted in their becoming Independents, or Congregationalists.

The Massachusetts Bay settlers may have been familiar with Ainsworth's psalter; but it is more probable that they used the Sternhold and Hopkins version, with which they would be even more familiar, to tunes from Day's books. Later settlers may have introduced tunes from the psalm books of Este and Ravenscroft.

Sad to say, the harsh treatment they had received in England did not teach the settlers at Cape Cod and Massachusetts Bay to be merciful to dissenters within their own groups. Their strict code, and the authoritarian attitude of their leaders, were never exceeded by the Roman church in its most despotic periods. The banishment of Roger Williams, the trial for sedition of Anne Hutchinson, the fining and banishment of

Baptists, the hanging of Quakers are only a few examples of cruel intolerance familiar to all who know early American history.

The formation of new religious groups, which was both the provocation and the result of Puritan harshness, together with the coming of the Dutch to what is now New York and the settlement of Swedes on the Delaware River, introduced new elements into Protestant worship. While the divergences were not great at the time, they were to have their effects upon future generations.

✤ THE BAY PSALM BOOK

Although there was no dearth of psalm books, the New England Puritans seemed to feel the need of yet another. The Ainsworth book, which had been brought over by the Pilgrim Fathers, had no appeal, sentimental or otherwise, for other groups of colonists. The Sternhold and Hopkins version may have become suspect because of its acceptance by members of the established church. Or perhaps all concerned would have been content to get along with the old psalm books had not three comparatively newcomers, John Eliot, Thomas Weld, and Richard Mather, decided to compile a new one. Whether these three clergymen undertook the work by invitation or on their own initiative is not known. The important fact is that, in 1640, their book appeared: *The Whole Booke of Psalmes faithfully translated into English Metre, whereunto is prefixed a discourse declaring not only the lawfullness, but also the necessity of the heavenly Ordinance of singing Scripture Psalms in the Churches of God.*

The "Bay Psalm Book," as the joint effort became known, had many defects. The chief purpose of the compilers was accuracy; that is, a close and faithful following of the words of the biblical version. This they achieved at the expense of beauty and good taste. From the point of view of a poet, it would be an understatement to describe the book as being uninspired.

Not only were tunes omitted, but no attempt was made to write the verses in such a fashion that all of them could be sung to old tunes. Users were referred to tunes in Ravenscroft's *The Whole Book of Psalms;* but this reference was of no help to those who did not possess the tune book or, possessing it, could not reconcile the meters of the tunes to the meters of some of the paraphrases.

As a direct result of the Bay Psalm Book, singing of metrical psalms deteriorated. Some tunes were forgotten because they could not be used with the new psalter, others were distorted and garbled by attempts to make them fit verses regardless of irregularities of meter.

In spite of the defects of the Bay Psalm Book, it had a remarkable history. It was the first complete book published in the colonies and it was as popular in the old country as it was in America. It ran to seventy editions in America, the last in 1773 (an astonishing run of one hundred and thirty-three years); eighteen editions in England, the last in 1754; and twenty-two editions in Scotland, the last in 1759.

Its popularity in America can be explained partly because of the fact that the Puritans discouraged (sometimes forcibly) the use of any other psalter, partly because its publication coincided with a prohibition of secular music. Its wide acceptance in England and Scotland can only be attributed to lack of discrimination on the part of many Nonconformists and stubborn resentment towards better versions on the grounds that they were recognized to some extent by the state church.

It was not until the ninth edition in 1698 that thirteen tunes, taken from Playford's *Introduction to the Skill of Musick,* were incorporated into the Bay Psalm Book. This edition also made history as the first book containing music to be printed in the colonies.

12

The

BAROQUE PERIOD

✤ THE NATURE OF BAROQUE MUSIC

The word "baroque," as originally used in connection with architecture, referred to a style marked by grandiosity, elaboration of design, and freedom of form. It has become customary to speak of painting and music of the period 1600–1750 as baroque; for, although the course of the arts cannot be said to have run parallel with that of architecture, it was marked by many of the same general characteristics.

Because of its extravagances and, in many cases, its absurdities, "baroque" was long a derogatory term, especially as used by the admirers of the earlier classic forms; but an impartial appraisal of the style by later generations has awakened an appreciation of its many merits.

It was less a revolt against the old, austere forms than an expression of the spirit of a new age, an age of ostentation, of lavishness and spectacular effects.

The tendency to depart from the polyphonic forms of music in the seventeenth century has been mentioned. The chordal style of composition, the movement towards a new concept of tonality that made for freer use of modulation and chromatics, were tentative steps that were to lead, eventually, to the baroque style. When we spoke of certain German composers bridging the gap between the polyphonists of Palestrina's time and Bach, we might have said that these musicians were establishing the baroque school in Germany.

Although the development of baroque music was primarily a secular movement, it influenced church music of the time and for centuries to come.

It had its beginnings in Italian opera at about the end of the sixteenth century. Many of its characteristics can be traced to innovations by Claudio Monteverdi (1567–1643) and his immediate followers. The recitative, the solo song and instrumental accompaniment were among the features that were soon to become familiar in secular and church music alike. Music on a grand scale for public entertainment, the interest of the nobility and the wealthy, the background of lavishly appointed drawing-rooms and ballrooms, make very significant mention of periods of study of foreign musicians in Italy.

The predomination of the homophonic style of music was the direct result of the rising popularity of recitative and aria. Interest was centered on one voice. The accompaniment was designed to support and enhance the solo voice rather than to compete with or distract from it. Even in choral passages, blocks of chords supporting the principal melody were found to produce more sensational *forte* effects than a number of interwoven melodic parts.

Contrapuntal passages were written in the newer style, and chords are to be found in polyphonic music; but, whereas chords in polyphonic music were incidental, so to speak, the result of several independent voices combining at certain points, in the newer style the voices became subordinate to predetermined harmonies and their freedom was restricted to sounds having definite relations to those harmonies.

Instrumental music received more attention from serious composers. Apart from their importance as members of the orchestra to accompany opera, certain instruments were developed as solo instruments. The floridness that marked vocal music was applied to the harpsichord by Domenico Scarlatti (1685–1757), François Couperin (1668–1733), and Jean Philippe Rameau (1683–1764); and to the stringed instruments by Arcangelo Corelli (1653–1713), and Antonio Vivaldi (c. 1680–1743).

The unaccompanied church music of the past gave way to compositions in which voices and instruments were wedded. The prejudice against instrumental music in church was broken down and, no doubt, an increase in the skill of the performers helped to break it down.

While the influence of the church modes remained strong, our present major and minor scales, with their more definite tonal centers, were quickly developed and much used.

As was discussed on pages 30–34, each of the church modes had its distinctive character. If one counts the number of tones from the beginning note to the other degrees of the scale, he finds that no two modes are identical. Moreover, the dominant does not always fall on the same degree of the scale.

In the newer tonality, every major and minor scale was, and is, constructed exactly like every other major and minor scale, and the dominant is always the perfect fifth above the tonic or starting note. One may change to another key, exactly like the original key in construction, by the simple expedient of establishing the new key through its dominant chord. (Because of the system of tuning, it was not possible to modulate extensively on keyboard instruments, but more will be said of that later.)

Uniform construction of scales meant that chords built on various degrees of the scale were the same in all keys. Instead of simultaneous progressions of single voices, composers concentrated on progressions of chords. Certain successions were favored, and parts must move in such a way as to sound the notes of a suitable succeeding chord, even if the progression was not melodious. In homophonic music, one often notices that a part repeats a single note several times, something that rarely occurred in polyphonic music in which each part was made as melodious as possible.

Prior to the baroque period, the most gifted composers had lavished their best on church music, since in that field lay the greatest opportunities. The *nuove musiche,* or " new music," shifted the emphasis to the secular. Composers kept their ears attuned to popular taste. It was from the public, rather than from the church, that the greatest rewards could be expected. There were few musicians writing exclusively for the church; and when they did turn their attention to worship music, it was natural that they should retain the same style and devices they used in the secular field.

The opera and the masque had their corresponding forms in the oratorio and the cantata.

The oratorio may be described as an opera without staging, costumes, or scenery. It is dramatic in form, requiring a large chorus, orchestra, and soloists for the character parts. Recitatives and florid arias with instrumental accompaniment abound for the soloists, and the chorus effects are massive. When, as is usually the case, the subject is a biblical one, the oratorio may be considered as religious, but scarcely as liturgical or worship music, since it could not be fitted into a church service.

The cantata is an oratorio on a small scale. It was originally secular, sometimes for only one voice with accompaniment. It was very popular in Italy and France and was cultivated by the best composers of the seventeenth century. Later, the sacred cantata was developed. In Germany it partook of the nature of worship music in that it was intended to induce an atmosphere of devotion, and it was interspersed with familiar chorals which the congregation often sang with the choir.

The anthem and the sung parts of the liturgy were no less affected by the baroque style. The austere and impersonal characteristics of the earlier motet and mass, so long insisted upon by ecclesiastical authorities and so greatly admired by purists of the present day, gave way to all the artifices of secular music.

Even the staid metrical psalm was not untouched by the spirit of the age, although, in this case, the attempt to transform the simple, straightforward melodies into florid passages was the work of amateurs and merely resulted in disfigurement.

Early baroque church music in Italy, while important because of its influence on worship music elsewhere, is not in itself important as far as modern Protestant church usage is concerned. Although the finest operatic composers of the time made contributions, and there was a surprisingly wide acceptance of *nuove musiche* in Italian churches, very little of it is heard today except, perhaps, the *Stabat Mater* by Pergolesi.

It may be more interesting and profitable, then, to review the development of baroque music in areas where it more directly affected Protestant church music.

✤ BAROQUE CHURCH MUSIC IN ENGLAND

The new era of worship music began in England after the restoration of the monarchy in 1660. It came about not by design but by force of circumstances.

The Commonwealth, although only of eleven years' duration, had brought about a clean break with the past. The peak of polyphonic music had been reached nearly half a century before the Puritan régime, and there had been a tendency to shift from modal music to a type that was a dim foreshadowing of modern harmony. Nevertheless, the old forms might have lingered longer had not the cessation of all church music except the metrical psalms broken continuity with the past.

For it must be remembered that church musicians, as well as church music, disappeared under the Commonwealth. Organists and choirmasters were unemployed; and many, becoming involved in politics (for it was difficult to remain neutral), were lost permanently to music. The choirs of cathedrals, chapels, and collegiate and parish churches were disbanded. There were active composers, for the Puritans were not averse to music as long as it was not associated with anything that would offend public morals; but worship music was a barren field for composition.

The re-establishment of the royal court under Charles II was accompanied by a reaction from the prim, cautious ways of the Puritans. Court and social life became gay and extravagant. There was much music; but, unlike Tudor times, art was not cultivated so much for itself as for a setting for the pomp and luxury of the social scene.

One of the first moves was an attempt to restore the elaborate cathedral services. This was more easily proposed than accomplished. Organists and choirmasters had to be found, and, while suitable men were available for the more important posts, many of the most capable organists of pre-Commonwealth days were missing. Some organs had been damaged and some destroyed by fanatics who had carried their prejudice farther than Cromwell intended they should.

But the most serious lack was that of choristers. Many of the men who had formerly sung in choirs had died or moved away; the voices of many others had deteriorated with age and disuse. There was not a single soprano available, since the voices of all former choir boys had changed. It is no overnight task to select boy choristers, cultivate their voices, and make them familiar with a liturgical service. Nor was there any inducement for parents to offer their children for cathedral service except that, in many cases, it would mean one mouth less to feed at home. Little thought was expended on the housing, nourishment, and education of choir boys.

Even the Chapel Royal, the most favored of institutions, had its difficulties. Captain Henry Cooke, who had once been a choir boy at the Chapel and later fought with the Royalist forces during the civil war, returned as master of the children. Only five former members of the choir returned—all of them men, of course. In recruiting boys, the Chapel Royal was in a more fortunate position than the cathedrals and collegiate churches. Service in the royal household, where living conditions were more tolerable than elsewhere, was more attractive; and Captain Cooke had the added privilege of going from cathedral to cathedral demanding the services of boys who had been trained by other choirmasters.

Education at the Chapel Royal was sketchy in all but one subject—music. The youths were taught not only to sing the service but to play instruments. The most talented were taught composition, and three of Captain Cooke's boys, Pelham Humfrey, John Blow, and Henry Purcell were to rank among the foremost composers of their generation.

Accompanied anthems and settings of the liturgy became the order of the day. The works of the older composers, such as Tallis and Byrd, were still sung; but a great many contemporary composers, good, bad, and indifferent, were busy supplying music that brought into play not only the organ but the orchestra. King Charles was proud of his string orchestra which, on many occasions, played with the choir of the Chapel

Royal, and was often augmented by other instruments for special occasions.

Few cathedrals could rival the Chapel Royal in providing orchestral accompaniments, but they did the best they could.

No such changes took place in the smaller parish and rural churches. The form of service prescribed by the Prayer Book was restored but, as in pre-Commonwealth days, it was generally said rather than sung. The music was that of the metrical psalms. Independent and Presbyterian churches were less active because of persecution, but the same paraphrases used by them were used in the Church of England.

Few small churches had ever had choirs, and the discouragement of such frivolities by the Puritans had not affected the music in such places. The wanton destruction of organs did make a difference, however. Many parish churches that had boasted organs (often poorly played) now had to get along without them. Organs were expensive and not easily replaced.

The publisher, Playford, sought to encourage singing in smaller churches by issuing, in 1671, *Psalms and Hymns in Solemn Music of four parts on the Common Tunes to the Psalms in Metre: Used in Parish Churches.* No doubt these settings were sung as anthems in some churches where four parts could be mustered, and perhaps some simple anthems were also sung; but the number of churches occupying the intermediate position between elaborate cathedral settings and plain, said services must have been relatively small.

If music in parish churches did not flourish, there were composers active in the creation of cathedral music that would find an important place in the parish churches of the future.

Henry Purcell (1658–1695) was one of the finest and certainly the most versatile composer of his time, and perhaps the greatest English composer of any age.

The first impressions of Purcell's music are of vitality and spontaneity. There is nothing labored about it, and its melodies attract the ear and remain in the listener's memory. Although his music can scarcely be considered a development or continuation of the style of his predecessors, he was influenced to no little extent by the traditions of English church musicians. He belongs to the newer school which was to reach a high peak with Bach and Handel; and he was well acquainted with and influenced by the works of Lully in France and Corelli in Italy, especially in his compositions for secular use.

Purcell was a prolific composer. If his church music seems a little theatrical compared with that of earlier generations, he was but following the general trend of his time. He had a remarkable skill in wedding words to music in such a way that they seemed predestined for each other.

His church works combined much of the polyphonic style with solid blocks of chords so well suited to the instrumental accompaniment (as in *Thy Word is a lantern*). Some of his solo passages are quite florid, with accompaniments such as had previously been considered only for operatic works (as in *Declare His honor*).

He was fond of verse anthems, consisting of passages for solo voices or quartets alternating with passages for full chorus and accompaniment. Not all of his anthems are well integrated. Some sections seem to have little to do with others, and there is lacking a smooth transition from one to another. In one of his best known anthems, *Rejoice in the Lord alway* (sometimes known as the Bell Anthem) the instrumental introduction and interludes have no definite relation to the anthem proper, either in style or time, and nothing is lost by omitting them.

Purcell was a master at developing the ground bass: that is, a phrase repeated over and over again in the bass, on which are superimposed melodic and harmonic variations in a manner that forms a continuous whole without any obvious dependence on the bass. His *Evening Hymn* is based on twenty-four repetitions of a short bass passage.

One wonders to what heights Purcell might have risen had he not died at the early age of thirty-six. Much of his music, and especially his church music, is as fresh and vigorous to modern ears as it was in his own day.

Pelham Humfrey (1647–1674) was among the very first boys to join the Chapel Royal after its re-establishment. By the time he was seventeen, his anthems were being sung. He was sent to France and Italy by Charles II, whose exile on the continent had led to his admiration of the dramatic, sometimes extravagant and always superficial, style of music that was in vogue there.

Humfrey seems to have acquired a foreign, foppish manner and a vanity that inclined him to disparage all musical efforts but his own.

Little of his music remains, since he died at the age of twenty-seven, before he had reached his full flower. Humfrey's influence remains, however, partly in the music of Purcell, who studied with him, and in works of other composers, which might never have been written without Humfrey's teaching and guidance.

John Blow (1648–1708), sometime organist of the Chapel Royal and Westminster Abbey, Michael Wise (1648–1687) a gentleman of the Chapel Royal and organist of Salisbury and St. Paul's (London) Cathedrals, and William Turner (1651–1740), who was a chorister all his life, all began their musical careers as choir boys under Captain Cooke and became noted composers of their generation.

During the last half of the seventeenth century, there was an influx of foreign musicians to England. After the death of Purcell, composition languished somewhat, and it seemed desirable to import music and musicians, especially in the secular field, who could supply the native lack.

Adult male sopranos began to appear in opera and concerts.

In the sixteenth century, the Spaniards had discovered a method whereby men could sing the soprano range, achieving good tone, by means of falsetto. The Sistine Choir of Rome used such singers, and soon after began to insure the supply of adult male sopranos (*castrati*) by means of a surgical operation which deprived them of some adult masculine qualities, including the changing of the voice. It was a convenient arrangement from a choirmaster's point of view, since it spared him the necessity of constantly replacing boys whose voices "broke" just when they had reached the period of their greatest usefulness.

Many operatic composers wrote the principal men's parts for men sopranos, who developed an amazing technic and virtuosity, and a vanity that would make the temperamental prima donna of today an amiable creature by comparison.

Male altos had always had their places in church choirs, the word "alto" meaning the highest part for a man's voice. They were, rarely, boys with unchanged voices; but generally men who, through long practice, had learned to retain the same quality and lower register of their boyish voices after their natural voices had become tenor or bass. Male altos, or counter-tenors as they are often called, are still important in choirs of boys and men in England and elsewhere. Their voices blend admirably with those of boy sopranos, the quality enables relatively few of them to balance the other parts, and they are capable of long service.

The large number of foreign musicians, their predilection for Italian operatic forms, the demand of male sopranos for more and more florid parts that would enable them to hold the center of the stage, resulted in radical changes in the music of England, changes that were to be reflected to a large extent in church music.

Arias of the period were so difficult and florid that some of them are beyond the capabilities of many good singers of the present time. There can be no objection to solos as long as they contribute to the whole musical work, but in the late seventeenth and early eighteenth centuries, the solo was the principal work. One often feels that the orchestra and chorus were present on sufferance, and with the stipulation that they did not detract from the soloist.

Purcell was competent to deal with the newer developments as we have remarked. Perhaps Humfrey, too, might have carried the newer trends so far forward as to offer serious competition to foreign musicians who were finding England a happy hunting ground. But both of these gifted men died before they reached their prime, and there remained no English composers with sufficient genius to carry on their work.

Of the foreign musicians who dominated English music at this period, only one made a worthwhile and lasting contribution.

George Frederic Handel (1685–1759) was a native of Halle, Saxony, and came to London in 1710, at the age of twenty-five. He showed a remarkable aptitude for music as a child, although his parents opposed the notion of his becoming a professional musician.

As a young man, he was a violinist in the orchestra of the opera house at Hamburg for a while, then went to Italy for further study. He became an accomplished harpsichordist and organist and learned thoroughly the Italian style of music, which was to be so prominent in all his composition.

Returning home, he became director of music at the court of George, Elector of Hanover. Life must have been very dull there for a self-willed, ambitious young man who had tasted the pleasures of Italian society and musical circles. Always an opportunist, he longed for a field in which to display and develop his talents, and London seemed to offer the most rewarding opportunities.

Englishmen have always reserved a warm spot in their hearts for Handel. He is remembered by most as a German-turned-English composer of sacred music. He never was a German as far as his style of music was concerned, and he never wrote any typically English music. He was a product of the Italian school, and remained so all his life. He was primarily a composer of secular music, turning to oratorio only when other fields ceased to be lucrative.

After a year in England, followed by a year at the court of the Elector, he again sought leave of absence and returned to London. Evidently he had no intention of returning to his job, and he was still in London when, much to his embarrassment, his employer became King George I of England. Fortunately, the king was mollified in time and forgave his musician's dereliction.

A protégé first of Queen Anne, then of King George, a friend of the nobility, a dominant figure among musicians, and a general favorite with concertgoers, Handel was for a number of years richly rewarded for his work. Concert halls were to be found all over London, and opera in the Italian style was immensely popular. Handel was kept busy writing operas, rehearsing singers, persuading soloists who had caught the public fancy to sing for him, and acting as comanager.

Handel was not without rivals in the production of opera, and it is not surprising that disloyalty among some of his friends and singers, and jealousy on the part of his competitors, led to adversities. Moreover, the popularity of Italian opera began to wane and Handel, unlike some of his rivals, stubbornly refused to adapt his composition to changing tastes.

In 1718, he was appointed *Kapellmeister* to the Duke of Chandos, who had a large estate and private chapel near Edgware. Here he composed some excellent church music, known as the Chandos anthems, and, among other things, a musical play called *Esther*.

Had he been satisfied to carry out his duties as a member of the duke's household, he might have kept busy, avoided disappointments, and still written the music for which he remains famous. But he was not temperamentally suited to a quiet life, and his obstinacy was such that he would not recognize the decline of Italian opera.

The reverses which he suffered led to his composition of oratorios. *Deborah* was written because he needed money badly enough to pander a little to changing tastes, and because oratorio was the only form of entertainment permitted at the Opera in Lent.

From that time on, although he stubbornly persisted in writing opera, his greatest success was in the field of oratorio. His most famous was, of course, the *Messiah,* which remains to this day the most frequently performed oratorio.

The *Messiah* is not so much greater than some of Handel's other oratorios as its popularity might indicate. It owes its pre-eminence to its subject, to its familiar text from the English Bible, and the fact that it is the most dramatic of Handel's works, sacred or secular. Those who decry the use of operatic music in church forget that some parts of the *Messiah,* which familiarity and tradition have sanctified as great and appropriate religious music, were as dramatic and operatic as anything could possibly be at the time they were written.

If Handel had written nothing else, the *Messiah* would have marked him as a musician who left a great heritage to church music; but in addition to many secular and instrumental works, he wrote twenty-six other oratorios (some of which should be heard oftener than they are) and a number of anthems.

✣ THE BAROQUE PERIOD IN GERMANY

Church music in Germany was not subject to the interruptions and sudden changes that took place in England. The Thirty Years' War (1618–1648), violent and disrupting though it was, could not destroy the firmly established tradition of Lutheran church music. Protestantism suffered reverses in many areas, but there were always large sections of the country where it flourished.

Nor was German church music dominated by Italian operatic forms. The large cities and the courts attracted a great many French and Italian musicians, mostly second-rate, who first created, then sought to satisfy, the public demand for opera. Native composers, however, never did write what amounted to a combination of operatic music and sacred words. Thanks to the continuity of the Lutheran tradition, there did not exist that vacuum which the Puritan influence had created in England, and there was less dependence upon composers whose first love was the opera.

Church music was not uninfluenced by the baroque style: indeed, German musicians who had studied in Italy began to apply the newer ideas to their composition years before the heyday of Italian opera in Germany. But the evolution, while steady, was gradual and unspectacular. Instead of subordinating church music to the operatic, the best composers selected what was fitting and appropriate from the secular field and adapted it to the requirements of church music, with no harmful results to either.

Heinrich Schütz, whose accomplishments were mentioned earlier, was the greatest writer of German choral music before Bach. Schütz wrote some opera, but he excelled in his Passion music. He used some devices borrowed from the opera, notably the recitative, but he was not sufficiently carried away by them to forsake the earnest simplicity which enhances religious music. Character parts were allotted to soloists, and many of the choruses were dramatic. There was no instrumental accompaniment except, perhaps, that of the organ.

Late in the seventeenth century, after Schütz, the texts for Passion music ceased to be strictly scriptural or liturgical. Narratives and dialogues were generally drawn from scriptural sources, but there was incorporated a great deal of verse that was appropriate to the theme or action being treated. Much of this verse was sung by the choir, but some was in the form of chorals sung by the congregation. Instrumental accompaniment, and even more dramatic choruses and arias appeared; yet, in spite of the fact that Passion music became, in effect, oratorio, it remained devotional.

The church cantata, intended primarily for worship music, was developed greatly during this period. It varied somewhat in form, sometimes using mostly solo voices, sometimes the entire choir, and being accompanied by a small orchestra or the organ, or both. It generally contained at least one choral for congregational singing. The cantata was of from ten to thirty-five minutes' duration, and was sung before the sermon in the Lutheran church. Its theme was generally that of the liturgical subject of the day.

Smaller forms, like the motet, were in use, but the more serious writers seemed to prefer the cantata as an outlet for their creative gifts.

Most of the great names between Schütz and Bach are those of organists and composers of organ music, and more will be said of them later in this chapter. There were, however, sound but less renowned writers who were concerned with the development of choral music: Reinhard

Keiser (1673–1739), Georg Teleman (1681–1767), Karl Graun (1698–1771), Johann Eberlin (1702–1762), and others.

Johann Sebastian Bach (1685–1750) brought the baroque style to its highest point of development.

He was born in Eisenach, in central Germany, in the same year that Handel was born. Although he studied with his father and, later, his elder brother, learning to play the violin, harpsichord, and organ, and singing as a boy soprano, his greatest accomplishments were self-taught. As a result of his studies and the stirrings of his creative mind, Bach envisioned possibilities which no teacher could have pointed out to him. Having learned all there was to be learned, he made that a point of departure.

Bach was just ten years old when his parents died, and he went to school at Ohrdruf, where his brother was organist. It was a Lutheran school; and the training there, added to the strong Lutheran background of the Bach family, might be said to have predestined Johann as primarily a church musician.

At the age of eighteen, he was appointed organist at the New Church in Arnstadt. Here he was constantly in trouble with the church authorities. He hated training the choir, he long overstayed a leave of absence granted him in order that he might go to Lübeck to hear Buxtehude, and he shocked his staid congregation by a style of organ playing that was beyond their powers to appreciate. His resignation, after four years of service, caused no regrets.

In 1707 and 1708, he was organist at Mühlhausen. It was there that he wrote his only cantata published during his lifetime: *Gott ist mein König*.

Bach reached maturity as a composer during his service at the court of Weimar during the years 1708–1717. His position was that of court organist and chamber musician. He perfected his playing on the organ and harpsichord and continued his study. (Like most masters, he ever remained a student.) Some of his finest organ works were composed during this period, and he wrote many cantatas for services in the chapel.

While Handel at the same age was an important figure, Bach's status was that of a servant. He wore the duke's livery, and enjoyed no privileges. His master took him on several short journeys, giving Bach opportunities of displaying his skill and increasing his fame as an organist. But the duke was not seeking to honor his musician as much as he was showing off a valuable possession.

Bach had several offers of other positions and probably would have left Weimar before he did had he not feared the duke's wrath. As it was, he was placed under arrest for a month when he finally asked leave to resign in 1717.

His new employer, Prince Leopold of Anhalt-Cöthen, treated Bach more as a friend than a servant; and in such a happy environment Johann Sebastian wrote some of his gayest and most lively music. Unfortunately, during his stay at Cöthen (1717–1723), Bach ceased to be a church musician, for the religion of the principality was Calvinism. Only the plainest hymn tunes were sung in the chapel: there were no cantatas to be written, no chorals to be made subjects of improvisation. Ironically, one of the foremost organists of his day had no organ of his own on which to play. His only public appearances as an organist came as the result of invitations to play in neighboring towns.

His compositions for orchestra, violin, and harpsichord, his development of keyboard technic, and his exploration of the possibilities of the tempered scale, important though they were, are not pertinent to a discussion of church music.

Partly because there was no Lutheran school in Cöthen to which he could send his children and, doubtless, because he was a church musician at heart and longed for the organ loft, Bach applied for the position of cantor at the *Thomasschule* in Leipzig. It is hard for us to imagine any committee failing to jump at the chance of securing Bach's services, but he was actually the third choice for the position, being appointed only after the two leading candidates found it impossible to accept.

Bach's duties included the training of the singers for the choirs of the four principal churches of Leipzig (a task which he disliked and often neglected), the supplying of a cantata for the *Thomaskirche* and *Nikolaikirche* on alternate Sundays, and the arrangement of music for services in both churches.

This was his greatest productive period. Countless cantatas were written for the church services, some of them put aside after their first performance, never to be heard again; five Passions, of which only the first and last (the *St. John* and the *St. Matthew*) survive; a few chorals and many harmonizations of chorals; most of the choral-preludes; and the *Mass in B minor,* which was never performed in its entirety during Bach's lifetime.

During most of his twenty-seven years at Leipzig, he was indefatigable as an organist, choirmaster, and teacher, gaining fame in all fields; yet, in addition to duties that would have exhausted the energies of a lesser man, he was prolific as a composer. He was never tempted into the field of opera ("pretty tunes," he called it), but used his gifts principally in building the immense structure of Lutheran church and organ music that surpasses all his other works, splendid as those works are admitted to be.

Bach was a simple, humble man. His music was composed and performed, not for self-aggrandizement but for service—service to his church and service to music. His career attests to his modesty. A man of his gifts need not have lived his life in comparative obscurity had he desired otherwise. His solid, Lutheran background is seldom obscured in his music. Again and again he turns to the simple choral for inspiration, not only in his vocal music but in his organ music as well. He beautifies, enriches, and elaborates it without sacrificing its essential simplicity. In every form that he used, and he invented few of his own, he began where other composers had left off, carrying the development to a point beyond the imagination and, at times, beyond the comprehension of his contemporaries.

The last few years of Bach's life contained elements of tragedy. It is not unusual for a genius to lose patience with the less inspired people with and for whom he works, and Bach was no exception. His misunderstandings with his employers placed his position in jeopardy on many occasions. During the last year, when he was ill and became blind, he must have known that the officials were impatient to replace him. When he died, on July 28, 1750, his successor was appointed before the funeral.

But what must have saddened him more than anything else was the fact that younger musicians, his own sons among them, were tiring of his style of music. No doubt they considered him "old-fashioned," not discerning that, far from belonging to a past generation, he was generations ahead of his time as far as music was concerned.

In fairness, it must be pointed out that Bach's works were not widely known. Only as an organist had he gained fame, and the art of a performer is transitory. Very few of his compositions were published. Perhaps few of his organ works were played by anyone but himself; and his vocal compositions, written chiefly for church use, were laid aside in manuscript form until they should be required again.

Bach and, indeed, most of his German predecessors and contemporaries, had little influence on Protestant church music outside Germany until long after they had passed on. For nearly a century, the manuscripts of works that make the name of Bach venerated among musicians lay gathering dust. One wonders if one of his successors at the *Thomaskirche* may have occasionally leafed through the pile of old music and, finding something that caught his fancy, revived briefly a cantata or a motet. Doubtless many were lost or destroyed, and we may be grateful for the rediscovery of so many after years of disuse.

✣ CHORALS, PSALMS, AND HYMNS

While the great musicians of the baroque period were developing the oratorio and the cantata, the anthem and the motet, worship music for the congregation was not being neglected. Perhaps psalmody and hymnody would have benefited from a little less attention in some quarters, for the attempts of well-meaning but incompetent persons to imbue simple tunes with the spirit of the age resulted in vulgarity and absurdity.

Something of the authoritarian policy that governed Catholic church music was badly needed in the "free" churches. The freedom of each church to follow its collective conscience was sound enough in theory, but it was soon discovered that there was no such thing as a collective conscience, or a collective opinion regarding the music of the church. Each individual interpreted the word "freedom" to mean that other members of the church were free to agree with his particular line of thought. People who might be capable of generosity and fair play in secular matters had no intention of budging an inch from their religious prejudices.

A review of this period, then, not only traces the progress of congregational singing, but reveals a belligerent bigotry on the part of many church people and an irresponsibility on the part of untrained amateur musicians, which are only too familiar to the student of church music of the mid-twentieth century.

Germany

In Germany, the metrical psalm and the choral developed together. The majority of capable musicians were Lutherans, since there was no call for their services in Calvinistic churches, but some of them had a part in the compilation of psalm books. Schütz, for instance, compiled a tune book for Becker's psalter, a collection that was widely used for more than fifty years. If some unworthy tunes crept into German psalters, time has drawn its curtain over them.

In 1722, a company of the Unitas Fratrum (Hussites) fled from persecution in their native Bohemia and Moravia and sought refuge in Saxony, founding the town of Herrnhut. The sect, which was by this time three hundred years old, had had no inconsiderable influence on German church music at the time of the Reformation; and more intimate contact led to a further and beneficial influence on the music of both the Reformed (Calvinistic) and Lutheran churches. These were the fathers of the group so favorably known on this continent as Moravians.

The choral, which differed from the metrical psalm chiefly in the fact that it was composed of "man-made" verses rather than psalm paraphrases, was never permitted to degenerate musically. The presence of so many sound men on Lutheran organ benches insured its quality. There were probably many tunes used for both chorals and psalms, as was the case in England and America. There was an exchange of tunes between the Calvinists and the Lutherans, until, finally, the choral became almost as integral a part of Calvinistic worship as of Lutheran.

The high standard of choral and psalm tunes in Germany reflects the importance placed upon congregational singing. They do not give the impression of having been dashed off at odd moments that the composers could spare from other forms of music. They are the products of churchmen; not necessarily those who wrote only church music, but certainly those who gave their whole and undivided attention to church music when they were writing it.

Nor were chorals written simply for the sake of writing. Like most of Bach's larger works, they were composed to meet a definite need, generally for new verses or for old ones for which there had been no tunes.

In the references at the end of this chapter will be found the names of many German composers and tune books covering this period, and these pretty well complete the list of chorals. Having supplied tunes for all the existing chorals (and each tune was almost inseparable from the choral for which it had been written), composers simply refrained from writing more.

Bach wrote only about thirty chorals, although he reharmonized hundreds. His harmonizations were for the use of the choir; for, while the congregation sang heartily, they sang in unison, thus providing opportunities for varied harmonies supplied by the choir or the organist or both, and for the interludes that became a distinct form in the choral-preludes.

The chorals were sung very slowly. In order to enjoy their full flavor, modern organists should play them at a tempo considerably slower than that generally used for hymns in this country.

Although we have mentioned a certain interdependence of non-liturgical and Lutheran churches in the matter of congregational tunes, it must not be imagined that serious differences in opinion did not occur. During Bach's short stay at Mühlhausen, his work was hampered by disputes among factions who wanted a great deal of music, very little music, and none at all. His career as a church musician was interrupted during his six years at Cöthen by the absence of any but simple psalm tunes in public worship. Nevertheless, the threat of Catholicism and a strong musical sense, shared by all Protestants, prevented squabbles from becoming as bitter and divisive as they were elsewhere.

England

It is to the Nonconformist (nonliturgical) groups that English-speaking peoples owe their hymnody. As they had been responsible for the introduction and development of metrical psalms in the sixteenth century, so, too, were they responsible for the introduction of hymns in the eighteenth.

New versions of psalm paraphrases continued to appear in England during the period under discussion, most of them sung to older tunes. The popularity of metrical psalms was so great that the Church of England had had to authorize (without recommending) their use. This grudging approval of one of the best versions of the day (that of Sternhold and Hopkins) led to many Calvinistic churches perversely choosing the inferior Bay Psalm Book in its place.

For twenty-five or thirty years after the Restoration of the monarchy, Nonconformists had to be very careful about singing anything, lest they betray to the authorities that they were worshiping contrary to the dictates of the established church. Nevertheless, they did sing; and some of them, known as Independents or Congregationalists, began to entertain more liberal views as to what constituted decorum in the matter of psalms and hymns.

One of their clergymen, the Reverend Isaac Watts (1674–1748), took very seriously the need for a better type of verse to be used in public worship. In 1707, he published a book of hymns, some of which were of such enduring worth that scarcely any hymnal in modern times omits them: "When I survey the wondrous Cross," "Joy to the world," "O God our help in ages past," "Jesus shall reign where'er the sun," "Lord of the worlds above," and "Give me the wings of faith to rise." Some of these hymns are still sung to tunes almost as old as the words themselves: *St. Anne* (Croft, 1708), *Darwall* (Darwall, 1770), *Rockingham* (Miller, 1790), *Duke Street* (Hatton, 1793), and *Wiltshire* (Smart, 1795).

The hymns of Watts were by no means the first to be written in English, but they formed the first considerable collection. No earlier and few later ones appealed so widely to churchmen. It is not surprising that Independent congregations sang no others for seventy years or so, or that Watts's hymns have retained their popularity after generations of hymn writers.

In 1719, Watts introduced psalm paraphrases written with much more freedom than those which were in use. He managed to express faithfully the sentiment of the psalms without following slavishly the prose text, and he enriched them for Christian people by references to New Testament thought. Following is the first verse of his paraphrase of Psalm 117:

> From all that dwell below the skies,
> Let the Creator's praise arise;
> Let the Redeemer's Name be sung
> Through every land, by every tongue.

It is unlikely that his psalms caught the public fancy as his hymns did. There was what amounted to a superstition about meddling with the words of Holy Writ, and Watts's somewhat free treatment placed his paraphrases under the awful heading of man-made verses. Among the stricter Independents, the Bay Psalm Book was used until well after the middle of the eighteenth century.

In the Church of England, the psalter of Sternhold and Hopkins, of which over six hundred editions had been issued, found a rival in that of Tate and Brady (1696). Of all the psalm books published in the seventeenth and eighteenth centuries, this one of Tate and Brady's is mentioned because many of its paraphrases are still popular: "Through all the changing scenes of life," "Ye boundless realms of joy," "As pants the hart for cooling streams," and others.

In cathedrals and churches with trained choirs, the metrical psalm was not considered essential or particularly desirable. It was included merely to please congregations. In smaller and rural churches, however, it still constituted the music of the service. It made little difference in some places whether the government was a monarchy or a commonwealth, for their simple music was acceptable in either case. Except in the choice of psalters, the singing in such established churches differed little from that of the Nonconformists.

Perhaps there was a stronger tendency to sing in harmony in the Church of England; and somewhat elaborate versions of psalm tunes, called reports, were sung when and where their use was feasible.

In the established church and, perhaps, in some Independent churches as well, an organ accompaniment might be played to the psalms, but it consisted only of the vocal harmony. Lacking both organs and organists of the quality found in Germany, the English were slow to develop free accompaniments.

Inspired by the example of Isaac Watts, churchmen began to write hymns, and a few of the more capable church musicians turned their attention to hymn tunes.

There remained groups among whom congregational singing made no progress, and others who strongly opposed it.

The Presbyterians, after 1650, had no tune book for their metrical psalter. Many of the old tunes were gradually forgotten, and only a very few (often poorly sung) remained in use.

Some Baptists would have no music at all; but, since each congregation was permitted to exercise its discretion in worship forms, there was singing in other churches.

The stricter Baptists objected to music on several grounds: congregational singing would enable unbelievers to take part in the service, the singing of "set" words was but a step from using "set" prayers, and pleasant tunes (like anything pleasant) were not consonant with worship.

Other congregations struck a sensible compromise, placing the psalms at the beginning and end of the service, thus enabling objectors to enter the church after the singing was over and to leave before it was resumed.

If the singing of psalms was a subject of disagreement, the introduction of hymns was the cause of even greater dissension. Congregations were split over the issue.

Judging from the reports of Baptist church conferences of this period, there seems to have been some difficulty with certain members who advocated instrumental music in the service. Such a suggestion was shocking to the stricter Baptists and, to keep the peace, such worldly music was officially frowned upon.

In the Rossendale valley in Lancashire, however, a community which had practiced music for two centuries joined the Baptists in 1720. They introduced their own tunes for voices and orchestra and carried music much farther forward than any other Nonconformist group. Their example was to be followed later in the century by many Baptist churches in England.

Mention must be made of the Wesley brothers, John (1703–1791) and Charles (1707–1788), and their contribution to English hymnody. Both were clergymen of the Church of England, and, in their student days, had been nicknamed "Methodists," a name adopted later by their followers who separated from the established church.

The Wesleys were musical. In 1735, they went to Georgia; and during their short stay there, they were deeply impressed by the doctrines and the music of the Moravians. After his return to England, John was in association with the Moravians there. It is known that a group of these expatriates from Herrnhut settled in Bradford, where their musical equipment included a fine organ; and no doubt the London Moravians, who were friends of John Wesley, were also active musically.

It is not because of their direct contribution to church music that the Wesleys are mentioned—although John did publish a tune book—but because, like Isaac Watts, they were writers of great hymns that gave inspiration to church musicians and led to the writing of some of our finest hymn tunes.

Both Wesleys wrote many hymns. Charles is said to have written over six thousand, many of which are still favorites. While older tunes, principally those of the metrical psalms, were sung to many of the hymns, tunes were written especially for many others. It is interesting to note that Handel wrote three tunes for the Wesleys, of which *Gopsal* is one.

American

The compilers of metrical psalters do not seem to have spared much thought on the tunes to which the paraphrases were to be sung. They assumed that, once the verses were written, people would sing them somehow. Unfortunately, they were too often right: people did sing them "somehow."

If ever a psalter needed a companion tune book, it was the Bay Psalm Book.

Tune books were scarce in New England. There must have remained many copies of Ainsworth's psalter with its thirty-nine tunes, but the Bay Psalm Book contained so many paraphrases in unusual meters that the older, discarded book did not meet the need. Moreover, it will be remembered that many of Ainsworth's tunes were drawn from French and Dutch sources, and their strangeness to English ears may have prevented them from becoming popular.

The only other tunes that the Puritans could draw upon were in English collections (Day, Ravenscroft, Este) and copies of these books were to be found only in the possession of individuals. Congregations singing the tunes learned them "by ear," either from the possessors of the books or, unfortunately, from others who had also learned them "by ear." Like the folk song and plainsong of medieval times, the psalm tune suffered from faults of memory; and what was intended to be the same tune might differ considerably in different localities.

To add to the confusion, most congregations abandoned any attempt to learn and preserve the tunes in their original forms. There were torturous expansions, contractions, and adaptations of tunes to fit meters for which they had never been intended. The changes were made at the whim of whoever was leading the singing, sometimes at the whims of the individual members of the congregation.

But the most pernicious habit was that of "ornamenting" tunes, a practice which had its origin in the old country and soon found favor in America. Reputable tune books contained helpful and legitimate instructions for singing; but others, pandering to the weaknesses of a large section of the public, gave directions for the use of trills, grace notes, passing notes, turns, and so forth. One seldom heard a long sustained note. It was butchered and mangled and divided into unseemly trills and running passages. The original notes were so far outnumbered by auxiliary notes that the melody of the tune was quite lost. It would have been bad enough if all members of the congregation had interpreted and sung the ornaments alike, but each one followed his own fancy.

It is surprising that the Calvinists, and especially the Puritans of New England, who had once made an issue of the plainness of their services and the simplicity of their lives, should have forsaken all dignity and seemliness in their singing at public worship.

Towards the end of the seventeenth century, the situation was so bad that there was a movement to abolish singing from the services. This drastic proposal was countered by a group of clergymen who advocated reform. There were many tracts published, and many sermons preached, on the desirability of "regular singing"; that is, the singing of the psalm tunes in their original forms.

Reforms were vigorously and bitterly opposed by many congregations who, perhaps, saw in the restoration of dignified singing the loss of their opportunities to "let themselves go." However, a number of tune books and singing instructors (notably those of Tufts in 1712, and Walter in 1721) began to have their effect. Before the middle of the eighteenth century, singing schools were numerous; and a general improvement in singing at public worship could be observed.

As in England, hymns were being used in addition to metrical psalms, especially the hymns of Isaac Watts.

During his visit to Georgia, John Wesley was influenced by the music of a group of Moravians who had settled there. As a result, he was arraigned by a grand jury in Savannah in 1737 on the charge of introducing unauthorized hymns and psalms into the services of the Anglican church. (He was still a minister of the Church of England.)

Soon after that time (in 1740) the Moravians moved to Pennsylvania, where was to be found none of the intolerance shown by the Anglicans in Georgia and the Puritans in New England. The Moravians had a fine musical tradition, as we have mentioned before—a tradition inherited from their Bohemian ancestors and modified and enriched by their association with their late neighbors in Germany.

These people were more or less musically self-contained. They imported musical instruments and publications from Europe, performances were given by choirs and orchestras in settlements other than their own, and there seemed to be no dearth of composers who wrote in the traditional style.

Although there was considerable activity in all Moravian settlements, Bethlehem was the musical center. In 1742, there was printed for the use of the Bethlehem congregation a collection of hymns called *Hirten Lieder von Bethlehem,* by Christopher Saur. Two years later, the *Collegium Musicum* was founded, and there were performed parts of several oratorios.

Moravians continued to compose liturgical services which were sung to the accompaniment of orchestra and organ. As early as 1756, Benjamin Franklin was moved to write of the excellent music at the church in Bethlehem. There seems no doubt that the music and performance were not only exceptional in America at the time but equal to almost anything that could be heard in Europe.

The influence of the Moravians on music in America was not as strong as we wish it might have been. In the first place, they were a separate people who had no extensive intercourse with English-speaking colonists; and then, too, their music was so far advanced that it could scarcely be appreciated, much less emulated, by outsiders.

Pennsylvania was the haven of more than one religious group who would have received unsympathetic treatment elsewhere. The Quakers, who were in the majority, did not favor music and discouraged public performances. However, they believed in freedom of conscience, and seemingly made no criticism of sects who used music in their services. Nor did they object to the musical activities of the Moravians in the secular field, since it was, for the most part, confined to Moravian communities.

Fifty years before the coming of the Moravians, Johannes Kelpius and a group of German and Swedish immigrants called Pietists had settled in Germantown, Pennsylvania. Kelpius and several of his companions wrote hymns and tunes, some of which still exist. This particular group of Pietists recognized the contribution that music could make to public worship. From the group came the congregation of the Gloria Dei Swedish Lutheran Church in Philadelphia, where, in 1703, was installed one of the first organs in a colonial church. Viols, oboes, trombones, and kettle drums also had their places in the service.

The Ephrata Cloister was an interesting, self-contained community of German Dunkers about fifty miles from Philadelphia, founded by Johann Conrad Beissel in 1725. The settlers became accustomed to supplying their own needs, and this applied to hymns and tunes. Beissel liked music and, although he had no technical training, wrote over a thousand hymns, and tunes in from two to seven parts. An Ephrata hymnal, *Gottliche Lieben Lobes Gethöne,* was published by Benjamin Franklin in 1730.

But most of the Ephrata hymns were in manuscript form, so beautifully copied and illuminated that they have become collectors' items. By his own acknowledgment, Beissel was no musician. His tunes are somewhat imitative of many others, his harmony and form purely instinctive. Yet, in the preface to the best known collection called, picturesquely, *The Songs of the Solitary and deserted Turtle-Dove, namely the Christian Church,* translated from the original German, he sets forth his views of harmony and seeks to establish a system whereby he and his associates might write their own hymn tunes.

The psalm and hymn tunes were all the church music that America could claim at this period; and, because the majority of the colonists were English, and the English standard of congregational singing was not high, the future looked bleak.

The music of the Church of England, conservative, regulated to a great extent by the authorities who had no real interest in music, made no

ne mechanism in good working order in churches that were poorly
. Yet, in the face of all these handicaps, the organists of the day
d to have performed brilliantly works that tax the ability of or-
of today, who have all the mechanical aids of the modern organ.
rgan music elsewhere lagged far behind that of Germany. When
d of the cathedral organists of England — Blow, Purcell, Clark, and
we must not think of them as comparing in skill with their counter-
of today, or even with some of the more obscure organists of their
ay in Germany and the Low Countries. They simply did not pos-
gans that permitted the development of great skill.
ter the Restoration in 1660, there was considerable activity in organ
g in England. Many instruments had been destroyed or damaged
the Civil War, many were rebuilt in order that they might con-
o the new system of tuning and serve the demands now being made
he organ as an accompanying instrument.
though most of the builders were Germans, they were not permit-
scope that they would have enjoyed in their own country. Most of
glish organs were comparatively small and without pedals. The
had not achieved the importance that it had in Germany. There
ot the music nor the performers to demand very much in the way
urces. Even the organ music of Purcell and Handel is not to be
red with that of their German contemporaries.
ance was in no better condition. Many composers wrote well for
rd instruments—Gigault, Marchand, Couperin, Daquin—but they
for the inferior organs of their time and are chiefly remembered for
arpsichord music.
he organ came to the American colonies at the beginning of the
enth century.
is said that the Episcopal church at Port Royal, Virginia, had an
in 1700; and in 1703, or earlier, one was in use at the Gloria Dei
h Lutheran Church in Philadelphia. An organ imported by
as Brattle was refused by the Independent church for which it was
ed and was installed in King's Chapel, Boston. (It is now in
hn's Chapel, Portsmouth, New Hampshire.) Instruments were
ally acquired by churches that wanted and could afford them, and
most often to be found in Anglican churches and among the foreign
s, such as the Lutherans and Moravians.
hese organs were small, probably averaging six or eight ranks of
and without pedals. Many of the early instruments had only one
al.
ost of the organs were imported, but as early as 1704 one was built
omas Witt at Philadelphia.
ne of the largest organs in America, that installed in Trinity

gains. The Moravians, the Dunkers, and the Lutherans were people apart; and neither their language, their customs, or their music were to affect the population in general for a long time to come.

If hymnody and psalmody reached their lowest point among the Puritan Nonconformists and their various offshoots, to the same people must be given credit for recognizing the chaotic condition and instituting steps for reform. They were far in advance of the people in the old country in this respect.

✳ THE ORGAN IN THE BAROQUE PERIOD

It was during the baroque period that the organ came into its own, both as a solo instrument and for accompaniment.

The long-standing prejudice against the organ was not without justification. We have mentioned that, for centuries, it was a loud, raucous instrument, with a clumsy mechanism capable of sounding not more than two notes simultaneously.

As pipes of lighter timbre were added, and stops were designed whereby the player could make a selection from various ranks of pipes, the tone was varied and modified; and as the keyboard became more compact and manageable, the instrument became more flexible under the hands of the performer.

But the chief factor in the development of the organ and other keyboard instruments was the modification of the scale and the resulting change in the system of tuning.

It will be remembered that, for centuries, the only pure consonants were considered to be the octave, fifth, and fourth. The vibrations of these intervals were in simple ratios to those of the fundamental sound ($2:1$, $3:2$, and $4:3$ respectively), and, as a result, many of the sounds of the harmonic series were in agreement.

As we stated in Chapter III, various methods were used to fill up the intervals between the fundamental and the fourth, and between the fifth and the octave. The scale attributed to Pythagoras gained greatest favor, and it was in common use until the sixteenth century.

Any of these sounds could be combined with its octave, its fifth (except B–F), and its fourth (except F–B), and the simple ratios were preserved. But the second, third, sixth, and seventh could not be combined with the fundamental.

It is wrong to assume that the scale of mode 2 (Hypodorian) was the same as our scale of A minor, or that mode 6 (Hypolydian) was the same as our scale of C major. They look the same on paper simply because we know no other way of writing them.

Harmony was out of the question as long as the Pythagorean scale was in use. One feels some sympathy for the ecclesiastical authorities when they protested the introduction of dissonances that must have threatened, at times, to become ear-splitting.

There were many experimenters who tried to find a scale that would provide more consonances. The only hope of success lay in devising a series of sounds whose vibrations would be in less complex ratios to those of the fundamental and to each other. It was such a scale that made possible the transition from modal music to that which was developed during the baroque period.

This new scale, first in a major then in a minor form, made chordal harmony possible. Thirds and sixths became not only tolerable but preferred consonances, although they were less desirable than the fourth, fifth, and octave as points of rest.

It would seem that nothing was now lacking for the development of *nuove musiche*. One might choose a sound of any pitch as a fundamental and adjust the voice or the strings of an instrument to appropriate intervals.

But this new scale, excellent though it was, presented some difficulties for the organ and other keyboard instruments. The keys were laid out very much as they are now, twelve to the octave; but the new musical system provided for many more sounds. E flat, for instance, would not serve for D sharp; and the same was true of other keys which do double or triple duty in our modern system.

Ex. 12:1

There were probably several methods of tuning keyboard instruments, but the most practical would be as in Example 12:1.

This system would permit the player to use the keys of C major and minor; the major keys of G, D, F, B flat, and E flat; and the minor keys of A, E, B, D, and G (but not in their later harmonic or melodic forms). Modulation had to be restricted to this group of keys. Vocal music that was accompanied on the organ must be sung in keys that could be accommodated on the organ.

The new tuning was not the result of a sudden change. There had been many advocates for some sort of reform in the past. We know that Adrian Willaert, whose duties included combining the two organs and two choirs at St. Mark's, Venice, felt the need of a system of tuning that would make his work practical.

Although Willaert was not the only or chie... ful system of tuning, it is significant that his pu... themselves with organs on which they could b... independent organ music. Andrea and Giovar... Merulo originated forms for the organ that re... technic. A great Italian of the next generatic... (1583–1643), organist at St. Peter's, Rome, carrie... farther. He took every advantage of the tonal... of his instrument, and the chromatic effects an... the freedom of the newer tuning permitted.

Organ music in Italy declined after Frescob... failure of Italian builders to keep pace with the...

It was Germany that benefited most from t... teenth-century Italian organ school and carried...

There had long been a great interest in the... mans. Much progress had been made by builde... what uninspired, school of playing had been esta... mann, Virdung, and Schlick in the early 1500's.

When Sweelinck, Hassler, and Schütz went... Gabrielis, they were already accomplished organ... standards. What they learned there, combined... and the much superior instruments of their own... lishment of the greatest school of organ playing... ever existed.

Of the many fine German organists who bri... Schütz and Bach, we may mention four outstandi... (c. 1605–1667) in Vienna, *Johann Reinken* (1... *Dietrich Buxtehude* (1637–1707) in Lübeck,... (1653–1706), chiefly in Nuremberg. When we re... these men that Bach derived most of his princip... many of his ideas of composition, we are better a... than through any detailed biographical sketches...

The organs on which they played, although... standards, were apparently quite adequate for p... and intricate organ music of the day. The tun... limitations we have mentioned above, was far i... systems and permitted the addition of mutatic... twelfth with which to brighten the tone. The... come an art, and the organs were well equipped...

The pedals were very short. They could l... toes, and there was no room to cross one foot ov... were often higher than the player's head and re... draw. No doubt it was difficult to maintain th...

Church, New York, in 1737, was a native product. It had three manuals and twenty-six stops.

Perhaps because of the difference in organs and in the skill of organists, much leeway was permitted in accompaniments. The organist (or harpsichordist) was provided with only a bass, above or below which were figures indicating the chords and their positions that were to serve as the accompaniment. From this *figured bass, thorough bass,* or *continuo,* the performer built up his part. If he were not expert, he could simply block in the chords as indicated; but organists prided themselves on their ability to provide elaborate accompaniments with nothing more to guide them than the figured bass.

Performers on keyboard instruments were, necessarily, expert in harmony, far more expert than their modern successors. No doubt some of their accompaniments were worked out beforehand, but the best of them preferred to extemporize the accompaniments during the performance. Very few instrumental parts of accompanied vocal works of that time are authentic in their modern published form. What we have are the interpretations of editors: the composers provided nothing more than the bass.

While some progress was being made elsewhere, Johann Sebastian Bach, unknown beyond the scene of his activity, was developing the art of organ playing and composition to a point that would have amazed his contemporaries in England, France, Italy, and America could they have known of his work. A hundred years later, when Bach's works were rediscovered, they were still far in advance of any other organ music that had been written to that time.

It was during Bach's time that great progress was made in the use of the tempered scale.

As we have pointed out, the "natural" major and minor scales contained thirty-five sounds within the octave. The problem of reducing all the necessary sounds to twelve, while retaining the possibilities of playing in any key, had engaged the minds of the best theorists. The solution was *equal temperament,* or a compromise scale. Each of the twelve sounds in the tempered scale was made to do duty for three sounds of the "natural" scale.

Perhaps a simple illustration will assist the layman in understanding the method of compromise.

Suppose it is decided to tile the floor of a room twelve feet wide with tiles one foot wide. Twelve tiles will be needed for each row. But if it is discovered that the room is only eleven feet and six inches wide, obviously the tiles will not fit. If the twelfth tile only is cut to fit, it will be rendered conspicuous by the fact that it is only half the width of the others. But if half an inch is cut from *every* tile, each tile will be *almost* one foot wide, the pattern will be preserved, and the eye will be satisfied.

Similarly, if we begin calculating true perfect fifths from C (G, D, A, E, B, F sharp or G flat, D flat, A flat, E flat, B flat, F), we will find that the last fifth (F–C) is too small to work into our pattern. The ear will not accept it. But if we reduce the other fifths slightly, we find that it is possible to space them evenly without departing perceptibly from their original forms.

Even a slight deviation in the pitch of one sound of the "natural" scale would have been unpleasant, but when the slight deviation was made in *all* sounds, the ear was satisfied, and a practical scale was the result.

Some musicians had been familiar with the theory of equal temperament long before Bach (Willaert, Zarlino, and Bull among many others), but Bach was the most zealous advocate of his day. He had his own harpsichords so tuned, and he wrote his two sets of preludes and fugues for the *Well-Tempered Clavier* to demonstrate the possibilities of the tempered scale.

It was not so easy to convert organ builders to the new theory, although a very few German organs had equal temperament before 1700. Bach himself wrote few organ pieces with a wide range of modulation, indicating that the organs he used were, for the most part, tuned in the old way.

Not until the last half of the nineteenth century did English builders adopt equal temperament to any great extent. In this, as in other respects, they lagged far behind the German organ builders, and the development of organ music in English-speaking countries was retarded.

✤ REFERENCES

Psalm and Hymn Tunes, Chorals

The following list is compiled from the indexes of several hymnals and is representative of tunes written during the period 1650–1750. Since there were many more tunes during this century than at any time prior to 1650, the list is selective.

Arne, Thomas, 1710–1778.
Bach, J. S., 1685–1750.
Barton's *Psalms,* 1706.
Bishop, John, 1665–1737.
Carey, Henry, c. 1692–1743.
Chetham's *Psalmody,* 1718.
Clark, Jeremiah, 1670–1707.
Clausener Gesangbuch, 1653.
Courteville, Raphael, c. 1675–1772.
Croft, William, 1678–1727.

Darmstadt *Gesangbuch,* 1698.
Darwall, John, 1731–1789.
Dresden *Gesangbuch,* 1694.
Freylinghausen's *Geistreiches Gesang-buch,* 1704.
Freylinghausen's *Neues Geistreiches Gesangbuch,* 1714.
Geistreiches Gesangbuch, Darmstadt, 1698.
Green's *A Book of Psalmody,* 1724.

Green's *Psalmody*, 1731.
Handel, G. F., 1685–1759.
Harmonischer Liederschatz, 1738.
Herbst, Martin, 1654–1681.
Himmels-Lust, 1679.
Howard, Samuel, 1710–1782.
Hymns and Sacred Poems, 1749.
Joseph, Georg, c. 1657.
Knapp, Wm., 1698–1768.
König's *Harmonischer Lieder Schatz*, 1738.
Lyra Davidica, 1708.
Mäyntzisch Gesangbuch, 1661.
Meiningisches Gesangbuch, 1693.
Meyer's *Seelenfreud*, 1692.
Münster *Gesangbuch*, 1677.
Musicalisch Handbuch, 1690.
Neander, Joachim, 1650–1680.
Nürnberg *Gesangbuch*, 1690.
Peter, Christoph, 1626–1669.

Playford's *Whole Book of Psalms*, 1677.
Psalmodia Sacra, Gotha, 1715.
Rogers, B., 1641–1698.
Rosseau, J. J., 1712–1778.
Sacred Harmony, Leeds, c. 1720.
Scheffler's *Heilige Seelenlust*, 1657.
Scheidt's *Tablaturbuch*, 1650.
Steiner, J. L., 1688–1761.
Störl's *Wurtemberg Gesangbuch*, 1710.
Straslund Gesangbuch, 1665.
Supplement to the New Version, 1708.
Tans'ur's *Compleat Melody*, 1734.
Tans'ur's *The Harmony of Sion*, 1734.
Thommen's *Christenschatz*, 1745.
Tochter Sion, Cologne, 1741.
Wainwright, John, 1723–1768.
Weale, W., d. 1727.
Wheall, Wm., 1690–1727.

Anthems, Motets, Oratorios

Asterisks denote oratorios and other extended choral works.

Alcock, John—
  Wherewithal shall a young man? [N]
Aldrich, H.—
  I am well pleased [N]
  O give thanks [N]
  Out of the deep [N]
  Thy Beauty, O Israel [N]
  We have heard with our ears [N]
Bach, J. S.—
  All music publishers' catalogues contain extensive lists.
Blow, J.—
  God is our hope and strength [N]
  I beheld, and lo! a great multitude [N]
  Lift up your heads [N]
  O God, my heart is ready [F]
  O God, wherefore art thou absent [N]
  Save me, O God [N]
  Sing we merrily [N]

  Thy hands have made me [F]
Boyce, Wm.—
  Blessed is he that considereth the poor [N]
  By the waters of Babylon [N]
  Here shall soft charity [N]
  I have surely built thee an house [N]
  O where shall wisdom [N]
  Pastoral Hymn, A [N]
  Save me, O God [F]
Clark (e), Jeremiah—
  How long wilt thou forget me? [N]
  I will love thee, O Lord [N]
  O Lord God of my salvation [N]
  Praise the Lord, O Jerusalem [N]
Creyghton, R.—
  Behold, now praise the Lord [N]
  I will arise [N]
  Praise the Lord, O my soul [N]
Croft, Wm.—
  Be merciful unto me, O Lord [N]

Cry aloud and shout [N]
God is gone up with a merry noise
  [N]
*I will alway give thanks [N]
*O Lord, rebuke me not [F]
*O Lord, thou hast searched me out
  [F]
Put me not to rebuke [N]
Graun, C. H.—
  Like as the hart [N]
  Rise again [F]
Greene, M.—
  *Arise, shine, O Zion [F]
  *Blessed are those that are undefiled
    [N]
  Let God arise [N]
  Let my complaint come before thee
    [F]
  Lord, let me know mine end [F]
  O God of my righteousness [N]
  O sing unto the Lord a new song
    [N]
  Thou, O God, art praised in Zion
    [N]
Handel, G. F.,
  *Chandos Anthems [N]
  *Coronation Anthems [N]
  I will lift up mine eyes [B]
  *Judas Maccabaeus [S]
  *Messiah [S]
  *Samson [S]
  *Ways of Zion do mourn, The [N]
  Most music publishers' catalogues
    contain more extensive lists.
Hayes, Wm.—
  Arise, ye people [N]
  Lord is good, The [N]
  Lord, thou hast been our refuge
    [N]
  O worship the Lord [N]
  Save, Lord, and hear us [N]
Humfrey (or Humphreys), Pelham—
  Haste thee, O God [N]
  Hear, O heavens [N]
  Like as the hart [N]
  Rejoice in the Lord [F]
  Thou art my King, O God [N]

Jackson, W.—
  Christ our Passover [N]
  *For joy let fertile valleys [N]
  Lord hear thee, The [N]
  We have heard with our ears [N]
Kent, J.—
  Hearken unto this, O man [N]
  Lord hath prepared, The [N]
  Lord is my Shepherd, The [N]
  My song shall be of mercy [N]
  *Who is this that cometh from
    Edom?* [N]
King, Charles—
  Hear, O Lord [N]
  Unto thee, O Lord [N]
  *Wherewithal shall a young man
    [N]
Leo, L.—
  Bow down thine ear [N]
  *God shall send forth [N]
Nares, J.
  Awake up, my glory [N]
  By the waters of Babylon [N]
  Call to remembrance [N]
  Lord, how long wilt thou be angry?
    [N]
  Souls of the righteous, The [N]
Purcell, Henry—
  *Behold, I bring you glad tidings
    [N]
  Bow down thine ear, O Lord [S]
  *My beloved spake [N]
  O Lord, our Governor [N]
  Rejoice in the Lord [F]
  Thy Word is a lantern [N]
  Who hath believed our report?
    [N]
Robinson, J.—
  Not unto us, O Lord [N]
Shepherd, John—
  Haste thee, O God [F]
Travers, J.—
  Ascribe unto the Lord [N]
  Keep, we beseech thee, O Lord
    [N]
  Ponder my words [N]

Turner, W.—
  Lift up your heads [N]
  Lord, thou hast been our refuge
    [N]
Weldon, J.—
  Hear my crying [F]
  In thee, O Lord [N]
  O God, thou hast cast us out [N]
  Who can tell how oft he offendeth?
    [N]

Wise, M.—
  Awake, put on thy strength [N]
  Awake up, my glory [N]
  Blessed is he [N]
  Prepare ye the way of the Lord
    [N]
  Thy beauty, O Israel [N]

13

THE CENTURY OF NEGLECT (1750~1850)

░░░

✣ THE DECLINE OF CHURCH MUSIC

After the middle of the eighteenth century, the development of music was completely divorced from the Church.

Two hundred years earlier, a composer could scarcely have become known as such unless he devoted his talents chiefly to church music. Secular music was intended only as a diversion, not to be taken seriously. A secular air had little chance of survival or recognition as serious music unless it was used as the cantus firmus for a motet. Even then, it must be disguised by a change of tempo and obscured by polyphony, lest it offend the ears of ecclesiastical authorities. Advances in the theory of music made in the secular field were considered illegitimate and in bad taste until, later (in some cases, very much later), they were recognized and grudgingly approved by the Church.

It is not suggested that early composers of note wrote church music almost exclusively because only in that field was there an outlet for their talents. Undoubtedly, there were some opportunists among them; but, for the most part, musicians found in the motet and the mass mediums for a sincere expression of genuine devotion to their religion. People in all walks of life were acutely conscious of the influence of the church, and the custom of offering their first and best to the church was deeply rooted.

During the baroque period, the emphasis shifted from church music to secular. The church no longer had exclusive possession of the facilities for the performance of good music. Nor were the churches the only buildings in which the public could conveniently congregate to hear music. Moreover, the respect for the church suffered some decrease as the awareness of the field of public entertainment increased. Some of the outstanding composers wrote little, if any, church music; others, like Purcell and Handel, divided their attention between the church and the world, with the balance in favor of the latter. The only great composer of the period to devote himself chiefly to worship music was Bach.

The century between the years 1750 and 1850, approximately, was a period of great musical progress. Even today it is considered by many to have been the golden age of music—the age of Gluck, Haydn, Mozart, Beethoven, Weber, Schubert, Schumann, Mendelssohn, and Chopin.

All of the advances were made in the secular field. The musical resources of the church had been explored and exploited: the caution and conservatism of the church were no longer restraints to experimental genius.

But, while little church music was written by the musical giants, their methods and technics were adopted to some extent by worthy but lesser composers who continued to write for the church.

The polyphonic style was generally abandoned except as it was used incidentally for effect. The homophonic style, featuring a melodic line with an accompaniment built upon basic chords, became highly developed.

Melodic lines, which were no longer required to conform to the restrictions of polyphony, became freer, clearer, simpler. As they gradually shed the somewhat artificial ornamentation of the baroque period, they assumed a warmth and beauty that had an instant appeal. Melodies were more definite than in earlier periods and were expressed in shorter and more regular phrases.

Harmony was remarkably simple at first. The complexities of Bach are nowhere to be found in the works of Haydn and Mozart. Common chords predominate, and even seventh chords occur infrequently. Form was regular and clear, modulation was still used only as a convenience for shifting from one key to another.

Beethoven was largely responsible for harmonic innovations. He and his contemporaries and successors introduced new chords and progressions, more seventh, ninth, and altered chords, more chromaticism.

Modulation was used for effect as well as for convenience, and there were passages in which tonality became indefinite.

It was upon the orchestra, the solo song, the piano, the opera, and chamber music that the musical talents of this century were lavished. There is nothing to indicate that composers were less religious than their forebears. Haydn, Mozart, Beethoven, and Schubert, among others, wrote oratorios, motets, masses, and other music on religious themes. Their music intended for the church was quite different from any church music that had been written before, just as their secular music differed from that of their predecessors. The Church rejected their offerings as being too worldly and lacking in seriousness! Her centuries-old passion for archaism has robbed us of the music of the masters, who might well have written more church music had they received any encouragement to do so. Let us hope that our self-righteousness compensates us for the loss as we listen to much of the drab, uninspired music that is heard in our churches.

Of the composers of music who found acceptance in Protestant churches, only the name of Mendelssohn would be recognized by musicians who are not especially interested in church music. The contribution of men who did write worship music must not be underestimated; but they were lesser men, bound by tradition and custom.

✤ PROTESTANT CHURCH MUSIC IN ENGLAND

The historical field as regards Protestant church music in America is now narrowed to English-speaking countries.

In Germany, which had taken the lead in the development of music for the reformed churches, there were no new advances. The peak had been reached with Bach. The excellent tradition of congregational singing was maintained, but there were very few new chorals written. With so many dignified hymns and tunes available, the Germans very sensibly considered it unnecessary to add more simply for the sake of having something new to sing. Organ music declined in the sense that nothing much was added to it, although organists were well supplied with music written in former years if they lacked the ability to compose their own. With the rest of Europe, the Germans turned their thoughts to secular music. They were more fortunate than their neighbors in that their church music was well provided for before their minds were diverted to other channels.

What happened to church music in England was, for a long time, significant to Americans; for the bonds of culture, custom, and language remained strong even after political ties were broken.

Although church music in England had not reached a state that justified church musicians resting on their oars, that is what they did. Some anthems were composed, some festival settings added to the Church of England liturgy, some hymn tunes written; but the chief developments were the breaking of some bad habits, an increased tolerance towards music on the part of Noncomformists, and attempts towards a more orderly use of the music that had been inherited from the baroque period. Church music had lost much of its importance. The English, like other people, associated music with concerts and entertainment.

Native musicians were eclipsed by foreigners—Germans, French, Italians, and Bohemians—whose mission was to offer musical entertainment as a means of livelihood. That is not to say that there were no capable English musicians. There were some who, under more favorable circumstances, might have made significant contributions to English music. But the public was enamored of foreign names and foreign reputations. (History was to repeat itself in America a century later, when the possession of a foreign name, genuine or assumed, was a prerequisite of acceptance in musical circles.)

A few English musicians, notably Thomas Attwood, went abroad to study, many more received their training from foreign musicians who had settled in England.

It was an age of child prodigies. Influenced, no doubt, by the phenomenal receptions of the two Mozart children, Wolfgang Amadeus and Maria Anna, parents and teachers pushed their gifted children and pupils before the public.

This apparent precocity is not to be regarded as an asset to English music, but as a reflection of the superficiality of the times. Child prodigies, however clever and dexterous, are immature; and the same may be said of the public that flocks to hear them. It was not music that people wanted to hear, but juvenile freaks.

In such an atmosphere, church music could make little real progress.

* THE CHURCH OF ENGLAND

The deterioration of the musical services of the church can best be appreciated by a consideration of what was taking place in English cathedrals.

Not only did composition languish; but the facilities for an adequate performance of the liturgical music were lacking, and this lack could not be compensated even by the competent organists who served in the cathedrals.

There was, in the first place, a dearth of music. Whether the libraries were depleted or merely neglected is not known. The choice of music to be used was not within the jurisdiction of the organist, but was the prerogative of the precentor (in this sense, a clergyman charged with the responsibility of music in a cathedral). Many of the precentors not only neglected their duties, but, by virtue of their authority, which they guarded jealously, prevented the organist from making good their neglect.

Alcock, at Lichfield, complained bitterly about the lack of music; Banks, at Rochester, notes that only two services and seven anthems had been sung (over and over again, of course) in twelve years!

Some cathedrals had no choirs at all, and the choral forces in others were scanty and uncertain.

The lot of choir boys was an appalling one. They were required to sing for daily services at the cathedral at hours which prevented their attendance at school, yet no provision was made for their education. Boy choristers at the Chapel Royal, where conditions were probably comparatively good, had lessons for an hour and a half on Wednesdays and Saturdays. With that admirable zeal that has inspired many a spinster to carry on single-handed crusades for reform, a certain Miss Maria Hackett harassed the authorities of every cathedral in England until she succeeded in improving the lot of the choir boys. One of her greatest victories was the extraction of a promise that *one hour a day* would be devoted to the general education of the boys of St. Paul's, of whom there were only eight. When it is considered that the remuneration averaged five pounds (less than twenty-five dollars) per boy per year, with no board or housing, perhaps the cathedral was extremely fortunate in attracting even eight boys for choir duty.

Probably regular rehearsals were held for the boys; but when their minds were allowed to lie fallow in every other respect, and they had no other occupation than that of practicing and singing the services for two or three hours a day, it is unlikely that they would turn out to be keen, intelligent students.

Rehearsals for the men of the choir were rare. Indeed, in many cathedrals, the presence of men was rare even at the chief service on Sunday morning. The parts other than the soprano were sung by minor canons of the cathedral, most of whom had parish churches of their own that required their presence at morning service. The organist frequently found himself supported by a handful of boys and two or three men. Even the precentor, who was nominally in charge of the music, was frequently absent.

At Hereford Cathedral, the anthem for Easter Day, 1833 (*Blessed be the God and Father*) was written by S. S. Wesley for sopranos in two parts and one bass (the latter the dean's butler, who was the only man in the choir). That this was not an unusual situation is proved by anthems by Wesley's predecessor, John Clarke-Whitfeld, for the same combination of voices.

Many of the same men served in the choirs of the Chapel Royal,

Westminster Abbey, and St. Paul's Cathedral. When services were held simultaneously at two of these churches, the men would hire substitutes to sing for them in one of the choirs. They often managed to save these deputies' fees by putting in an appearance at one church and, as soon as the anthem had been sung, rushing out to take their places in the choir of another.

Samuel Sebastian Wesley, who served as organist in four cathedrals (Hereford, Exeter, Winchester, and Gloucester), complained bitterly of the state of cathedral music and the conditions forced upon cathedral musicians. He is quoted, in *The Oxford Companion to Music,* as saying that a young musician taking service in a country cathedral is in a "painful and dangerous position." He speaks of the "mass of error and inferiority," which he considers "irremediable" because of the indifference, and even the hostility of the clergy towards organists who sought to improve conditions.

That a better standard of music prevailed in some of the larger parish churches is argued by the fact that several prominent organists (John Alcock and S. S. Wesley among them) resigned their cathedral positions to take service in such churches for a time. There, freed from officialdom, they were able to make a more telling contribution to the music and to gain some satisfaction from the improvements they were able to effect.

If music was in such a poor state in the cathedrals, it is not hard to imagine what it was like in rural parishes and small town churches which could not afford organs, competent musicians, or even much printed music.

Metrical psalms and, perhaps, occasional hymns, were sung in nearly all churches. Where there were organs, they would be used for accompaniment, played more often than not by amateurs who could pick out the tunes and a few odd notes to provide a rudimentary harmony. Very often the singing would be led by a precentor (in the Presbyterian rather than the cathedral sense), and the results would depend largely upon his skill or lack of it. A few people known to be good singers might be grouped together as a choir. Little or no attempt was made to chant the prose psalms or to sing the liturgy.

Parishes that had no organs, either because they had never possessed them, or because their instruments had worn out or been destroyed away back in the Commonwealth period, often allowed groups of amateur musicians to form little orchestras for the accompaniment of the metrical psalms and hymns. There was seldom any selection in the matter of instruments: whatever was available was used. Probably flutes, violins, and bass viols predominated, leaving the middle parts of the harmony weak.

It is interesting to note that bass instruments achieved a greater reputation for respectability than did others. The bass viol, in particular, enjoyed a sanctity comparable with that of a bishop, and was sometimes the *only* instrument in use in a church. In speculating on the reasons for the tolerance accorded bass instruments, one is reminded that there was still much music in use for which the composers had provided only the *continuo* as a basis for accompaniment. The instruments playing this part would take few liberties. On the other hand, music for instruments for which the composers had specified no definite parts might be improvised by the players or arranged by amateur musicians unskilled in instrumentation. The temptation to add ornaments and graces that would offer some scope for the instrumentalists, rather than to follow the voice parts, was too strong to be resisted.

It was their frivolity not only in the matter of music but in their conduct in church that earned the members of church orchestras the disapproval of both clergy and laity. Sharing with the choir the west gallery, behind the congregation, they too often regarded the services of the church as social gatherings. The music was the sole reason for their presence, and they were likely to disturb those parts of the service during which they were inactive. It is scarcely surprising that many of the clergy developed a strong prejudice against music and musicians.

Church orchestras did have the one redeeming feature of bringing amateur musicians together for the practice of their art. If they could have been disciplined and taught to regard music in the church in its proper perspective, they might have made a great and lasting contribution to worship music. Indeed, as late as 1922, the Archbishops' Committee on Music in Worship recommended the return of orchestras to village churches, no doubt believing that the manners of twentieth-century amateur musicians would show an improvement over those of their great-grandfathers.

In towns, the choirs often consisted of "charity children," which, in the idiom of the time and place, probably meant children from free schools or public institutions. These would have no musical training other than the rudiments which they learned at school, and it is unlikely that they added anything to the services but noise.

The scarcity of competent organists is reflected in the popularity of the so-called "barrel organ," which made its first appearance in the 1770's. Metal pins arranged on revolving barrels or drums operated the mechanism of the organ. Each barrel would play from six to ten hymn tunes, any of which could be selected. There might be half a dozen ranks of pipes which could be silenced or made active by means of stops. The cheaper models had not a full chromatic series and would play tunes in only two or three keys. Some had keyboards to be used instead of the barrel mechanism if an organist happened to be present; but, for the most part, these organs placed the music in the hands of anyone who could manipulate the simple controls. The playing of a barrel organ needed no more musicianship or discretion than the placing of a record on a modern record player and setting the mechanism in operation.

The popularity of the barrel organ was well deserved. It played the tunes much more accurately than many amateur organists were able to play them; and, in churches where there had been no organs, they delivered the congregations from the uncertainties and improprieties of church orchestras. That there were no competent musicians responsible for the music in these churches is to be deplored; but the barrel organs seldom displaced competent musicians or were installed in churches that were prepared to engage the services of organists.

There was a great deal of dissatisfaction with the music in established churches, and no group protested more vigorously than the clergy. Yet it was the clergy who, in the long run, were responsible for the deplorable conditions. Although "money" was a vulgar word in polite English circles, lack of money for the promotion of church music lay at the root of this particular evil. The bald, unpalatable fact is that the clergy, especially those of cathedrals, were far more anxious to appropriate available funds for their own stipends than to divert them to the music of the church. A canon might receive as much for three months' service in the cathedral as the combined salaries of the organist and choristers for a whole year (and this in addition to his annual stipend as rector or vicar of a parish church). Moreover, some of them were paid for singing the services without performing that duty or engaging substitutes to sing for them. The clergy in smaller parishes were, of course, powerless to do anything about the music in their churches; for their own stipends were pitifully small, and there were seldom sufficient funds to keep the churches in good repair, much less build organs or engage musicians.

Therefore, while the Church of England, through its bishops and higher clergy, complained about the state of church music, they lifted not one finger and expended not one pound to remedy conditions. Musicians, devoted to their art and to the church, were denied the authority to make improvements. Many gifted students, mindful of conditions under which musicians worked, were discouraged from entering the field of worship music.

✤ NONCONFORMIST WORSHIP MUSIC IN ENGLAND

In contrast to what was taking place in the Church of England, the interest of Nonconformists in worship music was encouraging. Lacking the musical traditions of the established church, the wealth of church music that had been accumulating for centuries, and the facilities for the adequate performance of fine music, they nevertheless showed a desire to make the most of their extremely slender resources. True, their zeal was sometimes attended by bigotry and bitterness, which is deplorable; but the fact that they were interested enough to quarrel about it argues an increased interest in music, even though it was sometimes accompanied by a decline of Christian charity.

Perhaps the greatest influence on Nonconformist music came from the Methodists.

The position of Methodism in the latter part of the eighteenth century was a peculiar one. It began as an evangelistic movement within the Church of England, although much disapproved by that body. The Wesley brothers (John and Charles senior) had no desire to form a new sect, but rather to effect a reform in the established church of which they were ordained priests. Successive steps towards separation may be said to have been the formulation of Articles of Religion in 1744, John Wesley's assumption of the authority of ordination in 1784 (an illegal proceeding which finally closed the door to hope of reconciliation with the bishops), and the first official Methodist Conference in 1791, just after Wesley's death, when the separation was made formal.

The Methodists' half century as continuing Anglicans had an important bearing on their attitude towards music as an accompaniment to worship. They had none of the Calvinistic conviction that music, apart from staid psalm tunes, was likely to corrupt the worshippers. They were accustomed to the services of the Church of England, where choirs and organs were considered desirable. Even George Whitefield, an early associate of the Wesleys who parted company from them to form a Calvinistic branch of Methodism, did not adopt the cautious Calvinistic attitude towards worship music.

The musical tendencies of some of the leading Methodist clergymen —the Wesleys, George Whitefield, and John Beaumont—served to inspire their followers.

The Methodists early profited from their founders' love of music, and their singing soon earned the grudging admiration of the Anglicans. Organists of the established church were quick to realize that congregational singing among the Methodists set a standard seldom, if ever, achieved in the Church of England. The clergy, less interested in music for its own sake, nevertheless saw in it one of the attractions that won followers for Methodism; and they began, at long last, to give serious thought to the restoration of congregational singing to its proper place in the services.

After the publication of John Wesley's tune book in 1742 (containing only melodies), a number of noted composers, including Handel, wrote tunes for Methodist hymnody. In 1821, Charles Wesley, Jr. revised his uncle's tune book, calling the revision *Sacred Harmony,* and adding figured basses to the melodies. Samuel, in 1828, published *Original Hymn Tunes adapted to every metre in the Collection of the Rev. John Wesley.*

The Methodists were greatly in need of new tunes, not because they rejected the old, but because their hymns were written in a wide variety of meters for which no tunes were available. Their leaders were too sound musicians to permit the distortion of traditional psalm tunes to fit new hymns.

Methodist tunes were inclined to be lively. For centuries, church authorities had urged the writing of syllabic music (one note to each syllable) in order that the sense of the words might not be lost. Methodist writers recognized no such limitations. Many of the tunes were florid: many were of the "fuguing" type; that is, containing imitative passages for various voices entering in succession. Sometimes the words of the last line were repeated over and over again by the men and women alternately. Refrains consisting chiefly of the word "Hallelujah" were often longer than the verses they followed. The rhythms were lively, and the tempo of hymn singing was much quicker than had previously been the case among church and chapel people. (John Wesley was known to deplore the old "drawling" style of singing hymn and psalm tunes.) All in all, the participation in the singing of a Methodist hymn could be an exciting experience.

The official conferences sought to regulate the performance of congregational singing to some extent. They decreed that the men should not sing the women's parts—would that their influence could be felt today!—and sought to combat the tendency towards ornamentation that the Methodists shared with other religious groups.

Choirs were used in early Methodist meeting houses. In addition to the hymns, anthems were sung, some borrowed from the repertoire of Anglican church music, others written by their own people. (John Beaumont published a book of anthems in 1793.)

Orchestras sometimes accompanied the choirs and might have received official approval from the conference had not the musicians forgotten their proper function and sought to prolong their performances at the expense of the sermon and other parts of the service. They became such a nuisance in time that, in 1805, the conference sought to end the use of all instruments except the bass viol.

Choirs and orchestras spent much time in the preparation of special programmes, or "sacred concerts," as they came to be known later. Solos and anthems were sung, and, according to an objection registered by the conference, there was a good deal of "fuguing," which, in this case, meant the singing of different words or syllables simultaneously by the various parts.

There must have been organs in some chapels, for the conference, in 1780, while refusing consent to the building of new ones, issued suggestions for the use of organs that were already installed. The controversy was renewed whenever a congregation wanted to have an organ and raised the necessary funds for its purchase. Protests came from some of their own members, from neighboring congregations, and from the conference. There were old, conservative die-hards who felt that the use of any instruments in public worship was unseemly, but there were also many Methodists and other Nonconformists who might have become reconciled to the use of organs for accompaniment only.

The church officials dreaded the appearance of organists who wanted to use their instruments as distractions from, rather than aids to, worship. A custom had arisen in the Anglican church of playing a long "voluntary" before the sermon, and this custom was adopted by many organists in Nonconformist churches. The chances of combining skillful performance, good taste, and brevity were remote. Capable organists were relatively scarce and there was little good music available to English organists; in addition, too many performers, like church orchestras, inclined to prolong their playing to the detriment of the service and the sermon. The opposition to organs was not entirely due to unreasonable prejudice on the part of the clergy and stricter members of the congregation: the organists themselves were to blame for much of it.

The effect of bright, congregational singing on attendance at Methodist chapels was not lost on other Nonconformist denominations.

The distrust of music as an aid to worship was, after all, a survival of the Reformation, when Calvinists had renounced everything that had a place in the services of the Catholic church. The continuing use of music among Anglicans and Lutherans was no recommendation, for their liturgical forms of service retained too many features of the old Catholic liturgy to be palatable.

The example of the Methodists was viewed in an entirely different light. Even before their separation from the Church of England, the followers of Wesley worshipped informally. Their difficulties with the Anglican hierarchy were sufficient to evoke the sympathy of other Protestant groups, all of whom had felt the weight of ecclesiastical authoritarianism at one time or another.

After their separation, the Methodists had a definite kinship with other Nonconformists. They had, in their services and in their theology, put aside all that was reminiscent of Catholicism; their leanings were definitely Calvinistic. Their attraction for great numbers of people won respect, and any means by which they attracted converts were not to be ignored.

There had been, since the beginning of the eighteenth century, a tendency among the Congregationalists and the Baptists to ease the restrictions on the music to be used in church. No doubt this tendency would have grown stronger in any case, but certainly the example of the Methodists gave it impetus.

Both Congregationalists and Baptists published tune books, perhaps the most noteworthy of which was Dr. John Rippon's *A Selection of Psalms and Hymn Tunes from the Best Authors,* published in 1791 and running into many editions. While remaining loyal to the metrical psalms, they made more and more use of hymns. The prejudice against "man-made" verses was breaking down.

The Congregationalists, in particular, were making some efforts to improve church music. Singing classes were organized, at first only here and there, but later among many local groups. Towards the end of the eighteenth century, even organs, which had long been anathema to Independents, began to make their appearance in some churches. At Surrey Chapel, London, organ and violin recitals of three or four hours' duration were sometimes played; and, while the attitude towards music in that church was unusually tolerant, it is evidence of the growing acceptance of music by the Congregationalists.

The use of music among the Baptists varied. Some congregations still opposed it, but others practiced it with enthusiasm. The Rossendale Valley group, mentioned before, not only performed music incidental to public worship but sang Handel's oratorios. Some of them participated in the Handel Festival at Westminster Abbey in 1784. All through the north of England music flourished in Baptist churches, serving not only as an accompaniment to worship but as a means of recreation as well. Singers and instrumentalists spent a great deal of time practicing, and those who possessed the skill asked no greater privilege than that of composing new music. One Thomas Jarman, for instance, wrote over six hundred hymn tunes and several anthems. A contribution to the cultural as well as to the religious life of simple village folk was the organization of some local music festivals.

Even the Presbyterians of Scotland did not remain untouched by the newer trend in congregational singing. It is said to have been introduced by English soldiers stationed in Aberdeen, one of whose number, Thomas Channon, was relieved of military duties in order that he might accept the invitation of several ministers to teach their congregations to sing. Channon formed choirs and revived part singing and was successful in abolishing graces and ornaments in the parishes in which he was active.

As early as 1755, Thomas Moore was engaged by the city officials of Glasgow to teach psalmody.

In 1820, R. A. Smith undertook the same duties in Scottish communities and later became choirmaster at St. George's, Edinburgh.

The movement did not meet with the popularity in Scotland that it enjoyed in England. Where teachers of psalmody were accepted, they generally brought about a better standard of singing than in England; but their field was relatively small.

It is ironical that the Nonconformists, who had rejected as worldly the fine music sung in the dignified settings of liturgical churches, not only admitted music of a more worldly type but allowed their choristers and instrumentalists to get entirely out of hand. Some of the disputes about music almost became brawls, and the feuds between musical and nonmusical factions make unpleasant reading.

Unsatisfactory as the situation was as regards both the standard of music and the manner of performing it, a real advance was made in removing prejudices, awakening a wider interest in worship music, and paving the way for better things to come.

✤ PROTESTANT CHURCH MUSIC IN AMERICA

In turning our thoughts back to the early history of America, it is difficult to know just when to stop thinking in terms of small, widely spread, underprivileged communities and begin to recognize the existence of centers that had achieved some social and cultural as well as commercial maturity. No doubt the realization of their altered status came as slowly to the urban dwellers of two centuries ago, for whom the growth from settlement to city was so gradual as to be imperceptible. Nevertheless, by 1750, the point in time at which we resume the story of Protestant worship music on this continent, several seaboard cities had assumed a commercial importance which rivalled that of European ports and were beginning to develop a sound cultural atmosphere.

That there was some taste for music other than that of public worship even before this time is indicated by records of concerts in Boston, New York, and Charleston, South Carolina in the 1730's. A ballad opera was performed in Charleston as early as 1735.

It was in communities such as these that the fight for "regular" singing of psalms and hymns was most successfully waged. Undoubtedly there were many urban dwellers who regretted the passing of the free and easy style of singing with its ornaments and graces, but here there were enough men of education and discernment to throw their weight in favor of dignity and decency in public worship. Here, too, were teachers capable of conducting singing classes along the lines laid out in *The Art of Singing Psalm Tunes* by John Tufts (1720), *The Grounds and Rules of Music Explained* by Thomas Walter (1721), and the many similar books that appeared from time to time, especially in New England.

Outside the cities, there were fewer opportunities for education and cultural advancement. What happened in Boston or New York was as remote to people living twenty miles from those cities as if it had happened in London or Paris. In the larger towns and villages, there were some voices that cried in the wilderness and received a response—musical missionaries from the cities or men with sound musical instincts who had managed to get hold of reliable singing instructors and to create an interest on the part of their neighbors.

In most rural communities and many small villages, however, the old, crudely embellished psalmody continued. It was not that the people in these places lacked instruction of a sort. Singing schools had become something of an institution which no community could do without; but whereas city-dwellers had sufficient diversion to permit them to take their singing lessons seriously, to rural folk the singing school was itself their chief diversion, a social pastime and recreation rather than an opportunity for learning. At many such gatherings, faulty methods of singing were encouraged rather than corrected by self-styled instructors who used books that pandered to the inclinations of the less musically educated. Not all singing instruction books were up to the standards set by Tufts and Walter. Besides those that advocated a continuation of "ornamentation," there were many "easy methods" which, like all easy methods before and since, were of little practical value.

The population of New England and the south in the pre-Revolutionary days was predominantly English and so was the music.

Church of England services were carried on in the old, traditional manner, often by capable organists who, discouraged by conditions at home and unable to meet the competition of foreign musicians, came to try their luck in the colonies. One of these, William Tuckey, became organist of Trinity Church, New York, in 1750, was one of the community's leading musicians for twenty-five years, and is credited with conducting the first colonial performance of Handel's *Messiah* (in abbreviated form) in 1770.

Immigrants from England kept the Nonconformists aware of trends in psalmody and hymnody in the old land; and the better educated collaborated with native Americans to improve congregational singing.

Public concerts, which are an indication of the improved musical atmosphere of the cities, may have owed something to the efforts of foreigners, as they did in England; but the colonial field was far less attractive than Europe for touring musicians. Gains in the performance and appreciation of music were due largely to the initiative of colonial musicians, aided by Englishmen who had been denied opportunities in their homeland because of the popular preference for foreigners.

The situation in Pennsylvania was quite different. Although the Quakers echewed music, we owe them a debt of gratitude for the hospitality and tolerance they accorded the music-loving peoples who settled among them. The Moravians, in particular, with their generations-old musical traditions, kept pace with developments in Europe and never allowed their music to decline. Although they kept pretty much to themselves, their neighbors could not help being aware of and influenced by their music. Thus we find that Philadelphia, in the 1750's, ranked with Boston and New York as a cultural center; and one of the earliest music schools was opened there by James Bremner in 1763.

The Revolutionary War threw American musicians more and more on their own resources. The wave of immigration from England abated, and those churchmen who did come over came with a far different attitude from that of their predecessors. Their presence was no longer a right, sometimes arrogantly exercised, but a privilege.

Immigration from other European countries increased, and music profited by it—but not church music. As we have seen, no advances in worship music were being made in Europe, and there was nothing new for the immigrants to bring with them. Lutheran congregations, for instance, increased greatly in numbers and swelled the volume of good, sound worship music; but their music was a heritage from a past generation, and it did not affect the English-speaking Americans who were not yet prepared to borrow from it.

What had been the Church of England, and was to be the Protestant Episcopal Church, lost in prestige and numbers. It is easy to understand that what had been the established church of a nation whose yoke had been recently and violently thrown off was regarded with suspicion. Many of its weaker members withdrew for reasons of patriotism or safety; many of the stronger ones, especially from the northeastern states, migrated to Canada in order that they might continue to live under the British crown.[1]

It was among the religious groups that stemmed from Calvinistic sources that most of the musical activity was to be found. We can no longer call them "Nonconformists" since, in the new republic, there were no official religious standards to which to conform. For want of a better term, we shall refer to them as "nonliturgical groups," although the description may not be strictly accurate in every case.

The development of music as an aid to worship ran parallel to what was taking place in England. There were no important additions, but there was the same striving for the establishment of a good standard of singing. There were also the charlatans who hampered progress.

[1] It is not generally realized that, early in the nineteenth century, the majority of the English-speaking population of Upper Canada, now Ontario, were people who had come from the United States. The British conquest of Canada had not been accomplished until 1759, and there had been no mad scramble of immigrants from the old country.

One of the most famous of the latter, and typical of his kind, was William Billings (1746–1800), a native of Boston and a tanner by trade. Like many others, he possessed a native talent for music, but not the patience and industry to develop it along sound lines. He must have heard and enjoyed a great deal of music, for his writings contain superficial similarities to other compositions of the time. He admits, in the preface to one of his books, to reading some treatises on harmony; but he dismisses as pedantic all generally accepted precepts and was firmly convinced that "Nature is the best dictator." Had he lived in an age of slogans, his might well have been: "Billings knows best."

Between the years 1770 and 1794, Billings published six music books, which contained commentaries on singing in their prefaces, and a great deal of music. He specialized in the so-called fuguing tunes, in which naive people thought they detected the influence of Handel; and it must be admitted that his melodies showed a great deal of spontaneity and originality. Certainly they proved attractive to great numbers of people who heard nothing but a bright tune with "lots of get" in it. Most of Billings' words were also original, and in these he was not so fortunate: his harmonies and rules of composition (still original) were decidedly unfortunate.

Billings was tremendously popular as a composer, and his style was widely imitated. There is no denying his sincerity or his right to compose as he wished, but it is regrettable that the more capable tune writers of his time did not share in his popularity. No musician took his work seriously, and Billings himself admitted that some of his tunes had not been worth printing: but the damage was done. He and his disciples made the task of the reformer much more difficult than it might otherwise have been.

Modern organists and choirmasters who complain of the clergy's poor taste in music—sometimes with justification—may be interested in knowing that, during the century of which we are writing, it was the clergy who led the crusade for better congregational singing. Many of the best tune books of the time were compiled either by ministers or by laymen working with the full support and encouragement of the clergy.

Early in the nineteenth century, there was a revulsion against fuguing tunes and ornamental singing in urban centers. Psalm tunes were sung as they were intended to be sung, and more dignified hymn tunes were given preference. Fuguing tunes remained in vogue in smaller places until the middle of the century, their popularity increasing as the distance from cities increased.

As part of the population shifted westwards, the pioneer conditions that had prevailed near the seaboard in the early colonial days were duplicated. Busy clearing and cultivating tracts of land, families were isolated for days or weeks at a time. Their loneliness and craving for companionship led to what became known as "camp meetings," occasional social gatherings where corporate worship was the chief occupation. Far removed from the ministrations of the regular clergy, leadership of these camp meetings or "revivals" was often undertaken by men whose credentials and qualifications were questionable. Their measure of success lay in their ability to work their listeners into a religious frenzy. People screamed, shouted, moaned, and wept. Although most of the meetings claimed to be under Methodist or Baptist auspices, there was little similarity to the worship of those two Protestant groups. Actually, the camp meetings led to the formation of a number of small sects, some of which adopted new titles, and some which claimed to be species of Methodists or Baptists.

There was no psalmody or hymnody suitable for this "old-time religion." For a while, the people used parts of the livelier hymn tunes, adding choruses or refrains in which the words "glory" and "hallelujah" were prominent. Sometimes, overtaken by what was called "the singing ecstasy," someone would improvise new verses and tunes.

This was too inviting a field for "composers" to neglect. It was not long before the itinerant singer accompanied the itinerant preacher, aiding in the incitement of the people to excessive emotional displays.

The next step was the publication of collections of these camp meeting songs, new and old. The most popular were Davisson's *Kentucky Harmony* (1820), Walker's *Southern Harmony* (1835), and White and King's *The Sacred Harp* (1844), the last of which was still going strong a century later.

One can understand the popularity of these "sacred songs" with uncritical, uneducated people for whom the camp meeting offered the only opportunity for whooping things up; but it is amazing that many of the songs, which have no appeal to either the literate or the musical, find a place among otherwise staid congregations under the classification of "good old hymns."

Meanwhile, a distinctive type of music had developed among the Negro population, chiefly in the South. The first Negroes were brought to America in 1619 so that by 1807, when the bill prohibiting the importation of slaves became effective, many of them were four, five, and six generations removed from their African ancestors. Two centuries in a new environment might well have eradicated nearly all traces of the musical peculiarities of their forebears had not new arrivals kept their music alive.

The slaves were a heterogenous people, originating in many parts of Africa, and there was a wide divergence in their language, customs, and music. "Negro music" cannot be applied as a comprehensive term. The singing of one cargo of slaves might sound very strange to another. The most common characteristics were a gapped scale, more often than not the pentatonic, and a strong sense of rhythm.

In addition to these varied sources, the slaves, always highly imitative, drew upon the music of their white masters and neighbors.

Negroes in America were early exposed to Christianity; some by being permitted a humble place in white men's churches, others through the efforts of missionaries. Whatever religion did for their masters, it brought some measure of comfort and hope to the slaves. Among themselves, they developed their own hymns or spiritual songs, using as texts words improvised on scriptural passages that appealed to their deeply emotional nature.

Many of the songs were first improvised by a leader, who sang a line or two and was answered by the chorus. There was often little relation between the words of one stanza and the next, but that seemed to matter little to the group waiting eagerly to raise their voices in the refrain. The melodies were often plaintive, generally vigorous, and there occurred unconscious reversions to primitive scales and rhythms.

It is noteworthy that, while their songs frequently reflected sadness, no note of bitterness, no suggestion of malice towards those who had enslaved them, was ever allowed to creep in.

The liveliness of the camp meeting hymn appealed to the Negroes— indeed, the whole atmosphere of the camp meeting found a ready response in them. On the whole, the revival type of song as improvised by the Negroes was a much better product than that of the whites, in that it contained elements of the musical gift that seems to be inherent in the African race.

✤ FESTIVALS AND CHORAL SOCIETIES

Nothing did more to further the cause of good choral music, in both Britain and America, than choir festivals and singing societies. They combined enthusiasm with good training and provided inspiration, not only for the participants but also for the crowds that gathered to hear them. Many oratorios and other large choral works were composed especially for such occasions.

It seems likely that, from quite early times, groups from two or three villages gathered once in a while for the purpose of singing together.

The practice of church choirs combining for such a purpose is recorded as early as 1655, when a yearly festival was inaugurated in London by the Corporation of the Sons of the Clergy. Since it had its beginning during the Commonwealth, the part played by music was very small. Later, however, there was a great deal of music and an orchestra was included. It was never a choral festival in the accepted sense, however, but rather a festival service.

Standard oratorios, as well as works commissioned for it, have always been featured in the Three Choirs Festival (the choirs being those of the cathedrals of Gloucester, Hereford, and Worcester) which has been held since 1724. It begins with a festival service and sermon on a Sunday, with the following four days devoted entirely to music.

The festivals at Birmingham from 1768, Norwich from 1770, Chester from 1772, and York from 1791 soon gained fame.

In Westminster Abbey, London, Handel commemorations in the four years beginning 1784, and in 1791, attracted the attention of the nation. A tremendous choir made up of singers from all parts of the country gathered to perform the works of the great German-English composer who, after his death, lost none of the prestige he enjoyed during his lifetime.

The United States was not far behind the old country in the formation of choral groups for special performances and they profited greatly by a strong German tradition added to their English choral heritage.

The *Collegium Musicum* of the Moravians, founded in 1744, was, in part, a choral group. Parts of several oratorios were performed very early; and Haydn's most famous ones, *The Creation* and *The Seasons,* were first sung in America at Bethlehem.

The Handel Society of Dartmouth College from 1780; the Harmonic Society of Fredericksburg, Virginia, from 1784; the Musical Society of Boston from 1785; the Musical Society of Stoughton, Massachusetts, about 1787; the Uranian Society of Philadelphia, from 1787; all flourished before the turn of the century.

On a more ambitious scale were the Handel and Haydn society of Boston, 1815; German *Männerchor* of Philadelphia, 1835; Chicago Sacred Music Society, 1842; *Deutsche Liederkranz* of New York, 1847, and the Milwaukee *Musikverein,* 1849.

Cincinnati was the scene of a great *Saengerfest* in 1849, in which most of the German singing societies participated.

Even the bald recital of these names tells an eloquent story of the spread of musical culture from the Atlantic to the Middle West, and of the enrichment of that culture by post-Revolutionary immigrants from continental Europe.

What did these choral societies and festivals, and the singing of oratorios, have to do with Protestant worship music? A great deal. In the first place, they represented the highest development of a tradition which had its roots in the congregational singing of Protestant churches. With few exceptions, the singers in these societies and festivals, apart from the soloists, were amateurs who had acquired a knowledge of and enthusiasm for part singing at their religious gatherings. With all its imperfections, congregational singing did prepare the more gifted for the musical discipline and better training that they received as members of the more advanced singing groups.

The debt that choral societies owed to congregational singing was amply repaid by the example and inspiration they provided, not only to their own but to all singers and by offsetting the pernicious singing practices that prevailed among so many congregations.

Choral groups for the purpose of singing more music than the worship services could permit sprang up in all settled parts of America, in England (especially in the north), and in Wales. Some were good, some not so good; but the more ardent choristers, especially when fortunate enough to have competent instructors, not only did their little bit towards maintaining and improving the standard of singing but derived immense pleasure from so doing.

❖ THE REVIVAL OF BACH

The importance of the rediscovery of Johann Sebastian Bach's music in the early nineteenth century, especially his organ and choral music, cannot be overestimated.

It is not clear how the old manuscripts, which had been gathering dust for over half a century, came to light. It would appear that one Karl Freidrich Horn, a German domiciled in London, was aware of them and perhaps had some of them in his possession; for his son, Charles Edward, was closely associated with a small group of Englishmen who were keenly interested in introducing the music of Bach to their fellow-countrymen.

Surrey Chapel, London, an Independent meetinghouse, was for some years the center of the revival. In 1808, the organist Benjamin Jacob was in correspondence with Samuel Wesley and William Crotch concerning the music of Bach; and in the following year, these three English organists began a long series of Bach recitals in the Surrey Chapel. The programmes often consisted of forty or fifty numbers and lasted three or four hours, yet the audiences were consistently large and appreciative.

It must have been no mean feat to play some of the tremendous organ works on an instrument of only thirteen stops and a pedal board of only an octave and a half. (Only one octave of independent pedal pipes was available. The rest of the notes were "borrowed.")

The recitals were not confined to Bach's organ works. Wesley himself played some of the violin sonatas.

Samuel Wesley and Charles Horn issued an edition of Bach's organ *Trios* in 1810, and one of *The Well-Tempered Clavier* in 1813. (This is the same Charles Edward Horn who emigrated to the United States about 1826, and became conductor of the Handel and Haydn Society in Boston.)

The Germans were even longer in discovering Bach. Felix Mendelssohn, from childhood an admirer of the neglected master, formed a small choir of sixteen voices in the year 1827 to practice the *Passion According to St. Matthew*. So great was the interest created among his friends and the friends of the singers that it was decided to perform the work at the *Singakademie* on a large scale. In 1829, the first public performance outside of Leipzig of the *Passion* since Bach's death was given, and hundreds of people were unable to gain admittance.

As a musician of international repute, Mendelssohn was able to carry on a missionary work on behalf of Bach more effectively than the little English group, who enjoyed considerably less prestige. Schumann became an early convert; and by the middle of the nineteenth century, Bach was a far greater figure than he had been when he was alive.

It takes but a moment's reflection to realize what a void there would be in present-day music, concert as well as worship, had it not been for the persistence and enthusiasm of the tiny Bach cult of a century and a half ago.

✤ WOMEN AS CHORISTERS

The presence of women in church choirs would have been considered unseemly two centuries ago. Never in history had they been permitted a voice in the government of the church, or a part in the performances of the services. Indeed, any activity that made her conspicuous (unless it was ruling a country) was likely to ruin a woman's reputation. Self-effacement was a condition of respectability.

It cannot be said that church music suffered because of the absence of women's voices. The soprano part was sung admirably by boys, or, rarely except in Italy, by *castrati;* the alto derived its name from the fact that it was the highest man's part, sung by men who had retained the ability to produce their upper tones with the same quality of voice as the boys. (They came to be called counter-tenors.) Some of the anthems in the reference list at the end of Chapter XII are for three voices —alto, tenor, and bass—and were intended to be sung by men only.

In the early eighteenth century, male sopranos and altos were preferred even in the field of opera; and, since the demand soon exceeded the supply, these men were able to sing pretty much on their own terms. When women were engaged for the opera, they required not only fine voices but a great deal of courage, for the public had a low regard for female entertainers.

We can imagine the Puritans' tight-lipped disapproval of these Jezebels, or of any woman who behaved in a manner that would attract attention to her: yet it was in chapels steeped in Puritan and Calvinistic tradition that women first appeared in choirs. Their admission must have caused much soul searching, much flaying of conscience, and much opposition, but it was accomplished.

For a long time, Calvinistic congregations were untroubled by the problem of choirs. Organized groups of singers smacked too much of the Catholic customs which they had renounced and presented the danger of monopolizing worship music to the exclusion of the congregation. Since the only permissible music was that of the metrical psalms, there was no need for choirs anyway.

Early in the history of Calvinism, psalm tunes in four parts were sometimes written and published; but these were not intended for public worship. The custom of singing in parts at social gatherings was popular, and it was probably thought that the provision of psalm tunes in harmony would remove the temptation to sing more worldly and lively airs in the home. Within the family circle, women were expected to sing their part (which was not the melody) ; in church, they sang in unison with the men, taking care to keep their voices discreetly modulated.

When four-part harmony and choirs were finally permitted in some chapels, there seemed no alternative but to swallow scruples and have the women sing the soprano part. (There seems to have been no shortage of male altos, and it was a long time before they were displaced by women.)

One can think of several reasons why the nonliturgical groups did not use boys for the soprano part. Choir boys were too reminiscent of the formal services of the liturgical churches; they required constant training, since the personnel of a boys' choir changes as voices change. There were probably few people in England, outside cathedrals and large churches, capable of refining boys' voices, and fewer still in America, where it was extremely difficult to maintain boy soprano sections even in Roman Catholic and Anglican churches.

To these practical reasons was added the consideration that many Calvinistic groups were chary of having unbelievers join in their psalms and hymns. While the children were scarcely unbelievers in the sense of having rejected the doctrines, they were too young to have made a confession of faith that would result in their full acceptance into the congregation.

Perhaps any or all of these reasons were used as excuses for using women instead of boy sopranos. The chief factor, seldom admitted, was the preservation of the pleasant, social atmosphere that had long marked the rehearsals of part-singers. It is not suggested that the men and women did not take their singing seriously, but the companionship, the conversation and exchange of gossip that preceded, interlarded and followed the singing, would be missed. The goings-on in some choir lofts were evidence that none of the social atmosphere was lost!

Whatever doubts the die-hards may have entertained regarding the propriety of women in choirs, all progress in the music of nonliturgical churches was made possible by mixed choirs. Choral societies, and those festivals that were not specifically under the auspices of Anglical cathedrals, had soprano sections made up chiefly or wholly of women.

Most tune books of the time, including those of William Billings, gave the part between the soprano and the tenor to men, and called them altos, counters, or counter-tenors. According to *The Oxford Companion to Music,* at the great Handel Commemoration in Westminster Abbey in 1784, all forty-five altos in the choir were men, although there were many women in the soprano section.

When women did begin singing a lower part, they were known as contraltos, a word that had a quite different meaning from alto at the time. An alto was one who sang the highest man's part; a contralto was a woman who sang the part below the highest, or soprano, part. Nowadays, the woman's part is known as the alto, a misnomer that has nothing to recommend it except long usage.

As late as 1883, forty-two of the fifty-nine altos in the Leeds Festival chorus were men.

In America, male altos have always been comparatively rare; although Billings' provision for them in the most widely circulated hymn books of the day indicates that they were to be found at least among the singers of fuguing tunes.

❖ THE ORGAN

The development of organ music in English-speaking countries continued to be retarded by the limitations of the instrument.

Although it is difficult to unearth authentic information, it is believed that some English organs—possibly only two or three—possessed some kind of pedal boards as early as the middle of the eighteenth century. It is just possible that in America, too, organs with pedals were built in obscure places by builders who had become accustomed to the contrivance in Germany. John Klemm, who installed the organ in the Moravian church in Bethlehem in 1746, and David Tenneberger, at one time associated with Klemm and a builder of organs in many of the thirteen colonies, were probably familiar with pedals, and may have used them to a limited extent.

Several English organs were fitted with pedals by 1790; although, in most cases, the pedals merely acted upon the manual keys, having no pipes of their own. There was no uniformity in the number of pedals. Some organs had an octave, some an octave and a half, and the organ at

St. Paul's, London, had two octaves. Very often the lowest pedal note was G (bottom line of the bass staff).

It was impossible to develop a good pedal technic with such a variety of keyboards. Many of the outstanding organists stubbornly refused to have anything to do with pedals.

As late as 1844, Mendelssohn had to cancel an organ recital in London because the organ on which he was to have played had insufficient pedals.

Many instruments had incomplete swell organs, some of the ranks of pipes lacking the bottom octave in the bass. (This condition is still found in some old organs.)

The missionary work of those who were trying to revive Bach's music was hampered by these incomplete organs that would not meet the demands of the performances.

On the other hand, English builders were among the first to devise mechanical improvements. Swell shutters in a crude form were known as early as 1712, pneumatic action in 1832, composition or combination pedals in 1809.

Organ building in the United States kept pace with developments in Europe. Improvements in action and voicing were borrowed from the English, and the features for which German organs had long been famous were introduced by immigrant builders from that country. The instrument at the South Reformed Church, in New York, was the first in America to have an independent pedal organ.

Congregations unable to afford pipe organs had their problems partly solved in 1840 with the invention of the harmonium, better known to later generations as the "parlor organ." It lacked much, but it was better than nothing at all for accompanying singing. It was much easier to play than a pipe organ and much more accessible to amateurs. Some well-known composers, recognizing the popularity and possibilities of the harmonium, wrote for it; and both Berlioz and Widor gave it some space in their treatises on instrumentation. It is almost extinct now, but it served its brief purpose as an aid in the promotion of congregational singing.

A variant of the harmonium was the melodeon, or American organ, in which the air was sucked through instead of blown into the reeds. Two-manual instruments with pedal boards were made available, the air being pumped by hand or, later, provided by electrically driven blowers. These instruments provided organists opportunities for practice when they did not have access to pipe organs.

The pumper was an indispensable personage in churches where there were pipe organs. Large organs required the services of two, three, or even more, without whose efforts the organist would have been helpless.

An important aid to organists was provided in 1811 by Vincent No-vello, a Roman Catholic organist who, forced to publish some of his own works, wrote out the complete organ part instead of merely the figured bass. The innovation was opposed by many organists capable of work-ing out their own accompaniments, but was received with gratitude by thousands of others who read figured bass with difficulty, if at all. The practice of printing organ accompaniments in full has prevailed ever since.

A contribution of equal value was that of J. A. Novello, son of Vin-cent, who published large quantities of choral music at low prices. Many choirs and choral societies that had previously sung from ill-written manu-scripts or from memory were now able, thanks to Novello's enterprise, to possess music libraries and extend their repertoires.

✤ REFERENCES

Psalm and Hymn Tunes

The selected list of sources given below refers the reader to various types of tunes written during the period 1750–1850, regardless of their merit. Not all tunes attributed to composers or collections mentioned here are recommended for use.

It will be noticed that there are fewer Germanic composers and tune books than appeared in previous lists. On the other hand, the inclusion of many American names and sources reflects increased activity on the part of the tune writers of this continent.

Although hymnals that have been consulted in the preparation of this list do not contain tunes from some of the early American collections, the names of such collections are included here for the convenience of readers who may have access to them.

Beaty, R. W., 1799–1883.
Beaumont, John, 1762–1822.
Billings' *Continental Harmony*, 1794.
Billings' *New England Psalm Singer*, 1770.
Billings' *Psalm Singers' Amusement*, 1781.
Billings' *Suffolk Harmony*, 1786.
Bremner's *Collection*, 1763.
Christian Lyre, The, 1832.
Clark, Thomas, 1775–1859.
Cooke, Robert, 1768–1814.

Cunningham's *A Selection of Psalm Tunes*, 1834.
Dougall, Neil, 1776–1862.
Edwards, J. D., 1805–1885.
Ett's *Cantica Sacra*, 1840.
Fawcett's *A New Set of Sacred Music*, c. 1822.
Filitz, F., 1804–1876.
Fink, Gottfried W., 1783–1846.
Flagg's *Collection of Best Psalm Tunes*, 1766.
Flemming, F. F., 1778–1813.

Gardiner's *Sacred Melodies,* 1812, 1815.
Harington, Henry, 1727–1816.
Harmonia Sacra, 1753.
Harrison, R., 1748–1810.
Hartig's *Vollständige Sammlung,* c. 1829.
Hatton, John, d. 1793 (?)
Havergal, William H., 1793–1870.
Haweis, Thomas, 1734–1820.
Haydn, Franz Josef, 1732–1809.
Haydn, Johann Michael, 1737–1806.
Hews, George, 1806–1873.
Holden, Oliver, 1765–1844.
Horsley, William, 1774–1858.
Hutcheson, Charles, 1792–1860.
Jackson, Thomas, 1715–1780.
Jones, William, 1726–1800.
Katholisches Gesangbuch, Vienna, 1778.
Knecht, Justin Heinrich, 1752–1817.
Kocher, Conrad, 1786–1872.
Law's *Collection of Best Tunes and Anthems,* 1779.
Law's *Select Harmony,* 1778.
Law's *Select Number of Plain Tunes,* 1767.
Lyon's *Urania,* 1761.
Madan, Martin, 1726–1790.
Marsh, Simeon Butler, 1798–1875.
Mason and Webb's *Cantica Laudis,* 1850.
Mason, Lowell, 1792–1872.
Mason's *Companion,* 1847.

Mason, Timothy Battle, 1801–1861.
Methfessel's *Lieder- und Commerbuch,* 1818.
Miller, Edward, 1731–1807.
Mills's *Caniadau Seion,* 1840.
Missouri Harmony, The, 1837.
Novello, F. Vincent, 1781–1861.
Oliver, Henry Kemble, 1800–1885.
Pleyel, Ignaz Josef, 1757–1831.
Psalmodia Evangelica, 1790.
Randall, John, 1715–1799.
Reinagle, Alexander Robert, 1799–1877.
Rheinhardt MSS, Uttingen, 1754.
Sacred Harmony, Leeds, 1720.
Sacred Harp, The, 1844.
Schulz, J. A. P., 1747–1800.
Shrubsole, William, 1760–1806.
Smart, George Thomas, 1776–1867.
Smith, Isaac, c. 1735–1800.
Stanley, Samuel, 1767–1822.
Stockton, John H., 1713–1777.
Turle, James, 1802–1882.
Union Harmony, The, Virginia, 1848.
Watson, James, 1816–1880.
Webb, George James, 1803–1887.
Webbe, Samuel, 1740–1816.
Werner's *Choralbuch,* 1815.
Western Lyre, The, Cincinnati, 1831.
Willis, Richard Storrs, 1810–1900.
Wilson, Hugh, 1766–1824.
Woodbury, Isaac Baker, 1819–1858.
Zeuner, Heinrich, early 19th cent.

Anthems, Motets, Oratorios

Asterisks denote oratorios and other extended choral works.

Arnold, Samuel—
  Who is this that cometh? [N]
Attwood, Thomas—
  Come, Holy Ghost [S]
  O God, who by the leading of a star [F]
  Teach me, O Lord [S]
  Turn thy face from my sins [F]

Battishill, Jonathan—
  Behold, how good and joyful [N]
  Call to remembrance [F]
  I will magnify thee, O God [N]
  O Lord, look down from heaven [N]
Beale, William—
  Bow down thine ear [N]

Beckwith, John C.—
  Lord is very great, The [N]
  My soul is weary of life [N]
Billings, William—
  A Virgin unspotted [B]
  Easter Anthem [S]
  I am the Rose of Sharon [S]
Bortnianski, Dimitri—
  Glory to God in heaven [F]
  Lord, to us be ever heeding (Cherubic Hymn) [B]
Camidge, J.—
  Lo! star-led chiefs [N]
Chard, G. W.—
  To celebrate thy praise [N]
Cherubini, L.—
  O strengthen, Lord [N]
  Praise ye the Lord [S]
Clarke-Whitfeld, J.—
  Behold, how good and joyful [N]
  Behold, now praise the Lord [N]
  Blessed is the man [N]
  Enter not into judgement [N]
  Hear, O thou Shepherd of Israel [N]
  I will alway give thinks [N]
  I will lift up mine eyes [N]
  O praise God in his holiness [N]
  Sing unto the Lord [N]
Crotch, William—
  Comfort, O Lord, the soul of thy servant [N]
  How dear are thy counsels [N]
  Methinks I hear the full celestial choir [S]
  O come hither and hearken [N]
  Prayer for peace [N]
  Sing we merrily [N]
Dupuis, T. S.—
  Not unto us, O Lord [N]
  O God, whose nature and property [N]
Ebdon, Thomas—
  Praised be the Lord daily [N]
Gauntlett, H. J.—
  I will go unto the altar of God [N]

This is the day the Lord hath made [N]
Thou wilt keep him in perfect peace [N]
Haydn, Franz Josef—
  Creation, The [S]
  Mass in D [S]
  Te Deum [F]
Haydn, Johann Michael—
  Passion Motets [S]
Hayes, Philip—
  Lord descended, The [N]
Himmel, F. H.—
  Father, I call to thee [F]
  Incline thine ear [F]
  O come, let us worship [N]
Horsley, William—
  Let thy merciful ears [N]
Lyon, James—
  Blessed be the Lord God of our fathers [N]
Mendelssohn, Felix—
  As the hart pants (Psalm 42) [S]
  Christus [S]
  Come, let us sing (Psalm 95) [S]
  Elijah [S]
  Hear my prayer [S]
  Hymn of Praise [S]
  In deep distress (Psalm 130) [N]
  Judge me, O God (Psalm 43) [S]
  Lord, how long wilt thou forget me (Psalm 13) [N]
  O praise the Lord [N]
  When Israel out of Egypt came [N]
Neukomm, S. R. von—
  Blessed is he that cometh [N]
Novello, Vincent—
  Blessed is the people [N]
  I will sing of mercy and judgement [N]
  Like as the hart [S]
  Lord is my strength, The [F]
  Pray for the peace of Jerusalem [N]
  There is a river [N]

Smith, John S.—
Almighty and everlasting God [N]
Come unto Me [N]
Spohr, Louis—
As pants the hart [S]
From the deep I called [N]
God is my Shepherd [N]
How lovely are thy dwellings fair [S]
Jehovah, Lord God of hosts [N]
Turle, James—
Almighty and most merciful God [N]
Arise, and help us [N]
Hear my crying, O God [N]
Lord that made heaven and earth, The [N]
This is the day which the Lord hath made [N]
Walmisley, T. A.—
*Lord shall comfort Zion, The [F]
Webbe, Samuel—
Christ being raised from the dead [N]

Wesley, Samuel (the elder) —
Behold, how good and joyful [N]
Sing aloud with gladness [N]
Thou art a priest for ever [N]
Thou, O God, art praised in Sion [N]
When Israel came out of Egypt [N]
Wesley, Samuel Sebastian—
All go unto one place [N]
Ascribe unto the Lord [N]
Blessed be the God and Father [N]
Face of the Lord, The [F]
God be merciful unto us [N]
Lead me, Lord [F]
Let us now praise famous men [N]
O Lord, thou art my God [N]
To my request and earnest cry [N]
Wash me thoroughly from my wickedness [S]
Wilderness, The [N]

14

THE LATE
NINETEENTH CENTURY

❖ A GENERAL APPRAISAL

The last half of the nineteenth century, which we associate with amazing progress in science, industry, and commerce, with great statesmen and preachers, with the flowering of philosophies and institutions which we still cherish, was a period of mediocrity in the field of arts. The leadership which English-speaking peoples exercised in other fields was lacking: indeed, they lagged far behind their contemporaries of continental Europe, especially in music.

The failure of our musicians to scale the heights attained by Europeans—Brahms, Wagner, Verdi, and others—was due to a complex set of circumstances which would require a complete book to analyse. Long neglect of native music and musicians in Britain, lack of tradition in America, preoccupation of both peoples with such practical things as politics, industry, and commerce, were all contributing factors. The characteristic conventionality and reserve of the British, inherited by a large section of the population of the United States, restrained composers from making daring innovations and breaking new ground. They were good craftsmen and excellent followers along paths that had been clearly defined by others, but they were incapable of making successful and significant explorations away from the beaten track.

The social atmosphere was not such as would inspire a creative musician—indeed, it may be said that there was scarcely any musical atmosphere at all. Music was not part of the people's lives as it was in continental Europe. It is true that there were festivals and singing schools conducted in a staid, formal, almost self-conscious manner, but there were not the spontaneous little fiestas that sprang into being whenever a group of Italians or Bohemians got together.

In short, there was no *hunger* for music. Our grandparents could take it or leave it alone. They left alone, almost severely, music with an intellectual appeal and found their pleasure in ear-tickling melodies that they could hum when they wanted to.

If composers who attempted serious music failed to arouse a public at home or abroad, those who wrote in a lighter vein were more fortunate, and it is by the music of these latter that we judge the Victorians. Their efforts must not be disparaged. Their harmony and form were good, their melodies were attractive. If the general effect was romantic and sentimental and lacking in depth, appealing wholly to the ear and not at all to the intellect, it must be remembered that in no other way could they have awakened public interest in music of a better type than that of the so-called music halls. If what they offered was not the best, it was certainly not the worst.

Theodore Finney, in *A History of Music,* refers to the late nineteenth century as a period of adolescence in American music, and the products of American composers as "people's music." He could have said the same of British music. Indeed, continental Europe had its musical adolescents and composers who wrote for them; but it also had what English-speaking countries lacked—a musically mature public sufficiently large to support and encourage composers of serious, intellectual music.

British and American music of the late nineteenth century was, then, a reflection of its time and locale, and that is all that one can expect from any art. In its own peculiar ways, it was as important in the development of music as organum and ars nova. As with these, it was an expression of the times; as with these, too, it will merge (is, indeed, now merging) into something better and more mature.

❖ THE OXFORD MOVEMENT

A century after the Wesley brothers laid the foundation for Methodism at Oxford University, another group in the same university began the Tractarian, or Oxford movement.

Like Methodism, the Oxford movement, begun in 1833, was intended as a reform within the Church of England. Unlike the Wesleys, who had strong evangelistic and Calvinistic leanings, the Tractarians inclined toward the Roman Catholic Church. Both movements met with strong opposition; but, whereas the Methodists were eventually frozen out of the Anglican Church, the Tractarians remained as the High Church, or Anglo-Catholic, party (although such prominent leaders as John Henry Newman and Frederick William Faber renounced their Anglican orders and were ordained into the Roman Catholic priesthood).

The Tractarians, while less concerned with music than the Wesleyans had been, had just as great an influence on worship music, although of a different type. They sought to restore dignity to public worship by improving the cathedral services and by introducing cathedral practice in modified form to parish churches.

In many places where the music had been confined to hymns or metrical psalms and possibly the chanting of the canticles at Matins and Evensong the prose psalms were now chanted. The intoning of the responses, the introduction of anthems and sung settings of the communion service soon followed. Ritual and ceremony increased. Choirs, which had occupied a modest position in the gallery, often at the rear of the church, were now surpliced and placed in the chancel. There was a general tendency towards using choirs of boys and men, following the traditional cathedral practice.

Whatever else may be said about the Oxford movement, and the Low, or Evangelical, party of the church had a great many critical things to say, it did achieve its purpose of restoring dignity. There was a general renascence of cathedral music; and in most parish churches, a far better standard than had existed before. The new position and dignity of the choir resulted in a better behaved and better disciplined body of singers and, consequently, a better performance.

Although they were concerned wholly with the Church of England, the influence of the Tractarians is felt by all Protestants. An attempt to delete some of their hymns from any Protestant hymnal would meet with general opposition. Newman's "Lead, kindly light" and "Praise to the Holiest in the height"; Faber's "Faith of our fathers"; "Hark, hark, my soul," and "Souls of men, why will ye scatter"; and John Keble's "New every morning," "Sun of my soul," and "Blest are the pure in heart" are among the many hymns we think of in connection with the Oxford movement which have become the property of all Protestants.

Like the Wesleyans before them, the Anglicans began to realize, somewhat belatedly, the value of congregational singing as a means of encouraging general participation in public worship. That so many fine hymns were written in the nineteenth century was due to the great need for additions to hymnody—or perhaps it would be more accurate to say that it was due to the realization of a need that had long existed.

There were not a great many hymns of enduring quality. Hymn writing was a comparatively new art. It was less than a century and a half since Isaac Watts had published his collection, and such "man-made" verses had been accepted for an even shorter time. There had been writers of religious verse before Watts but, because of a general prejudice, little of their work survived as hymns. There had been hymn writers after Watts, too, but only a small percentage of their hymns had qualities that make for survival.

Some of the metrical psalms remained and were given a place in the hymnody of the time, but many others were too crudely and awkwardly phrased to serve as expressions of nineteenth-century praise. Hymns of nonliturgical groups employed many meters, some of which invited a musical treatment inconsistent with the dignity that had become the goal of the Tractarians.

Among the outstanding and prolific writers of late nineteenth-century hymns were clergymen. In addition to the leaders of the Oxford movement, whom we have mentioned, Sabine Baring-Gould, William Walsham How, and John Ellerton wrote hymns that were typically Victorian. All of them are represented in almost any hymnal. They combined the staid, regular meters of the old psalm paraphrases with the deft phraseology of contemporary poets typified by Tennyson.

The increase in the number of hymns created a demand for tunes to which they could be sung; and there arose a veritable host of tune writers.

Many of the metrical psalm tunes survived, as they survive today, being used not only for psalm paraphrases but also for hymns of the same meters. The list of hymn tune sources at the end of Chapter X, containing the names of psalm books as far back as the sixteenth century, was compiled from modern hymnals. All these tunes were current in the 1800's.

Available, too, were some of the German choral tunes, but only some of them. As it has been mentioned, Victorian hymn writers showed a decided preference for uncomplicated meters, and only such German tunes as agreed with the metrical patterns could be used. It was not until after the middle of the century that writers like Catherine Winkworth gave us such beautiful translations from the German as "Deck thyself, my soul, with gladness"; "Now thank we all our God" and "Praise to the Lord, the Almighty, the King of creation," thus enabling us to use tunes of less familiar meters: *Schmücke Dich, Nun Danket* and *Lobe Den Herren*.

Tunes of the eighteenth century, by men such as Croft and Darwall, whose style the best of the Victorians adopted, were not numerous.

A comparison of the majority of Victorian tunes with those that survived from the periods of the Reformation and the eighteenth century, and with such German tunes as had found their way into English usage, reveals many similarities. The melodic lines were well rounded and perhaps a little more spontaneous; although where would one find brighter melodies than those of *St. Michael (Old 134th)*: "Revive thy work, O Lord" which came to us from the Genevan Psalter of 1551; *Darwall:* "Rejoice, the Lord is King" from 1770; or *Franconia:* "Blest are the pure in heart" from a German tune book of 1738? The rhythms tend to be more regular and conservative than even some of the early psalm tunes and chorals.

There are a few harmonic devices used that were unknown to hymn tune writers of a century earlier, but seldom are they extreme. There are scores of tunes in which there is no more than simple transient modulation through a related key, and the melodies depart from the sounds of the original scale only insofar as they are required to do so by the modulation. This is not chromaticism. Very few of the tunes that retained popularity were chromatic in the sense that they introduced notes foreign to the scale.

Many composers succeeded in writing bass parts which added vigor to the tunes; and others, notably J. B. Dykes, treated their inner parts with a freedom that had been unknown since polyphonic days. In consequence, part singers hailed with enthusiasm these tunes which gave them such interesting parts to sing. Altos, tenors, and basses invariably put forth their best efforts when singing tunes like *Melitia:* "Eternal Father, strong to save" and *Gerontius:* "Praise to the Holiest" by Dykes; and *Dalkeith:* "Weary of earth" by Thomas Hewlett. They are inclined to resent the singing of such tunes in unison, since the loss of the inner parts considerably weakens the effect.

Church composers were using, in modest forms, the latest developments in music—developments made possible by the experimentation of Haydn and Mozart, Beethoven and Brahms, in larger and more complex forms. That the same musical devices used for sentimental and romantic secular music were used for church music does not necessarily mean that all church music was sentimental and romantic. Certainly, many of the Victorian tunes met the Tractarians' specifications for dignity and vigor.

It is not to be supposed that the writing of hymns and tunes was confined to adherents of the Oxford movement. Churchmen of all stamps, High and Low, Anglican and Nonconformist, having been given the lead by the Tractarians, contributed largely to hymnody.

The Reverend John Bacchus Dykes (1823–1876) stands out as one whose tunes are the most numerous in almost any Protestant hymnal. If the reader will look up the hymns set to Dykes's tunes in his own hymnal, he will conclude that they are indispensable, at least for the present.

Four successive organists of St. Paul's Cathedral, London—Thomas Attwood, John Goss, John Stainer, and George C. Martin—were among the leading church music composers.

Stainer (1840–1901) had a happy knack of treating sympathetically the words for which he was composing. Enjoying as he did more prestige than any other church musician of his generation, he was able to exercise a wide influence in the improvement of church music. Not content with raising the music of St. Paul's to a high standard, he took a great interest in the music of parish churches. Much of his work was written for amateur choirs and congregational singing, and he did an invaluable work as editor of hymnals and psalters.

William Henry Monk (1823–1889), who wrote many hymn tunes, made his greatest contribution as editor of *Hymns Ancient and Modern,* which appeared in its first edition in 1861. This was not a great hymnal, certainly not worthy of the veneration paid it by the majority of the English public; but it was the means of spreading and popularizing the Victorian hymn. It proved to be of the greatest value in the promotion of congregational singing, chiefly among Anglicans, but among other groups as well. Considering that over sixty million copies were sold in its first fifty-three years, it is not surprising that most of its tunes are still current in England, and many of them in America. The number of people who have learned to sing parts from "Hymns A. & M." is incalculable.

While it is not difficult to make a good case for the better type of Victorian hymn tune, it must be admitted that some of them were pretty sticky and sentimental. Others were incredibly dull. Perhaps the percentage of poorer tunes was no greater than in earlier times. Our veneration of the past is generally due to the fact that only the best examples survive: the poorer examples gradually languished and finally died with the passage of time. The poorer examples of Victorian hymns have not had time to die. A hundred years from now, when all trace of them has disappeared, people will judge the Victorian era by its best features and perhaps conclude that its hymnody was not as bad as some of our present-day critics would have us believe.

If, as a result of the Oxford movement, congregational singing was encouraged and raised to a higher standard by the provision of new hymns and tunes, the people's participation in other parts of the service was made more difficult.

It had been the custom in most parish churches to read the prose psalms, minister and congregation taking alternate verses. The canticles at Morning and Evening Prayer were also read in some places, although, since they were used every Sunday, thus offering an opportunity for the people to become familiar with them, they were generally chanted by choir and congregation. In many parish churches, the custom of chanting the psalms was now adopted, and the output of chants was almost as great as that of hymn tunes. The experiment was not invariably a happy one.

There was not, and never had been, any generally accepted method of pointing the psalms. A choirmaster would decide what syllables were to be stressed and what words would be sung to certain notes and mark the choristers' prayer books accordingly. Since the direction of choirs was often in the hands of amateurs, some of the pointing was strange indeed. Moreover, a parish choir would sing any particular psalm infrequently, and therefore seldom chanted with any degree of confidence. The congregation, with no visual aids, had no alternative but to remain silent.

In 1837, Robert Janes published the first-known set of instructions for pointing, but most churches preferred the systems that had become traditional with them. During the half century that followed, pointed psalters were prepared by several capable clergymen and church musicians working together, and the results were good. However, there has never been any uniformity in the manner of pointing. A misconception of the principles of chanting leads to a jerky, spasmodic rendering instead of an easy flow of words and melody. Lack of any kind of instruction leaves the people mute during a part of the service that is traditionally theirs.

The attempts of overambitious, unprepared choirs to sing the responses and the communion service also tended to silence the congregation. John Stainer and others did yeoman service in preparing psalters and service books for the guidance of choirs that were attempting choral services, but the books were variously interpreted. A score of competent instructors moving from parish to parish would have accomplished in a decade what a century has failed to accomplish.

It must not be supposed that these changes were accepted meekly by all churches in the Anglican communion. In the United States and Canada, as well as in Great Britain, surpliced choirs, sung services, and the extension of ritual caused much dissension in many parish churches. These outward signs were construed by many Evangelical churchmen as steps towards Rome, and the transition of such men as Newman and Faber from Anglo-Catholicism to Roman Catholicism seemed to support their contention.

✤ CONGREGATIONAL SINGING IN NONLITURGICAL CHURCHES

While nonliturgical groups, both in Britain and America, benefited as much as did their Anglican neighbors from the wave of hymn writing that resulted from the Oxford movement, the need for additions to their hymnody was less pressing.

Congregational singing had flourished for a long time, as we remarked in earlier chapters. As restrictions were gradually removed and singing in harmony was permitted, not only the choir sang the parts but most of the congregation as well. There were plenty of hymn and tune books and, while most of them were of an ephemeral nature, they were popular in their day.

Through most of the nineteenth century, singing schools continued to provide recreation and instruction. The calibre of the instructors and the methods they used were generally improved. From the ranks of men and women who learned to read the parts of hymn tunes and choruses came amateur conductors and composers and a few who were inspired to study music seriously.

No movement becomes popular without the efforts of zealous and dedicated leaders; and nonliturgical bodies, especially the longer established ones, were fortunate in that many of their spiritual leaders were among the most ardent advocates of congregational singing.

We read of a blind Congregational minister, the Reverend John Waite, who went from town to town in England encouraging and instructing singing classes where they existed, and organizing them where they did not. In addition to the time and inconvenience such missionary journeys must have cost him, he prepared a set of tune books with staff notation for those able to read it and an added system of numerals for the assistance of beginners.

The Congregationalists enjoyed the services of some excellent organists and composers. For example, Dr. H. J. Gauntlett (1805–1876), who wrote many hymn tunes in the best Victorian style—he claimed to have written ten thousand!—served for some time as organist at Union Chapel, Islington. It is almost certain that he wrote and used some of his tunes there and introduced others of the contemporary Anglican school.

Hymn singing was not the greatest musical accomplishment of the Union Chapel congregation. A singing class (or psalmody school, as they called it) was conducted there for many years; and it was reported that, at one time, nearly three hundred members were actually paying for instruction. In the 1870's (perhaps even a little earlier) congregations of as many as a thousand people regularly sang anthems at the Sunday services—not particularly simple anthems, but those which a modern, well-trained choir would sing only after some rehearsal. On Christmas Day, the congregation sang parts of Handel's *Messiah*.

While conditions at Union Chapel were unusually favorable to music, the congregation there was by no means the only one that sang anthems. Performances varied in quality with the amount and quality of the instruction received at local singing schools. Perhaps some congregations would have been better advised to confine their efforts to less ambitious music, but the general standard of singing was better than fair.

The change in attitude of this one-time Puritan body was completed soon after the middle of the century, when many chapels began chanting the prose psalms. Some of the larger chapel congregations used the Anglican chant before it was much used in many Anglican parish churches. That they used it more intelligently was due to the fact that they had better instructors than the smaller Anglican churches could afford. Chanting was not confined to choirs in Congregational churches: it was shared by the whole body of worshippers, as it should be.

Some of the larger congregations were prosperous enough to publish music, and from this source came the London house of Curwen and Sons. This firm is mentioned because its founder, like the Novellos half a century earlier, established it primarily as a service rather than a business.

The Reverend James Curwen (1816–1880) was one of the many clergymen who were promoting congregational singing. Like his fellows, he issued tune books, anthem collections, and instruction books, but his most important work was the perfecting of a system that would assist people who found the orthodox method of reading music difficult.

From time immemorial there have been codes intended to designate the pitch and duration of notes. The conventional system of notation is itself a code designed to end all codes; but, among amateurs, auxiliary systems still persist.

Since the seventeenth century, and perhaps even earlier, a *sol-fa* system had been in vogue among amateur musicians in England and had received some recognition from professionals. Briefly, it consisted of representing the various degrees of the scale by certain syllables. Its use had been advocated by Campian and Playford early in the seventeenth century, and it was the method used in many instruction books two hundred years later. Because it was especially popular in the north of England, it became known as the Lancashire sol-fa; although by the middle of the nineteenth century it was more used in America than in Britain.

The first edition of the Bay Psalm Book to contain music (1709) had sol-fa symbols under the staff notation; the *Western Lyre* in 1831, and the *Missouri Harmony* in 1837, were still using it. *The Sacred Harp* (1844) and *The Social Harp* (1866), both published in Philadelphia, were about the last collections to contain vestiges of Lancashire sol-fa. The Americans displayed some ingenuity in combining sol-fa and the staff notation. Notes of various shapes (triangular, round, square and diamond) were made to represent the sol-fa syllables and written on the regular staff. Reading this "buckwheat notation," as it was called, a singer could disregard the position of a note on the staff and recognize its pitch solely by its shape. Buckwheat notation is still found in the most recent editions of *The Sacred Harp* and in some other hymnals in use in the southern United States.

Despite its popularity, the Lancashire sol-fa had many serious defects and limitations. When Curwen discovered a Miss Sarah Ann Glover using new and original principles in the teaching of sol-fa, principles that insured a more accurate and intelligent reading of the music, he became not only a convert but an apostle. Between Miss Glover and Curwen, the system known as the *tonic sol-fa* was perfected.

Solmization was the means by which the art of part singing was propagated, not only in the psalmody classes but also in schools. Curwen's improvements gave it the advantage of enabling instructors and school teachers without conspicuous musical gifts to develop proficiency in their pupils. A competent musician, after having organized a singing class, might leave it in the hands of an intelligent local instructor, who could be taught the principles of tonic sol-fa in a comparatively short time. There were hundreds of these instructors, who might be called lay musicians, carrying the rudiments of music to a field much larger than the professional musician was able or willing to cultivate.

Curwen was almost forced into publishing, since his efforts created a tremendous demand for music noted in his new system, and other publishers could not be expected to produce in large quantities something that was in an experimental stage. Curwen produced music of all sorts—hymn tunes, chants, anthems, and even oratorios—in tonic sol-fa, and on the foundation of that system the present house was built.

Today there is enough vocal music published in tonic sol-fa to make choirs quite independent of staff notation if they are not acquainted with the latter. The system remains popular in British schools and with some choirs. It never entirely displaced the older type of solmization in the United States; although it was widely used, and is still taught, in some schools. It is used in many Canadian schools, where the English influence in music remains strong.

Other nonliturgical sects, notably the Baptists and Methodists, were influenced by the hymns associated with the Oxford movement, the singing school, and the popularity of tonic sol-fa. There was a general "toning down" of hymn singing—more refinement and, unfortunately, less exuberance.

Even the Presbyterians, both in England and Scotland, became more liberal in their views on church music, permitting the introduction of choirs and organs late in the nineteenth century. It is interesting to note that English organists, choirmasters, and hymnal editors had to be imported into Scotland, native church musicians having become almost extinct in the centuries during which the precentor reigned supreme.

The trend of worship music in the United States followed that of Britain to a large extent, although there was considerably less use of the Anglican chant. There were a number of American hymn tune writers who, while following the general style of the Victorian hymn, wrote tunes that were less stereotyped. Timothy Battle Mason (1801–1861), John Zundel (1815–1882), Isaac Woodbury (1819–1858), Samuel A. Ward (1847–1903), and John Gower (1855–?) are not likely to be remembered for long, but they have left tunes we would not like to be without.

On the other hand, a great many writers of hymns and tunes, no doubt impressed by the popularity of the rollicking camp meeting hymns, took a definite step in that direction. Both words and music lacked the vitality that had marked earlier colonial hymnody. The late nineteenth-century "gospel hymn" reflected a disturbing self-centeredness. While one would hesitate to call it self-idolatry, certainly the individual had become the focal point, and his welfare the be-all and end-all.

It was not to be expected that such a shifting of emphasis from God to the individual would inspire great hymns. The best of the gospel hymns are blighted by this altered perspective; the poorest are mere doggerel written in a sentimental style which often borders on the maudlin, and with refrains calculated to drive home the main theme.

The tunes are seldom more worthy than the words. The melodies lack character, the rhythms are of the toe-tapping varieties that seldom suit the words, and the harmonies are elementary.

Although gospel hymns found favor chiefly among people who were familiar with the camp meeting background, and among splinter groups from longer-established denominations, many tunes by William Bradbury, P. P. Bliss, William J. Kirkpatrick, W. H. Doane, G. F. Root, and others are to be found in the hymnals of more conservative denominations who would not have tolerated them at one time. Such hymns can attract only the uncritical. By every standard by which a hymn can be judged, they are poor; and support for them would be weakened if the people who sing them would examine them more thoughtfully.

Camp meeting methods of conversion were raised to a much higher level by the evangelistic campaigns of Dwight Lyman Moody (1837–1899) throughout the United States and in Canada, Mexico, and Great Britain. Whatever one thinks of Moody, one cannot help but admire his sincerity and his ability. His was the greatest evangelistic mission since that of the Wesleys. With him on his campaigns was Ira David Sankey (1840–1908), who led the singing and supplied the music. Sankey's hymns were generally of the gospel type, and the chief essential was that they should be "rousing." They met with instant favor and, although they fulfilled the purpose for which they were intended, they lowered the standard of congregational singing. While Sankey's hymns are given much of the credit for the success of the evangelistic tours, it is probable that a man of Moody's sincerity and compelling presence would have achieved the same results had he used any kind of hymns or no hymns at all.

Lesser evangelists followed the example of Moody, all accompanied by musicians of sorts who played the role of Sankey.

In 1865, William Booth began the Salvation Army in London, and the organization was established in the United States fifteen years later. Again one's admiration for a movement and its founder is tempered by a regret that it was deemed necessary to adopt a poor type of music. "Why should the devil have all the good tunes?" Booth is reported to have asked. Alas, it was not the good tunes that the Army purloined from the devil!

There were new sects springing up everywhere, and never a sect without its amateur hymn writers. A good hymn or a good tune, like anything else well done, appears deceptively easy; and hundreds of people with scarcely any elementary training rushed in where many capable poets and musicians hesitated to tread. A number of publishing houses existed, and still exist, solely because of the tremendous sales of what they choose to call "sacred songs."

The state of church music in Canada was somewhat peculiar. In the Church of England, which was, naturally, very strong, English influence predominated. Because of the small and widely scattered population, there were few facilities for choral services outside the larger cities. The services were generally "low," that is, plain and mostly said, not always from choice but from necessity. The most important posts were held by English organists and English clergymen.

The nonliturgical evangelists first came to Canada, not from the old country but from the United States. Unfortunately, they did not bring with them the hymnody of the early colonial churches nor the most capable musicians of their own time. The songs of the camp meeting and the revival and, later, the gospel hymn were the mainstays of congregational singing. When ministers from Britain finally arrived, somewhat belatedly, they must have been astonished by the kind of music their congregations sang. To this day it is difficult to convince many Canadians (and perhaps Americans, too) that gospel songs are not "good old Methodist hymns." Methodists may have had a hand in introducing such tunes, but they are not the hymns of Wesley. Continuing Methodists, and those who have merged into the United Church of Canada, are trying to live down this not wholly deserved reputation by decreasing the percentage of weak hymns with every revision of their hymnary.

✤ ANTHEMS AND LARGER CHORAL WORKS

There was a time when a composer of anthems and motets would consider his works to have a large circulation if they were sung in a score of cathedrals and churches. Long after psalm and hymn books and music for secular use were published in some volume, printed copies of choral music beyond the scope of the congregational singing were difficult to obtain. Manuscript copies and limited published editions were expensive. While there was a scarcity, it was hardly a shortage; for there were not enough choirs capable of singing such works to create a demand that would justify publication.

The scarcity became a shortage when singing schools advanced beyond the teaching of hymns, and large numbers of people began to participate in choral festivals. The cost of what music was available was prohibitive. In many cases, only the conductor's copy of a work was in score; and from that copy the singers would be taught aurally, or manuscript copies of the separate parts would be furnished them.

This was the situation that prompted the Novellos to publish cheaper editions of choral works; although a number of Nonconformist churches had to go into the publishing business in a modest way in order to insure the circulation of music by their own composers.

While credit must be given to nonliturgical groups for promoting the singing of anthems where they had rarely been sung before, it must be remembered that the thousands of people affected by their singing schools constituted a small percentage of the population of England. The vast majority of the people were members of the Church of England and, apart from the cathedrals and a few of the larger churches, no pretense was made to provide music on the scale that was being attempted by their Nonconformist neighbors.

The Oxford movement changed all that.

As we have mentioned, the influence of the Tractarians resulted in surpliced choirs and choral or semi-choral services in hundreds of parish churches. Having learned a quasi-cathedral service, the choirs desired to go a step further and sing anthems in the cathedral style, often before they had mastered the arts of chanting and hymn singing. It was to meet this need, coupled with a good prospect of having their work published, that an army of anthem writers, almost equaling in number the hymn writers, arose.

Although it was primarily to meet the demand of Church of England choirs that the wave of anthem writing gained force, lines of demarcation between Anglican and Nonconformist, British and American worship music quickly disappeared. Good anthems became the property of all denominations on both sides of the Atlantic, regardless of by whom they were written.

The manifest intention of the composers of this period was to supply anthems that were attractive, singable, within the capabilities of amateur choirs, and not inconsistent with cathedral tradition. Some were wholly successful, others partially, many not at all.

In most cases, the harmonies were well done; in fact, many anthems strongly resemble the careful, conservative sort of thing that a harmony student would write for an examination. They show no imagination or originality. They are correct—almost painfully so!—but lifeless. The melodies, if such they can be called, seem made to fit predetermined successions of chords. Curiously enough, these dull little compositions earned a nod of approval from many church musicians of their day. In an age when drabness was so often considered a mark of respectability, the writing of a melody was almost as reprehensible as wearing a red dress.

Before long, even the most staid composers were making some concession to melody, but cautiously. Many an anthem starts out with an attractive melodic phrase or two, but the inspiration quickly fails, and the rest of the piece is disappointing. This is particularly true of settings of the canticles: they have to be completed, and the gift of melody runs out before the words.

It can be imagined with what raising of eyebrows the conservative element greeted the works of composers who, going to the other extreme, did not care very much whether their anthems were sung in cathedrals or not as long as they gave enjoyment and some measure of inspiration to choirs and congregations of parish churches. J. H. Maunder, for instance, may have been regarded as superficial, but he could never be called dull. He wrote, frankly and unashamedly, for the people. His anthems were within the capabilities of fair amateur choirs willing to put a little work on them, and capable of being understood and appreciated by congregations who listened to them. They were melodious, the organ accompaniments were such as to interest the amateur organist without taxing his ability, and there were little parts for soloists. Maunder was also fond of interpolating a little section in six-eight time that invariably charmed the singers. He showed much skill in his harmonies: a student could use them as models without acquiring a single fault. Indeed, his harmonies were quite conventional, but he used them more attractively than his more conservative contemporaries. Light though his work was, it carried a certain conviction—a great deal of conviction, in fact, to thousands of choristers who looked forward with eagerness to practicing such anthems as *Christians, awake* and *Praise the Lord, O Jerusalem.*

There were many composers who followed Maunder's style, some running into the twentieth century. Roland Smart and Edmund Turner became widely known for a type of anthem similar to, but with less immediate appeal than, those of Maunder.

An amazing feat was that of Caleb Simper, who wrote anthems as fast as Gauntlett wrote hymn tunes, but with less satisfactory results. A copy of one of his anthems, dated 1915, indicates that the sale of his church music compositions exceeded seven million copies, which must be almost a record. When one adds his chants, settings of the canticles, communion services, carols, hymns, cantatas, and organ pieces to his long list of anthems, it can only be assumed that he borrowed mass production methods from industry. The tremendous popularity of his works is no compliment to the church-going public of at least thirty countries in which they were circulated. His writing is spiritless and tedious. The melodies are forced, the harmonies commonplace. Each anthem is so like a thousand others of the same type that it has not the slightest distinctive feature by which it can be remembered. In spite of all this, one cannot truthfully say that Simper's works are bad: they are simply banal. Yet scores of choirs (perhaps one might safely say "hundreds," in consideration of the seven millions circulation) seized upon them avidly, wasting time in rehearsal under the delusion that a good performance would redeem a trite anthem. And all this while a treasure-store of better church music was being made available by publishers!

Not all the best composers of the day were dull. Church musicians whose works are to be found in the repertoire of cathedral and parish church alike sometimes combined a gift for melody with dignity and restraint. Curiously enough, it was this saving gift of melody, even in tastefully composed anthems, that caused such men as Stainer and Dykes to be classed as second-rate by so-called purists. In an age when the public fancy was captured by melody, when, even in the field of intellectual music, the great composers gave much care to the perfecting of melodic phrases, the introduction of anything that would appeal to the ears of churchgoers was considered as a lowering of standards.

For perhaps the first time, the anthem conveyed some meaning to the congregation. Whatever the merits of the older, the less melodic church music, it was, from the point of view of the layman, a meaningless succession of chords. Apparently it did not matter whether the anthem was remembered by the people or not, although the clergy would not have cared to think that their sermons made such a fleeting impression. Now, however, the worshippers began to hear things in the anthem that they could remember. Melodic phrases would recur later and remind the people of the words with which they were associated. It may be argued by some people that these melodies are scarcely worth remembering (although that is a debatable question); but if the anthem is of any value in the service, surely it is better for the congregation to remember these unpretentious themes than to remember nothing at all.

The anthem changed considerably in form. It became exceptional to write longer anthems as continuous, unbroken units unrelieved by contrasts in tonality, time, and mood. There were little sections or movements with more definite relationships to each other than had been the case in the past and approached and quitted more gracefully.

Some shorter anthems needed no other contrast than that provided by transient modulation; others begin with solos, the melodies of which are repeated in harmonized form by the full choir. A conventional form begins and ends with bright movements, with a quieter section for solo or choir between. A favorite device with Stainer was to use a spirited movement for the first half of an anthem, following it with a quiet ending—for example, *I am Alpha and Omega* and *Ye shall dwell in the land.*

Solo voices were used more freely than in the past. Such anthems as Roberts's *Seek ye the Lord* and Shelley's *Hark, hark, my soul* might be said to be miniature concertos, the principal duty of the choir being to provide a background for the soloist.

There was a tendency towards the dramatic, to vary the mood of the music to suit the words. As in medieval times mystery plays were enacted to enable the people to visualize the gospel narratives, so a few Victorian composers drove home the significance of the texts by dramatization that appealed to the aural sense.

The oratorio and the cantata flourished. The choral festivals in England were the inspiration of some of the larger works; but as the capabilities and confidence of church choirs increased, many cantatas which made more modest demands on the singers were written. Much of what has been said about the Victorian anthem applies to the lesser of the Victorian cantatas. Although there is little in most of them that is likely to survive for long, they were, for the most part, bright, well written, and mildly inspiring. A few retain their popularity: every Lent, throughout English-speaking countries, choirs still sing Maunder's *Penitence, Pardon and Peace* and *From Olivet to Calvary,* and, more particularly, Stainer's *The Crucifixion.* People who like only fine music do not go to hear these performances, but thousands of others derive real benefit from listening to the simple, effective expositions of the Passion narrative.

While a great many church music composers of this period may be judged fairly by their work, there is more than a suspicion that some of the better ones allowed themselves to be underrated by sacrificing their musical aspirations to the public need. Between their ideals and the popular taste there was a great gulf. In order to raise the general standard of church music, of which the public was becoming increasingly conscious, these composers had to forego the pedestals of greatness or near greatness and retreat to a position where they could lead the people forward rather than beckon them vainly from afar. To them is due much more respect than they usually receive. Thanks to their missionary work, a few composers towards the end of the century (such as Samuel Coleridge-Taylor and Charles Villiers Stanford) were able to write with some individuality and with a fair prospect of having their work accepted.

✤ FOREIGN INFLUENCE ON CHURCH MUSIC

All composers are influenced by the works of other creative musicians, past and present, with which they may be familiar. Some are frankly imitative, but even those who display originality follow some patterns that have been established by others. It is a far cry from a Beethoven symphony to a hymn tune or simple anthem; yet church music (or any music) reflects, in small ways, the advances that are made by great musicians. Certain harmonic progressions, certain positions of chords, certain forms that were once unheard of, are made acceptable by musicians whose judgment and authority are not questioned.

Early in the nineteenth century, the worship music of the English-speaking countries was affected only in a general way by developments in the larger field of music. Conservatism prompted church musicians to turn to the past for inspiration and example. Foreign musicians had little interest in our worship music; and, certainly, we should expect little contribution from them in a field that was particularly our own.

The outlook became less insular as some of the larger choral works of European composers became known; and as, especially in the United States, there developed a much closer association between native church musicians and their contemporaries in and from France, Germany and, to a lesser extent, Italy.

In the first half of the nineteenth century, two contemporary foreign-born musicians, Mendelssohn and Louis Spohr, made a great impression in Britain and the United States. Not only their oratorios but, especially in the case of Mendelssohn, shorter choral works became well known. Since there was a definite kinship between their composition and the English traditional idiom, perhaps their immediate acceptance was not surprising.

But as the century passed the halfway mark, festivals and choral societies began to feature the larger works of composers who had no national or religious kinship with the Anglo-Saxon world—composers who spoke a musical language which, while quite familiar in the secular field, was foreign to British and American expression of religious themes. The oratorios and cantatas of Berlioz, Liszt, Brahms, Franck, Saint-Saëns, Dubois, Gounod, Dvořák, and Perosi, most of which were performed in both Britain and the United States widened the horizons of our own composers.

The introduction of these new works did not, happily, lead to foreign domination, as was the case with music in England in the eighteenth century. The oratorios of Handel and Mendelssohn retained their popularity and contemporary composers received every encouragement. Costa, Sullivan, Macfarren, Stainer, Mackenzie, Cowen, Stanford, Parry, and Elgar in Britain added much to their musical stature by their oratorios; Paine, Parker, Buck, and Shelley were among the important American composers of larger choral forms.

The greatest and most valuable influence of contemporary foreign musicians was exerted through personal association with our church musicians. Americans, chiefly, enjoyed this association. British churchmen, conservative and confident in their own traditions, felt less need of outside influence in the field of composition; and the condition of their organs was not such as would enable them to profit by the example of European organists.

Americans were, at this time, acutely conscious of their cultural deficiencies. They were, indeed, inclined to exaggerate their artistic shortcomings and to overlook the accomplishments of their own people. There was a popular impression that all good art came from Europe, and the work of many Americans was underrated because they could not boast European training.

The number of American students in Europe during the latter part of the nineteenth century cannot be estimated, but it must have been large.

Church musicians who intended to study abroad went chiefly to Germany and France, and their primary interests were the organ, theory, and composition.

There were several reasons why they did not go to England, famed for its choral tradition though it was. In the first place, the English choral tradition was well established in the United States and was being kept alive by many excellent English church musicians who emigrated to America. English teachers of theory and composition were far too insular in their outlook to offer anything new to Americans, who had rubbed shoulders with European musicians who had taken up residence in the New World. The limitations of British organs with abbreviated pedal boards, and very few of them tuned to equal temperament, offered no inducement to student organists. British organ music tended to be dull and ponderous, and British organists had no ambition or opportunities to bcome virtuosi.

Germany attracted many American organ students. The reputation that had long been enjoyed by German organs and organists was being maintained in the nineteenth century by such men as Adolf Hesse (1809–1863), Gustav Merkel (1827–1885), G. W. Fink (1831–1911), Julius Reubke (1834–1858), Josef Rheinberger (1839–1901), and E. R. Flugel (1844–1912). One could be sure of a sound, classical training there; and in Leipzig especially, famed for its organists before the time of Bach, the very atmosphere would be conducive to study. Germany had the advantage of being one of the great Protestant centers of music, where

American students would find music and the method of performing it pertinent to their future as church musicians.

A school of an entirely different type was that of the French and Belgian organists centered in Paris. Developed centuries later than in Germany, organ building, composition, and playing made phenomenal strides in France during the entire nineteenth century.

As was to be expected, the musical expression of a volatile people like the French little resembled that of the more phlegmatic Germans. To German and English ears, the airiness of French organ music bordered on the frivolous, and there was more than a hint of garishness in its climactic passages. Actually, the French were not deficient in musical intelligence, earnestness, and dignity. They simply expressed themselves in another idiom. French people could listen to French music with much the same reactions that Germans listened to German music; but whereas the performing and hearing of organ music was something of a rite to Germans, to the French it was a pleasure.

The French organs were admirably designed for the expression of French composers and organists. Diapason ranks, with which British and American ears are so familiar as the foundation of organ tone, were given far less prominence on French organs. On the other hand, the large proportion of finely voiced reeds, while lacking something of the solidity of the diapasons, lent themselves to brilliant effects for which earlier composers and organists had not striven. The organ became a concert instrument while losing none of its value as an aid to worship.

An American organist, deciding whether to study in France or Germany, could not fail to be impressed by the reputation and prestige of such French (or Belgian) organists as Alexandre Boëly (1785–1858), Lefébure-Wély (1817–1869), Charles Gounod (1818–1893), César Franck (1822–1890), Nicholas Lemmens (1823–1881), César Salomé (1834–1896), Camille Saint-Saëns (1835–1921), Theodore Dubois (1837–1894), Alexandre Guilmant (1837–1911), Eugene Gigout (1844–1925), and Charles Marie Widor (1844–1937). Some of these men were not only organists and composers for the organ, but acknowledged masters in other fields of music. Their versatility and their broad conceptions were rarely matched by organists elsewhere. Moreover, their understanding was not limited to their own idiom. The works of Bach, for instance, "discovered" first by Boëly, are nowhere more assiduously studied or carefully performed than in France.

In order to impress the reader with the fact that American organists who studied abroad were not lesser musicians who returned and lost themselves on obscure organ benches, a few should be mentioned: James Cutler Parker (1828–1916), Horatio Palmer (1834–1907), B. J. Lang (1837–1909), John Knowles Paine (1837–1906), Dudley Buck (1839–

1909), Fenelon Rice (1841–1901), Elbridge Whiting (1842–1923), Homer Bartlett (1846–1920), E. M. Bowman (1848–1913), Frank Gleason (1848–1903), Clarence Eddy (1851–1937), A. A. Stanley (1851–1932), George W. Chadwick (1854–1931), R. Huntingdon Woodman (1861–1943), and Horatio Parker (1863–1919). Samuel P. Warren (1841–1915) was a Canadian who, after studying in Germany, settled in New York. Augustus Vogt (1861–1926), another Canadian, studied in Leipzig and was later active in Toronto where he founded the famous Mendelssohn Choir.

These men, upon their return to America, were among the foremost organists and choirmasters and the most noted educators in the field of music. The knowledge and skill which they acquired abroad was transmitted to their pupils, many of whom became equally prominent in both concert and worship music.

No small factor in American progress has been the assimilation of people from foreign lands who, in return for a welcome and a home, have contributed their skills and crafts and intellects to the common weal. Something has already been said of the contributions of immigrants to American music. The nineteenth century saw a continuance of those contributions. Among newcomers who were prominent in the cause of choral music and composition were Leo Kofler (1837–1908), Max Vogrich (1852–1916), Eduardo Marzo (1852–1920), Max Spicker (1858–1912), John Lund (1859–1925), and Louis Victor Saar (1868–1937).

It would be wrong to overemphasize the influence of foreign musicians on American music, especially worship music. There were no revolutionary changes; indeed, some of our best worship music has come from American composers who never left their own country. Nevertheless, the influence is there, subtly manifested in many small ways. A musician acquires traits from his teacher and his teacher's teacher just as surely as he inherits characteristics from his father and his grandfather; and, as more freedom is exercised in church music, the broader perspective will become more evident.

❖ REFERENCES

Psalm and Hymn Tunes

Some of the composers mentioned below have done nothing to enhance worship music. Their tunes provide a means of comparison with better examples, and illustrate the type of gospel hymn that was becoming popular.

Baker, Henry, 1835–1910.
Baker, Henry Williams, 1821–1877.
Baring-Gould, Sabine, 1834–1924.
Barnby, Joseph, 1838–1896.
Bliss, Philipp, 1838–1876.
Bowdler, Cyril W., 1839–1918.
Bradbury, W. B., 1816–1888.
Brown, Arthur Henry, 1830–1926.
Calkin, J. Baptiste, 1827–1905.
Cobb, G. F., 1838–1904.
Converse, Charles C., 1834–1918.
Cottman, Arthur, 1842–1879.
Cutler, Henry S., 1824–1902.
Doane, W. H., 1832–1916.
Dykes, John B., 1823–1876.
Elliott, James W., 1833–1915.
Elvey, G. J., 1816–1893.
Ewing, Alexander, 1830–1895.
Fisher, W. G., 1835–1912.
Gauntlett, H. J., 1805–1876.
Gilbert, Walter B., 1829–1910.
Goss, John, 1800–1880.
Gould, J. E., 1822–1875.
Gounod, Charles, 1818–1893.
Gower, J. H., b. 1855.
Hartsough, Lewis, 1828–1919.
Havergal, Francis R., 1836–1879.
Hayne, L. G., 1836–1883.
Hemy, Henri, 1818–1888.
Hervey, F. A. G., 1846–1910.
Hewlett, Thomas, 1845–1874.
Hopkins, Edward John, 1818–1901.
Irons, H. S., 1834–1905.
Jackson, Robert, 1840–1914.
Jeffrey, J. A., 1851–1928.
Jenner, H. L., 1820–1898.
Jude, W. H., 1851–1902.
Kirkpatrick, W. J., 1838–1921.
Lahee, Henry, 1826–1912.
Langran, James, 1835–1909.

Llyfr Tonau Cynulleidfaol, 1859.
Lowry, Robert, 1826–1899.
Lutkin, Peter C., 1858–1931.
Maclagan, W. D., 1826–1910.
Maker, F. C., 1844–1927.
Martin, George C., 1844–1916.
Matthews, T. R., 1826–1910.
Monk, W. H., 1823–1889.
Nevin, George Balch, 1859–1933.
Oakeley, H. S., 1830–1903.
Ouseley, F. A. G., 1825–1889.
Parker, Horatio W., 1863–1919.
Parry, C. H. H., 1848–1918.
Parry, Joseph, 1841–1903.
Patton, Arthur, 1853–1892.
Peace, Albert L., 1844–1912.
Plymouth Collection, New York, 1855.
Pritchard, Rowland, 1811–1887.
Purday, Charles H., 1799–1855.
Redhead, Richard, 1820–1901.
Redner, Lewis H., 1831–1908.
Root, George F., 1820–1895.
Sankey, Ira D., 1840–1908.
Scholefield, Clement C., 1839–1904.
Schulthes, Wilhelm, 1816–1879.
Sherwin, William Fisk, 1826–1888.
Smart, Henry T., 1813–1879.
Smith, H. P., 1825–1898.
Somervell, Arthur, 1863–1937.
Southgate, Thomas, 1814–1868.
Stainer, John, 1840–1901.
Steggall, Charles, 1826–1905.
Straub, Solomon, 1842–1899.
Sullivan, Arthur S., 1842–1900.
Thompson, William J., 1847–1909.
Uglow, James, 1814–1894.
Walch, James, 1837–1901.
Ward, Samuel A., 1847–1903.
Wesley, S. S., 1810–1876.
Zundel, John, 1815–1882.

Anthems, Cantatas, etc.

Composers of church music in the late nineteenth century were so
numerous that a great deal of space would be required to list even half

of them.   The list below is not claimed to be the best that can be compiled, but it is representative.

Generally speaking, the list includes composers who were active in the nineteenth century even though much of their best work may have been done in the twentieth.   All of these works were considered good by our grandfathers, and many of them are still great favorites with many choirs.

Asterisks denote oratorios and other extended choral works.

Alcock, W. G.—
 Benedictus [F]
 Give ear, O ye heavens [N]
 *God is our refuge [N]
 He that spared not his own Son [N]
 When thou turnest away from ill [F]
Armes, P.—
 *I will sing a new song [N]
 Rejoice in the Lord [N]
 There is sprung up a light [N]
Baker, H.—
 Mine eyes look unto thee [N]
Barnby, Joseph—
 All thy works praise thee [N]
 As we have borne the image of the earthy [N]
 Awake up, my glory [S]
 Drop down, ye heavens [N]
 O how amiable are thy dwellings [N]
 O Lord, how manifold are thy works [S]
 Sweet is thy mercy [S]
Bartlett, Homer N.—
 Bethlehem [S]
 Hail the King [S]
Bradford, J.—
 Let us now go even unto Bethlehem [N]
 We have seen his star [N]
Brewer, A. H.—
 As the earth bringeth forth her bud [N]
 Bow down thine ear [N]
 *God within [N]

Let the people praise thee [N]
 Prevent us, O Lord [N]
Bridge, J. C.—
 Be joyful in God [N]
 Christ is risen [N]
Bridge, John F.—
 Behold my servant [N]
 Blessed be the Lord God [N]
 Christ became obedient unto death [N]
 Great and marvellous [N]
 May the Lord bless thee [N]
 When I was young, I sought wisdom [N]
Brown, Arthur Henry—
 Angel said unto them, The [N]
 Give the King thy judgements [N]
 Praise God! the One, thrice Holy [F]
Buck Dudley—
 Christ our Passover [S]
 *Christ the Victor [S]
 *Coming of the King, The [S]
 Darkly rose the guilty morning [S]
 Fear not ye, O Israel [S]
 He shall come down like rain [S]
 My faith looks up to thee [S]
 Virgin's lullaby, The [S]
Bunnett, E.—
 Blessed be thou [N]
 If we believe that Jesus died [N]
 In the beginning was the Word [N]
Caldicott, A. J.—
 Behold, how good and joyful [N]
 If I go not away [N]

Calkin, J. Baptiste—
*Behold now, praise ye the Lord [N]
I will magnify thee [N]
Lord redeemeth the soul, The [N]
O send out thy light [F]
Whoso hath this world's goods [N]

Chadwick, G. W.—
Morn's roseate hues [N]
Savior, again to thy dear Name [N]
Sun of my soul [N]

Clarke, J. H.—
Be thou my judge [N]
I have set God always before me [N]
Out of the deep [N]
They that go down to the sea in ships [N]

Churchill, Norman—
Abide with me [B]
Come, let us join our cheerful songs [B]

Coombs, C. W.—
As it began to dawn [S]
At the feet of the Master [B]
Brightest and best [S]
Joyous peal, ye Christmas Bells! [S]
Lord is my strength, The [B]
Where is He? [S]

Coward, H.—
Behold, how good a thing it is [N]
Lord, thou art good [N]

Dykes, J. B.—
Reproaches, The [N]
These are they which came [N]

Elvey, G. J.—
Arise, shine [S]
Christ is risen [S]
Daughters of Jerusalem [N]
Hark those voices sweetly blending [N]
In that day shall this song be sung [N]

Whom have I in heaven [N]

Foote, A.—
God is our refuge and strength [N]

Foster, Myles B.—
Let not your heart be troubled [N]
*My heart is inditing [N]
Now know I that the Lord helpeth [N]
O for a closer walk with God [S]
O God, who is like unto thee [N]
*Seed-time and harvest [S]
There were shepherds [S]
While all things were in quiet silence [N]

Gadsby, H.—
Except the Lord build the house [N]
He is risen [F]
I will lay me down in peace [S]
O Lord, our Governor [S]
Ponder my words [N]

Garrett, G. M.—
In humble faith and holy love [S]
It shall come to pass [N]
Our soul on God with patience waits [N]
Prepare ye the way of the Lord [S]
Thy mercy, Lord [N]

Gaul, A. R.—
*Holy City, The [S]
I heard a voice from heaven [N]
O God, who hast prepared [B]
Remember now thy Creator [N]
*Ruth [S]
Thine is the kingdom [S]

Gauntlett, H. J.—
I will go unto the altar of God [N]
Thou wilt keep him in perfect peace [N]

Gilbert, W. B.—
Our conversation is in heaven [N]

Gilchrist, W. W.—

Except the Lord build the house
[S]
I heard the voice of Jesus say [S]
Gladstone, F. E.—
Bring unto the Lord, O ye mighty
[N]
He that spared not his own son
[N]
Thou art worthy, O Lord [N]
Goss, John—
*And kings shall be thy nursing
fathers* [N]
Behold, I bring you good tidings
[F]
Christ our Passover [F]
Forsake me not [N]
God so loved the world [N]
O Savior of the world [S]
O taste and see [S]
Wilderness, The [N]
Gounod, Charles—
As the hart pants [N]
Ave Verum [S]
By Babylon's wave [S]
Come unto him [S]
Gallia [S]
Messe solenelle (St. Cecilia) [S]
Redemption, The [S]
Send out thy light [S]
Gray, Alan—
Angel of the Lord, The [N]
Communion Service in G [F]
Jerusalem on high [F]
Thou shalt show me the path of life
[N]
Harwood, Basil—
Heavy heart, A [N]
I am the living Bread [F]
Jesu, thy boundless love to me
[N]
O sacred banquet [F]
This day Christ is born [N]
Ye choirs of new Jerusalem [N]
Hiles, H.—
Blessed are the merciful [S]
Gracious and righteous is the Lord
[N]

If any man sin [N]
Lord is my light, The [F]
Wherewithal shall a young man
[N]
Hopkins, E. J.—
God, who commanded the light
[N]
I will wash my hands [N]
Try me, O God [N]
Iliffe, F.—
Blow up the trumpet [N]
Jesu, lover of my soul [N]
Worship and praise the Lord [N]
Jordan, J.—
Lost sheep, The [S]
Kitson, C. H.—
Holy Father, cheer our way [N]
King all glorious [N]
Lloyd, C. H.—
Art thou weary [N]
Beloved, it is well [N]
Give the Lord the honor due [N]
Righteous live for evermore, The
[N]
Lutkin, Peter C.—
Christians, awake [Gray, New
York]
Knight of Bethlehem, The [Gray]
Lord bless you and keep you, The
[S]
*O Brightness of the Immortal
Father's face* [Gray]
Thine, O Lord, is the greatness
[Gray]
Macfarren, G. A.—
Behold the tabernacle [N]
Day in thy courts, A [S]
I will look unto the Lord [N]
Lord is my shepherd, The [S]
Remember me [N]
Maker, F. C.
Arise, shine, for thy light is come
[F]
Awake, thou that sleepest [S]
Fear not, O land [B]
I will extol thee [N]
One soweth, another reapeth [N]

Thou crownest the year [S]

Mann, A. H.—
God be merciful unto us [N]
O love the Lord [N]

Marchant, A. W.—
Blessed are they that dwell [N]
Hear me when I call [N]
Strife is o'er, The [N]

Martin, G. C.—
As it began to dawn [N]
Great day of the Lord is near, The
[N]
Hail, gladdening Light! [N]
O be joyful in the Lord [N]
Save us, O Lord, while waking
[N]
Whoso dwelleth under the defence
[N]

Maunder, J. H.—
Christians, awake [N]
Penitence, Pardon and Peace [S]
Praise the Lord, O Jerusalem [N]
Sing to the Lord of harvest [N]
Song of Thanksgiving, A [N]
While the earth remaineth [N]

Naylor, C. L.—
God that madest earth [N]
Lead, kindly light [N]
Through the day thy love [N]

Oakeley, H. S.—
Behold now, praise the Lord [N]
Evening and morning [S]
Whatsoever is born of God [N]

Ouseley, F. A. G.—
All the kings of the earth [N]
Lord is King, The [N]
O Lord, thou art my God [N]
Salvation of the righteous, The
[N]
They that wait upon the Lord [N]
Whom have I in heaven but thee
[N]

Palme, Rudolph—
*Cause is thine, Lord Jesus Christ,
The* [F]
God so loved the world [F]
Lift us your heads [F]

Parker, Horatio W.—
Bow down thine ear [S]
Come, see the place where Jesus lay
[S]
Grant, we beseech thee [B]
Holy Child, The [S]
In heavenly love abiding [N]
Light's glittering morn [S]
Lord is my Light, The [S]
Now sinks the sun [N]

Parratt, W.—
Death and life [N]
Face of death, The [N]

Parry, C. H. H.—
God is our hope [N]
Hear my words, ye people [N]
Prevent us, O Lord [N]

Parry, J. H.—
I will magnify thee [N]

Rea, W.—
My soul truly waiteth [N]
Souls of the righteous [N]

Redhead, R.—
Lord of the harvest [N]
Who are these like stars appearing
[N]

Roberts, J. V.—
*Behold, I send the promise of my
Father* [N]
Lord shall be thy confidence, The
[N]
Lord, we pray thee [N]
Peace I leave with you [B]
Peace, perfect peace [S]
Seek ye the Lord [S]

Rogers, J. H.—
Beloved, if God so loved us [S]
Be ye therefore followers of God
[S]
Doth not Wisdom cry [S]
Lift up your heads [S]
Man of Nazareth, The [S]
Now if Christ be preached [S]
Search me, O God [S]
Sing, O sing this blessed morn [S]

Salter, Sumner—
Lord is my light, The [S]

Two harvests [B]
Weary of earth [N]
West, John E.—
All people that on earth do dwell [N]
Lord is exalted, The [S]
Most glorious Lord of life [N]
O come, Redeemer of mankind [N]
O Trinity of blessed light [N]
Woods and every sweet-smelling tree, The [S]
White, J.—
Have mercy upon me, O God [N]
Ye choirs of new Jerusalem [N]
Whiting, A.—
Give ear, O Shepherd of Israel [N]
Williams, C. Lee—
Come, Holy Ghost [N]
Day thou gavest, The [N]

Last Night of Bethany [N]
Thou wilt keep him in perfect peace [S]
Wolstenholme, W.—
Lord hath chosen Zion, The [N]
Now if Christ be preached [N]
O that men would praise the Lord [N]
Woodman, R. H.—
Blow ye the trumpet in Zion [S]
Fear not thou [S]
God so loved the world [S]
I will be glad and rejoice [S]
Lord is my rock, The [S]
Woodward, H. H.—
Behold, the days come [S]
Comes, at times, a stillness [N]
Radiant morn, The [S]
Rejoice greatly [F]
Sun shall be no more thy light, The [S]

15

THE PRESENT STATE
OF WORSHIP MUSIC

‡‡‡‡‡‡‡‡‡‡‡‡‡‡‡‡‡‡‡‡‡‡‡‡‡‡‡‡‡‡‡‡‡‡‡‡

❖ LOST OPPORTUNITIES

Never has so much good music been available to so many people as in this mid-twentieth century. Broadcasting and extensive catalogues of "classical" recordings make it possible to hear the best performances of the best music in even the smallest and most isolated communities.

The teaching of music has become so general that every child who attends school learns at least the rudiments, and opportunities for more advanced study are almost unlimited. Music publishers have made available to us, at small cost, the scores of masterworks covering some four centuries.

If our forefathers could have stretched their imaginations to the point of envisaging the general state of music in the twentieth century, they would have predicted that church music would be of a standard seldom approached and never surpassed by former generations. They associated only the best with public worship; and they would have argued that, since the best of our secular music was of such a high standard, the standard of our worship music must be higher still.

Their expectations might be at least partially fulfilled if they could hear a service in one of a small minority of our churches. They might hear an organ voluntary, well chosen and well played, which created an atmosphere of quiet and worship; a congregation singing devotional hymns to tunes that enhanced the spirit of the words; a well-trained choir singing an anthem consonant with the theme of the service and conveying some meaning to the people; in a liturgical church, chanting that was a leisurely, flowing utterance of the words without distortion of the prose rhythm; and, finally, an organ postlude that preserved the atmosphere created at the beginning of the service and maintained throughout.

It is to such churches that our thoughts turn when we seek reassurance concerning the state of worship music. Here, we hear examples of the best music of all ages; and if the works of composers of our own time are not often done, we have a reasonable hope that they soon will be.

But while it would be wrong to underrate the advances which are being made here and there, it would be foolish to deny that very little of what might be termed worship music, or even good music, is heard in the vast majority of our churches.

The typical service begins with the organist playing something like the *Melody in F* or *Angels' Serenade,* with the tremulant very much in evidence; or, as a special treat, he may select from his classical repertoire Handel's *Largo,* which is considered appropriate for almost any occasion. There may be one good hymn—a metrical psalm, a German choral tune, or something from the Victorians. Almost certainly there will be a gospel hymn and at least one of a rollicking character more often associated with Saturday night than Sunday morning. Any chanting is likely to consist of frantically hurried recitations alternated with stiff, unnatural sections of the chant in strict time, the sense and beauty of the words being entirely destroyed in the process. The anthem may be one of those that are run off the presses of our lesser publishers in as great volume as our metropolitan newspapers, but with less intellectual content. Perhaps the big moment arrives when the soloist, assuming a conspicuous position and carefully looking around the church to make sure that no one's attention is diverted elsewhere, sings *Open the Gates of the Temple* or *The Stranger of Galilee.* Having succeeded in destroying the effects of devotional prayers and a good sermon, the organist triumphantly plays the people out with a march that makes the windows rattle.

Unfortunately, this description of service music is not exaggerated. Nor is the type confined to small rural churches. I have examined service lists of large city churches which have included every item that I have mentioned. The reader who remains incredulous will have no difficulty in verifying my statements in almost any community in the United States or Canada.

Who and what are responsible for the disturbing state of present-day church music?

Some students will affirm that there has been a steady decline since the sixteenth century, reminding us of the transfer of initiative from church musicians to secular during the baroque period, of the discouragement of all but the simplest worship music by the Calvinists and the Puritans, and of the barren century which we have called, in Chapter 13, the century of neglect. The implication is that we are the innocent and helpless victims of the neglect of former generations.

Nothing could be farther from the truth. The decline is admitted, but it has not been steady. There have been periods when it has been checked, and there have been renascent periods when some ground has been recovered. The widespread interest in choral music during the Victorian era, and the valiant attempts to raise the general standard of music extended into the early years of our own century. It is true that the nineteenth century was not marked by great church music, but the trend was certainly upwards. Had we possessed the energy and initiative exercised in the fields of industry and commerce, we would have taken up where the Victorians left off and made church music of the mid-twentieth century a glorious thing. We have muffed the chance.

The churchgoing public is often made the scapegoat by clergy and church musicians. Our congregations are charged with being apathetic towards good music. It is said that the poor, transient, "popular" tunes with which their ears are assailed from all quarters spoil them for the type of worship music which idealists advocate.

Doubtless there are thousands of people who love syrupy organ solos, sentimental or rollicking hymns, superficial anthems, and vocal solos that do nothing for anyone but the soloists. But many ministers seem to regard such music as normal, and many church musicians spend time in preparing it without protest. The congregations do not demand such music: in fact, individual members would very soon be put in their places if they sought to interfere. But since the music is chosen and presumably approved by the minister or organist or both, whose responsibility it is, musically illiterate congregations may be excused for supposing that it is good and suitable.

The world does not today corrupt the music of the church. The efforts of secular musicians to improve the public taste put the church to shame. Whereas, early in this century, comparatively few people heard good music, fifty years later it is heard by incalculable numbers. This immense, scattered audience had to be wooed and won. If broadcasting companies and record manufacturers had suspended operations until the public demanded good music, they would have waited in vain.

Nor does "popular" music influence worship music overmuch. Its styles are not followed by the church, and the type of church music of which I am speaking would be repudiated by "popular" musicians.

Clergymen and organists who use poor music for fear of offending public taste might be surprised at the number of people who remain away from church because of the music. It may be difficult to defend these delinquents, but it is not hard to understand their reluctance to attend churches where the quality of the music destroys any good that they may receive from other parts of the service and leaves them irritated and disturbed.

No, we cannot honestly blame our negligent ancestors or a musically illiterate people for the state of present-day church music. The onus must be placed where it belongs—on the clergy, who are responsible for everything connected with public worship; and on church musicians, who are charged with leadership in their own field.

As we review the development of church music in this twentieth century, we shall have cause to be grateful to both clergy and church musicians who have done much to further the cause of good music. We shall also have cause to regret the negligence of many of both groups who have betrayed their trust and permitted worship music to fall to a level lower than in any period in church history.

✤ MUSIC FOR THE CONGREGATION

Since congregational singing has been the foundation and strength of Protestant church music from the time of Calvin and Luther, it has served in any period as a fair index of the general state of worship music.

If we seek common ground on which all present-day schools of hymnody occasionally meet, we find that hymns of the so-called Victorian type are still the most widely accepted.

Many tunes in use sixty years ago are seldom, if ever, sung now. Granted that some of them were dull and labored, finding acceptance only because of the need for new hymn tunes at the time, it is hard to say why others were dropped from the majority of hymnals. They may have been too closely associated with hymns that have fallen out of favor, but in most cases they simply lacked the indefinable qualities that appeal to an unpredictable public taste.

The more recent tunes of this type were subjected to intense competition from the moment they were conceived, not only from the Victorian hymn tunes whose popularity was already well established but from other types which were becoming familiar and gaining favor. A few survive, but most of them had a short life.

Nevertheless, scores of Victorian hymns are still widely sung. Whether they deserve this popularity or not is beside the point. They are contained in hymnals of all denominations and of all types. Efforts to supplant them have not succeeded, and are not likely to succeed. A hymn book without such tunes as, for instance, Dykes's *Nicaea:* "Holy, holy, holy," Monk's *Eventide:* "Abide with me," and Barnby's *Evening:* "Now the day is over," would be considered incomplete. Apart from long association of words and music, there is an affinity between some hymns and tunes that is lost when other tunes are substituted.

We can retrace our steps still another century, to the eighteenth, without losing touch with the hymnody of most of the Christian denominations that flourish in our own day. Miller's *Rockingham:* "When I survey the wondrous Cross"; Darwall's tune that bears his name, sung to "Rejoice, the Lord is King"; Croft's *St. Anne:* "O God, our help in ages past" and *Hanover:* "O worship the King" are still among the best loved hymns and tunes of the English-speaking world.

A few German chorals that were among the first translated into English and an ever dwindling number of metrical psalms pretty well complete the hymnody that belongs to the whole body of Protestantism.

Once we leave this common ground, we discover hymns developed and used by some Protestant bodies and not others.

Beginning at one extreme, we have plainsong tunes which, because of their association with the Roman liturgy, were first avoided, then forgotten by Protestants. Their revival was due to certain groups connected with the Oxford movement, but they appeared in very few hymnals until the early part of this century. Some of these tunes, when well sung, are beautiful and well worth study. In the nineteenth century they remained the property of a small cult. Very few choirmasters and singing school instructors were familiar with them. The chances of awakening the interest of the public were as remote as the prospect of carrying on an ordinary conversation in Elizabethan English.

Some well-intentioned musicians, hoping to interest congregations, arranged a few plainsong melodies in strict rhythm, providing each note with an accompanying chord in the manner of modern harmony. ("O come, O come, Emmanuel" is a survival of this experiment.) They only succeeded in ruining the chances of the melody being sung in its proper form.

Plainsong tunes now appear in the hymnals of liturgical churches, and of a few nonliturgical churches where they are seldom, if ever, used. They remain strange to the ears of the majority of people. Whether they will become familiar or not depends upon the missionary zeal of those who advocate their use. It is unlikely that they will ever become popular, although they deserve a place in modern hymnody.

We sing a great many tunes that have been borrowed from other centuries and other peoples.

Tunes from German psalm and hymn books, to which references have been made at the ends of several chapters, were almost unknown in Britain and the United States a century ago, although Moravian, Lutheran, and German Evangelical immigrants to America sang them. Since then, we have drawn heavily upon this fruitful source, and our hymnody has been enriched in consequence.

Other borrowings, especially from the traditional melodies of other peoples, have not always been happy. Folk music is something like humor in that some of it can be appreciated by everybody, but much of it has a limited appeal.

Much folk music has no charm except for the people among whose forebears it originated. The many English traditional melodies that have been revived and pressed into service as hymn tunes may or may not catch on in Britain, but they certainly have no future in America. There are exceptions, of course, and such examples as *Royal Oak:* "All things bright and beautiful" and *Terra Beata:* "This is my Father's world," should be mentioned.

The same may be said of traditional melodies of other peoples. They speak to us in a language and of an age and background quite outside our experience. The quaint qualities that endear them to others are lost on us. Again there are exceptions—two traditional Irish tunes: *St. Finian:* "Go, labor on" and *Slane:* "Lord of all hopefulness."

The trouble is that the delvers into the past seldom know when to stop. They discover priceless examples of some period and locality and are not content until they have presented the world with everything they can find, whether it measures up to the original discovery or not. The words "old" and "traditional" have become hallowed. As long as a piece of music is Old English or Old French or Old Something, we are expected to subdue our critical faculties. Our hopeful expectations are not always realized.

Our inability to share certain experiences is brought home to us when we regard the practice, happily not widespread as yet, of adapting American Negro melodies to what we regard as more conventional forms. We can sense, to some extent, how spirituals affect the Negroes: we must regard with a feeling akin to awe any music, however foreign to us, that can so deeply move a people. But it does not and cannot so move us; not because of any deficiencies on its part, but because our natures and background and traditions have not supplied us with that indefinable something that responds to such music. It is an idiom strange to us, and it will not serve to express our aspirations as a result of its original form being disguised and distorted.

Leaving the field of borrowed and adapted music, we find that composers of original hymn tunes have not been lacking. Many of them have slavishly followed the style that gained popularity last century. Some of their work has been commonplace; some good, but not distinctive. It is pretty hard to achieve distinction in an idiom that has been worked over for more than a century by literally hundreds of tune writers. If no one ever writes another hymn tune in the Victorian style, we shall still have more than enough for our needs.

But there have also been experimenters. What their experiments have been worth, it is hard to say as yet. Certainly they have been intertesting and praiseworthy; but a hymn tune, in order to be considered good, needs more than the approval of musicians. It needs those qualities that make people want to sing it, and no one knows whether or not it has those qualities until it has been introduced to the public. Few tunes written during this century have been submitted to popular judgment. They appear in one or two hymnals as a result of pressure on the part of some members of the compiling committees who see possibilities for them. They will not be included in any other hymnals until they have proved to be fairly popular with people on whom they have first been tried. Even if they are accepted, they may wait years until other denominations revise their hymnals.

The most prominent schools of hymn tune writers have gone to the past for their inspiration: the British to folk tunes, both British and American to modal music. That does not mean that their tunes sound altogether like something from the past. They are not intended to. What the better composers have done is to make modal harmony the basis of their work, combining it with many of the arts and skills that musicians have acquired since the transition to baroque music.

The future of this type of tune depends on the ability of its proponents to convert public taste. At present, people react to it as they react to anything strange. The harmonies, the melodic intervals, and the indefinite tonality disturb them. Many of the tunes seem out of character with the words. It is difficult to sing words of a joyful or hopeful nature to tunes that have a decided minor flavor. Of course, the tunes are not always minor in the sense that they are based on our modern minor scale (although they sometimes are) but they have the same effect upon the uninitiated. The tune to a bright and joyful hymn is apt to sound very much like that of a Lenten or funeral hymn; and the general verdict, rightly or wrongly, is: "Doleful!" No doubt a distinction can be recognized by a connoisseur of modal music, but how many of us are connoisseurs?

It is characteristic of church musicians (but none the less disappointing) that, in writing hymn tunes, they have turned their faces to the past and their backs to the present. The developments that have taken place, and are taking place, in secular music are calmly ignored. The harmonies of the concert hall, to which our ears have become accustomed, are not, apparently, for the church.

In spite of the fact that we have so many popular hymn tunes, and that the chances of a new tune displacing a long-established one are slim, some of the contemporary tunes seem destined for general acceptance in time. No one can predict which ones will survive, the public fancy being, as we have said, unpredictable; but there are some tunes which, while close enough to a familiar idiom to be attractive, have features that set them apart from the ordinary and appeal to musician and laymen alike. The following tunes of various styles are among those gaining favor: Vaughan Williams' *Down Ampney:* "Come down, O Love divine" (written in 1906); Martin Shaw's *High Road:* "Let all the world in every corner sing" (1915); John Ireland's *Love Unknown:* "My song is love unknown" (1925); Healey Willan's *Stella Orientis:* "Brightest and best of the sons of the morning" (1927); Gordon Slater's *St. Botolph:* "Jesu, the very thought of thee" (1930); Anna J. Morse's *Consecration:* "O Love that will not let me go" (1941) and David McK. Williams' *Canticum Refectionis:* "This is the hour of banquet and of song" (1941). They appear now in few hymnals; but it is to be hoped that, when new books are compiled and old ones revised, they will be given serious consideration.

There is an increasing use of faux bourdon and descant arrangements of hymn tunes, particularly in Britain and Canada.

The term "faux bourdon" or "faburden" has meant various things in various periods. As we have seen, in the fourteenth century it was a "false bass" obtained from the inversion of an artificial triad. Today, it is a hymn tune rearranged with the melody in the tenor and a secondary melody in the soprano. The bass may be the same as in the original form of the tune, or the original harmonies may be altered somewhat, but certainly there is no "false" bass.

Such arrangements dating from the seventeenth century or earlier are not faux bourdons in the modern sense, although they are effectively used as such. In those days it was normal to allot the melody to the tenor: the soprano was not intended to be melodious, but simply to fill out the harmony as the alto and tenor do in modern hymn tunes. As faux bourdons are written now, the counter-melody in the soprano is often as attractive as the original melody. The reader who wishes to study the form will find the best examples among those of the Shaw brothers, Martin and Geoffrey, and Healey Willan.

Descants, more widely used than faux bourdons because they can be made effective with fewer resources, are more or less independent melodies sung by the sopranos while the other parts (and the congregation) sing the melody of the hymn tune in unison.

Too many people are writing descants these days. By this I do not mean that there is an oversupply, but that uninspired musicians, recognizing the trend, are laboriously stringing together successions of notes selected from the chords of hymn tunes, and producing unmelodious upper parts which they call descants.

If the arranger chooses to confine his material to the harmonies of the hymn tune and have the organist play the tune in its original form as an accompaniment, he requires some ingenuity to make his descant interesting. Some tunes lend themselves to such treatment without alteration of harmonies, but most do not.

The most attractive descants are those by arrangers who have extended their resources, not merely for the sake of altering the harmonies, but in order to gain freedom in writing the counter-melodies. Perhaps the outstanding writer of descants was Geoffrey Shaw, who wrote many of them. His soprano parts are melodious and spontaneous, rivalling the original tune melodies in interest. The accompaniments are free and interesting, but so admirably conceived that they do not distract those who are singing the original tune. The reader who would study descants can find no better examples than those in Shaw's collections.[1]

The judicious use of descants does much to brighten hymn singing. Provided the people know the tune and are willing to sing it, they enjoy carrying their part against the descant.

When it is not practicable to sing faux bourdons or descants, either because the sopranos have not been trained to sing them or because there is no choir present, the arrangements offer the organist opportunities to vary his accompaniment to hymns. The modern development of these forms is a distinct gain.

The possibilities of free organ accompaniments are recognized by some composers who provide two versions of their tunes: a four-part arrangement for verses to be sung in harmony, and a unison version with an independent accompaniment to be used for certain other verses. (Examples: Vaughan Williams' *Sine Nomine:* "For all the saints" and, earlier and better known, Goss's *Praise, My Soul:* "Praise, my soul, the King of heaven.") Many tunes are being written to be sung in unison throughout, a more varied harmony than would ordinarily be supplied for voice parts being provided by the organ accompaniment.

People who are concerned about church music generally confine serious discussion of hymns to the types that we have mentioned so far in this section. That is understandable, if unrealistic. It is human nature to dwell upon pleasant and hopeful things and to exclude abuses

---

[1] *Thirty-Six Descants for Use with the English Hymnal* (London: Oxford University Press, 1934) ; *The Descant Hymn Tune Book,* Books I and II (London: Novello and Company) .

from our minds. But it would be folly to pretend that Victorian hymns, plainsong, modal harmonies, German chorals, metrical psalms, folk tunes, and traditional melodies constitute the rule rather than the exception in worship music. We defeat our purpose by arguing the merits of one against the others if we remain oblivious to the fact that all are being threatened by a travesty of hymnody that combines the worst in verse and music with sentiments that fall far short of the spirit of worship.

In this age of compromise, when everyone is careful not to say anything that will offend a large section of the public, lovers of church music have too long remained silent upon this subject. We cannot continue to remain aloof from it. It has invaded the precincts of the temple. We must convert or be converted. There is no neutral ground.

The "gospel" and "revival" hymns that gained currency in the nineteenth century were not long excluded from churches with traditions of sound hymnody. Why it should have been thought necessary to find room for them in new editions of hymnals that had previously been devoted to something much better is a mystery. Certainly the responsibility for their inclusion rests with the governing bodies of the various churches. One cannot believe that Anglican, Lutheran, and Presbyterian congregations, for instance, expressed a desire to sing such hymns. And no church musician worthy of the name would lend his support.

After fifty years or so, compiling committees, like the sorcerer's apprentice, having said the magic word that permitted these unworthy hymns to inundate their hymnals, would very much like to find some way of getting them out again. But congregations, whose taste for this kind of hymn was deliberately fostered by church authorities, are reluctant to see them go. They have been singing them ever since their Sunday School days, and developed a sentimental attachment for them that comes from association, rather than from either words or music. (We must still call these compositions hymns for want of a more exact term, just as we call a child's drawing a picture without implying that it is comparable to a fine painting.)

There were churchmen in the nineteenth century who fondly hoped that the gospel hymn was a passing fad. If it survived very long, they argued, it would be subjected to improvements and refinements that would cause it to lose its identity and merge with a better type.

The contrary is true. Not only does the gospel type of hymn remain lusty: additions to it become worse year by year. It has reached such a low level that one hesitates to insult the memory of earlier gospel tune writers such as Bradbury and Doane by classifying them among modern contributors.

Self-centeredness remains the theme of the verses. There is expressed the same wishful thinking, the same conviction that the individual need only sit and wait for the glories, which he has done nothing to deserve. There is the same negative attitude: as long as we refrain from doing evil, there is no call for us to take any positive action towards spiritual improvement. The emphasis is placed on God's promises to man: the conditions and the responsibilities of man are glossed over.

A more recent type of verse deals with trivial personal experiences that can be shared by anyone with the weakest imagination. There is no contemplation of things Divine. The writers are earthbound.

I have described the verses rather than the tunes because most people are more capable of appraising words than music. The tunes are as pointless, as devoid of imagination and skill, as the verses. Any untrained person with an average ear for music could sit down at the piano and "compose" an acceptable gospel tune. Touched up a little, it would break no rule except that of good taste.

The hold that these intellectual and musical trifles has taken on the public is amazing and disturbing. Congregations, whose response to a fairly good hymn is slight, will sing gospel hymns with enthusiasm and vigor. They will quite as vigorously defend these trifles on the grounds that the Divine Name is mentioned therein and that, therefore, they carry the weight of Holy Writ and deserve the same veneration.

Few Protestant denominations can adopt a superior attitude and claim that the gospel hymn is confined to intellectually inferior groups or recently formed sects. Nor can the clergy claim that they are badgered by their congregations into singing gospel songs.

I knew an Anglican bishop, rather proud of his culture, who had a decided weakness for these hymns. I have heard clergymen of all denominations refer to them as "grand old hymns." On the other hand, I have known some Baptists, who generally receive much of the blame for the deterioration of church music, express concern about that deterioration.

We have seen in earlier chapters that, left to themselves, church people are apt to play havoc with worship music. Who would have guessed, soon after the Reformation, that the plain, austere manner of singing the metrical psalms would have been succeeded by fuguing tunes, the use of graces and ornaments, and other devices that robbed congregational singing of all dignity and reverence?

The return to worthy congregational music was long and difficult. It was accomplished, not by prohibitions, but by patient education. The movement received its inspiration from the clergy—from men like Watts, the Wesleys, and Curwen in Britain; Symes, Walter, and Eliot in America. It was accomplished chiefly through the singing school which flourished at the beginning of this century.

It is significant that, in the late nineteenth century, the gospel hymn and the camp meeting hymn made headway chiefly in areas where no singing schools conducted by competent instructors existed, and that their acceptance elsewhere coincided with the decline of group instruction.

The breaking up of the singing schools was due largely to competition of interests. It will be remembered that, especially in small and rural communities, they served not only for instruction but as social gatherings as well. There people met their neighbors and, with them, made their own entertainment; there, too, many a young man and maiden hied themselves for the pleasure of each other's company before, during, and after the singing. The wonders of our fathers' age—the stereopticon, the talking machine, the movies, improved roads and means of transportation that made it easier for road shows and stock companies to play small towns—all attracted many people who had formerly depended on gatherings like singing schools to fill some of their leisure time. Later on, player-pianos, automobiles, the radio and, recently, television provided the public with entertainment without requiring any effort on their part.

We cannot blame those charged with the responsibility of worship music for the counter-attractions that drew people from singing schools. Nor can we blame them for a lack of foresight and an ignorance of the history of church music that prevented them from realizing what neglect would do to congregational singing. But, as interest declined, as congregations showed less and less inclination to sing anything but poor hymns that could be learned without thought or effort, some definite steps might have been taken to halt the decline.

Instead of taking remedial steps that had proved so effective only a few decades ago, the clergy and church musicians not only surrendered after the feeblest of struggles but actually contributed to the decline.

In order to entice people to mid-week and mission services, ministers held out the bait of "hearty singing"; and in order to keep their promise, they chose the worst of hymns. Since their parishioners could not be expected to suppose that a hymn suitable for Wednesday was not equally suitable for Sunday, they began to expect some of the same type of music at the regular services.

Many clergymen, fond of the sound of their own voices, robbed congregational singing of its importance by hacking stanzas from hymns, or even omitting a hymn, in order that they might preach longer without lengthening the service. Many of these abbreviations, made on the spur of the moment, had the same effect on the hymn as the omission of two or three paragraphs would have had on the meaning of the sermon.

In the meantime, organists and choirmasters devoted their whole attention to music for the organ and choir. There are few choirs that sing hymns really well, and few organists who consider the playing of hymn tunes worthy of thought or practice.

That, unfortunately, is the present state of congregational worship music. What can be done to improve it is a subject that must be reserved for the next chapter.

✢ MUSIC FOR THE CHOIR

It is not surprising that church music composers writing for the choir have followed the same trends that mark their music for congregational singing. So close is the parallel that the general plan of the discussion "Music for the Congregation" may well serve for this one.

Anthems of the nineteenth century, and those of this century that follow the same general style, are still the most widely sung. Although one would have supposed that our fathers' and grandfathers' generations provided a surfeit of this type of music, the output has not ceased. Many of the compositions are such faint shadows of better works of the same type that one wonders how they came to be published. The idiom is so familiar now that almost any musician could turn them out by the ream were there any point in doing so.

Some of the most successful composers who might be said to belong to the nineteenth century school wrote much of their music in the twentieth. Choosing at random from many names, we find that Alfred Hollins lived until 1942 and was very active in the 1920's, and the popular J. H. Maunder was writing anthems until nearly 1920. Although, in America, we are apt to think of Harry Rowe Shelley as belonging to a past generation, he lived until 1947. Will C. Macfarlane belongs more to this century than to the last.

A few composers have written anthems Victorian in content (harmonic progressions, for example) but certainly not in spirit. They have not been afraid to abandon the genteel reserve of the Victorians, but have borrowed freely from the dramatic effects of secular music without making their work incongruous for church use. Since an exhaustive review of twentieth-century choral music would require a book in itself, it is practicable to cite only one or two examples. For the type of anthem under consideration, I recommend a reading of two works by John E. West: *O come, Redeemer of mankind* and *All people that on earth do dwell*. The free use of the organ, alternating at times with full, unaccompanied choral passages, West's unquestioned gift of melody, and the climactic *fortissimo* passages for voices and organ, make these truly festival anthems.

There are no sharp lines dividing schools and periods. Composition in one style does not suddenly cease, to be superseded at once by another. There is always a great deal of overlapping. While it is possible to make some sort of classification of music of the remote past because the chaff has been winnowed out, in the case of more recent music we are barely past seeding time. Another generation must reap the harvest and do the winnowing, leaving still another generation unaware of the many experiments and abortive trends which we cannot recognize as such.

Thus, while what we may call an extension of the Victorian school was very active during the first half of the present century, even before the close of the nineteenth century some composers were breaking away from a style that had become almost stereotyped. They formed no definite school, for most of them were working independently. Their departures from the conventional were not, at first, radical; but each added some individuality to his compositions that set them just a little apart from the others. Perhaps a hundred years from now a coalescence of these individual types will be known as the twentieth-century school; but for the present, our best composers retain their identity of style.

Among the earliest composers who left the beaten track were Charles Villiers Stanford (1852–1924) and Peter Christian Lutkin (1858–1938).

A number of church musicians who showed great promise last century fulfilled that promise in this.

T. Tertius Noble (b. 1867), whose long career was about equally divided between English cathedrals (Ely and York Minster) and St. Thomas's Church, New York, made contributions that are likely to endure as long as the works of any church composer in history.

Edward C. Bairstow (1874–1946), Noble's successor at York Minster, makes great use of the organ in his choral music. It is not so much an accompanying instrument as a partner with the smoothly flowing voices of the choir. There are few solid, supporting chords; but, rather, independent organ passages that lend color and effect. Bairstow recognizes no limits where modulation is concerned. He has a fine sense of tonality, and the organ parts are worthy of the best orchestral composers. The organist must be skillful in order to play his anthems: if he is imaginative as well, he can make them works of art.

Born also in or near the 1870's were several composers of note who, while engaged chiefly in other fields of music, made significant contributions to the church: Walford Davies (1869–1941), Gustav Holst (1874–1934), Ralph Vaughan Williams (1872–1958), and John Ireland (b. 1879). Samuel Coleridge-Taylor (1875–1912) might easily have been numbered among these had his career been longer.

Americans were also numbered among the church musicians who were seeking to break new ground. Clarence Dickinson (b. 1873), Louis Victor Saar (1868–1937), Nathaniel Dett (1882–1943) are names picked at random from a long list.

One is encouraged to be hopeful concerning the state of choral music when, on seeking to compile a list of contemporary composers worthy of note, he discovers that there are far more than he has space to catalogue. Examples of their work are mentioned in references at the end of this chapter.

These composers depart from the norm of their Victorian predecessors in various ways. Some lean toward modal harmony, some English writers are influenced by the folk music of their country, others are not unmindful of the trend of modern secular music. It is doubtful that the best ones are following any pattern except as laid out by themselves. Their expression is the result of a multitude of coalescing impressions.

In addition to the harmonic content, which may be quaint in the sense that it flavors of the past, or somewhat rugged and even harsh as the composer seeks to face forward, modern anthems differ from those of the past century in form.

While contemporary composers have by no means wholly deserted the form which achieves contrast by changes of key, rhythm, tempo, and mood, the tendency is towards works of single movements with dependence upon changes of intensity and tonality for contrast.

Prominent today are anthems which depend for interest on varied treatment of a repeated theme. Very often the melody is sung first by the whole or part of the choir in unison, then in harmony, then in unison with a free and often massive organ accompaniment. Because of the hymn-like repetition, some genius is required to avoid monotony, and the more skilled composers are careful to write good melodies and somewhat free organ accompaniments that complement the voice parts. As might be expected with any popular form, scores of composers with no genius are turning out compositions of this kind; and a style that can be most interesting in the hands of Henry Ley or Eric Thiman proves to be very dull indeed when less skillfully treated.

Another type of anthem gaining in favor is that for voices in unison, with or without an occasional descant and, generally, with an effective and free accompaniment.

Unison anthems and services are, of course, a boon to choirs which are poorly balanced as to part singers. They must be carefully rehearsed in order to be effective. They are far too good to be treated casually. In many places where they are within the capabilities of the choir, their use is precluded by the lack of competent organists. The accompaniments are not such as can be played by any pianist-turned-organist who can be pressed into service. They require good technic and good taste; and, for the young organist who must divert some of his attention to conducting the choir while playing, careful practice.

The revival of old melodies and folk tunes, and subjecting them to modern treatment, has been both well and badly done.   In choral music, as in hymn tunes, the words "old" and "traditional" are often permitted to blunt our powers of discrimination.   There are, however, many beautiful melodies borrowed from other times and peoples which have been treated in such a way as to add beauty to beauty.   Pearsall's arrangement of *In dulci jubilo,* Baker's setting of the old French carol, *Whence is that goodly fragrance,* Ley's treatment of *The strife is o'er* by Vulpius, are all good examples in various styles.

Some church musicians have done their best work in this field.   Clarence Dickinson, for instance, has made splendid arrangements of many folk and traditional melodies that would have remained unknown to us but for his efforts.   A quarter of a century ago, choirs began singing music from the Russian church which had been made available to them by Winfred Douglas and others.   Much valuable work is being done in this field.

A type of choral arrangement that should be approached cautiously is that of the Negro spiritual.   Too many spirituals have been desecrated by thoughtless people who do not catch their spirit.   We can accept with confidence arrangements by Negroes who combine a deep understanding of the music of their race with a sound musicianship: Dett's *Listen to the lambs,* Burleigh's *My Lord, what a morning,* and Dawson's *There is a balm in Gilead.*   But even these should not be added to a choir's repertoire without some consideration.   The fact that they express the fervor and aspirations of Negroes does not guarantee that they express the feelings of other people.   Unless they can be sung *and heard* with the devotion and reverence that inspired them, they should not be used as worship music.   One of the most tasteless and blasphemous acts of which singers are guilty is the singing of the livelier spirituals in a manner calculated to make the audience smile or chuckle.

The bright side of contemporary church choral music has now been presented.   If that were the whole story, our fears for the future would be allayed.   But the fact is that, in spite of all the good choral music that is available and being made available, it is being sung by only a minority of our Protestant church choirs.

One reason is that contemporary composers make demands that few modern choirs are able to meet—although choirs of forty or fifty years ago would have met them.   I am not suggesting that the skill and potentiality of present-day choristers fall short of those of their predecessors. It is not ability in which choristers fall short, but interest.

Forty years ago, most churches had full choir lofts and full programmes of choral music.   Choirs that had liturgical services and anthems to prepare, not only for Sunday services but for certain weekday festivals and observances as well, were often on duty eight or ten hours a week. In nonliturgical churches, where there was less service music, the choirs were generally busy preparing cantatas and oratorios in addition to hymns and anthems.

There were, of course, reasons for all this, some idealistic, some practical.

Church attendance was better than it is today. Perhaps no more people went to church, but they went oftener. There was not much else to do on Sunday. Fewer cars, poorer roads, and shorter weekends than we have now gave people little incentive to travel. What diversions there were in the home were not considered suitable for Sunday.

Our loyalty and devotion to religion have not been proof against the changed conditions and increased distractions of the mid-twentieth century. Whether or not the clergy have been caught napping, it is hard to say; but the fact remains that excuses for not attending church which would have been unacceptable forty years ago are considered quite valid today.

Much of our population is on the move during weekends. Even many of those who remain at home are kept from church by the expectation of visitors. Radio and television programmes are largely responsible for sparse attendance at evening services. People may be as religious as ever, but they are not willing to sacrifice motor trips and programmes for church attendance.

All this has a direct bearing on the music of the church. Choristers and people who might, under other conditions, make good choristers are also owners of cars, radio and television sets, and are quite as susceptible to their attraction. Obviously, no choir can meet exacting musical standards if its personnel varies from Sunday to Sunday. And in the case of choristers, there is the added problem of enticing them away from other interests some time during the week for rehearsals.

Whereas people used to pay fees to be taught part-singing (as we read in the last chapter), it is now exceedingly difficult to persuade them to attend choir practice where they may receive instruction free. Hundreds of choirmasters spend hours at the telephone every week, almost pleading with choristers to attend rehearsals in order that, perhaps, sixty percent of them may be present and more or less prepared on Sunday.

The situation is such that a choirmaster cannot choose his singers: he takes what he can get. People who at one time would not have been accepted for choir duty are now eagerly sought in order to avoid the embarrassment of empty choir lofts. Even if they did turn out fairly regularly, they are incapable of singing much of the good choral music without intensive training.

There is no time for training. The pressure of "getting something ready for Sunday" is so great that choristers are seldom taught even how to use their voices. Except from the very best choirs, one seldom hears a good quality of tone; and range becomes more limited year by year.

We find, then, choir lofts half or two-thirds full of people who are not always qualified to give the lead in worship music, hymns indifferently sung, anthems ill-prepared or warmed over from a week ago. Few choirmasters dare announce ahead of time what music is to be used at a service, as was once the custom. They cannot make a tentative choice until the last rehearsal or a final choice until they survey their choral forces five minutes before the service is to begin.

In seeking an easy way out, too many choirs have recourse to a type of chorus they can sing without much trouble (although it is not suitable to be sung at all) and the "sacred solo."

Choruses of this nature express the same weak sentiments as the poorer gospel hymns, and the music is as weak as the sentiments. The harmonies are extremely simple, chromaticism appears at its worst, and long series of thirds and sixths over an almost stationary bass abound. They are about the poorest musical offering that one could present to his God. They are not as widely used as hymns of the same type, but several publishers find it profitable to deal in them exclusively. Quite apart from their slight musical content, they have no qualities to inspire and uplift. They tend to detract from, rather than contribute to, the act of worship.

Solos, even good ones, are hard to fit into the framework of public worship. It is no easy task for the most modest of soloists to submerge his or her personality and self-consciousness, or for the congregation to regard the singer as their spokesman for the moment rather than an individual. The common practice of placing the soloist in a conspicuous position before the congregation makes it impossible for all but the most seasoned singer to lead the thoughts of the people Godwards.

Yet, the solo has become one of the features of the service in most Protestant churches; and, because very few church choir soloists possess the qualities that would enable them to make their offering an act of worship on the part of themselves and the congregation, this feature generally falls to the level of entertainment.

There are very few solos that can be classed as worship music when sung under the most favorable conditions. It is a field that has not attracted church musicians. Most of the "sacred songs" are the works of composers who write in an idiom associated with the ballad or drawing-room songs. Even when the words are good, the music lacks the flavor of the church. The accompaniments are written for the piano, and it is difficult for the organist to make them sound well. Some trouble and thought would be required to adapt these accompaniments to the organ, and the majority of them are not worth the effort.

Words from Scriptures and good poems apparently do not inspire a great many writers of sacred solos. The cheapest, most transparent verses are often used—rather worse than one finds on the most sentimental greeting cards. Here, again, are expressed fanciful, immature experiences that the writers endeavor to translate into something resembling spirituality.

There are good solos, of course; but not nearly as many as publishers' lists would indicate. Most of them are seldom heard. Few singers are capable of interpreting them in the spirit intended by the composers.

It is possible to end this section on a more cheerful note by turning our attention to choral groups whose influence extends to the public at large.

While choirs seldom have time these days to prepare oratorios and cantatas or anything else beyond the minimum requirements of the Sunday services, and choral societies made up of members of various church choirs have almost ceased to exist, the miracles of radio and high-fidelity recordings make it possible for people from coast to coast to hear fine performances of good choral music.

The frequent radio performances of the Westminster Choir (John Finley Williamson, conductor) with the New York Philharmonic Orchestra, the Schola Cantorum (Hugh Ross), the Robert Shaw Chorale, and other similar organizations have been heard by scores of thousands. F. Melius Christiansen's work with the St. Olaf Choir School has been outstanding. The Westminster Choir and the St. Olaf Choir, although very different in production, interpretation, and performance, have been of great value in bringing good music to thousands of people all over the country.

There are other outstanding choirs and schools which merit our attention: The Hymn Society of America, The National Fellowship of Methodist Musicians (publishers of the successful magazine *Music Ministry*), and the School of Sacred Music, Union Theological School, New York. As these choirs have become familiar to all American lovers of good music, so the Toronto Mendelssohn Choir (Walter Susskind) has won the proprietary interest of all Canadians.

Unique among choral groups in its appeal to the public is the Mormon Tabernacle Choir of Salt Lake City (J. Spencer Cornwall conductor until 1957, Richard P. Condie since 1957). Until 1929, it was one of many good choirs with a long and honorable history, but with only a regional appeal. During the past thirty years, its unbroken series of weekly broadcasts has brought it within earshot of every home in America. Besides the pleasure and inspiration that the Mormon Tabernacle Choir broadcasts have brought many people, they have proved two valuable points: first, that public interest in choral music can be sustained by a wide variety of schools, types, and periods; second, that it is still possible to achieve all this with devoted volunteers.

Good choirs and good choral music are not enough to persuade broadcasting and record companies to invest time and money in making them available to the public. They must be convinced of a public demand and response, and the fact that they are so convinced should encourage church musicians to greater efforts in restoring worship music to its proper place and standard.

Another advantage of recorded performances lies in the opportunities offered for study. People in small communities used to sing in choirs for years without hearing any other good choir, amateur choirmasters learned and interpreted the music and trained their choirs with nothing to guide them but the printed page. Today, organists and choirmasters and singers can hear how some of the best organists, choirmasters, and choirs perform church music. The experience of hearing a record is not quite as valuable as attending a rehearsal of a first-rate choir, where one could observe the methods of the choirmaster and learn *how* he achieves his results; but repeated, attentive hearings of a work are almost equivalent to a course of lessons from leaders in the field of choral music.

I recommend a study of the following recordings of the Mormon Tabernacle Choir because of the wide variety of music, because it is a choir devoted primarily to music for public worship, and because many of the numbers are within the capabilities of average singers. Even those works beyond the reach of average choirs serve as models of balance, tone, interpretation and general technic.

Concert of Sacred Music—Columbia ML 5048
Songs of Faith and Devotion—Columbia ML 5203
The Lord is my Shepherd—Columbia ML 5302
Christmas Carols—Columbia ML 5222
The Beloved Choruses (with the Philadelphia Orchestra, Eugene Ormandy conducting) —Columbia ML 5364

Those who train boys' voices, whether for schools or church choirs, will find much pleasure and instruction, as well as fine examples of voice production for their choristers, from the following records:

A Festival of Lessons and Carols by the Choir of King's College, Cambridge—Westminster WP 6036
St. Paul's Cathedral Choir—Angel 35138 and 35139

✣ ORGANS, ORGANISTS, AND ORGAN MUSIC

While builders of organs make improvements to the instrument on their own initiative, a generation of fine organists, such as arose in the last half of the nineteenth century, spurs them on to greater efforts. The artist, exploring and finally mastering the possibilities of his instrument, becomes aware of its limitations, and demands of the craftsman more resources and facilities. As the builder meets and often surpasses these demands, he, in turn, opens a field for not-so-great organists who find it much easier to play effectively on modern organs than they would on the instruments of a century ago.

In the early 1900's, the popularity of the organ and the supply of players was increasing. A new generation had arisen, yielding nothing in skill and artistry to their immediate predecessors.

Few basic changes were taking place in German and French types of organs. The tonal qualities and balance had long been established, and the improvements were more generally confined to the mechanism and improved devices for the convenience of the organist.

In England, there was more rebuilding than building. The inadequacy of English organs to meet the requirements of organ music of the late 1800's was painfully apparent. Very few organs had complete pedal boards or independent pedal sections, and many of them were not tuned to equal temperament. Perhaps the playing of concert organists like W. T. Best, who used instruments modern in their time, did much to create a demand for more versatile organs. Possibly the installing of many new and modern instruments in Scotland (thanks to the generosity of Andrew Carnegie and the recently liberalized views of the Presbyterian Church) provided a comparison that made the need for improvement apparent.

English builders had long displayed some ingenuity in devising mechanical improvements. The swell shutter and the combination piston had made the management of the organ easier. The susceptibility of the pneumatic action to dampness and changes of temperature was more than offset by the flexibility it offered in comparison with the old tracker actions which, especially on larger organs, were heavy and tiresome. The tonal properties of most old English organs were excellent, and they were well worth saving; although the obstacles to be overcome in redesigning them were great.

The increased importance of the organ, not only as a solo instrument but also as a partner in choral works, was made possible by this process of modernization. The careers of scores of English organists such as Charles Macpherson (1870–1927), Harvey Grace (1874–1944), and Hylton Stewart (1884–1932) were enhanced by the improvements to the organ.

The case in America was far different. The majority of our present-day organs were yet to be built at the beginning of this century. True, there were many organs in the east, but the word "old" has not the same connotations in America as it has in Europe. We do not build organs to last for centuries. Our entire history lies in a period of progress and constant change. We are prepared to have them become obsolete and replaced within two or three generations. While our old organs could be more easily modernized than the much older organs of England, many congregations, in preference to this course, planned to scrap them and replace them with new ones. This course, combined with the continuing expansion of the population, provided plenty of work for organ builders. While organs with tracker and pneumatic actions, short keyboards, and abbreviated ranks of pipes are scarcely rare as yet, there are not many of them.

The concert tours of famous European organists and the frequent recitals of some of our own best organists increased public interest to such an extent that several larger cities built municipal instruments, and engaged municipal organists. One of these concert organists was Edwin Lemare (1865–1934), a sound musician who, quite properly considering his position, played for the entertainment of the people. He transcribed all kinds of music for the organ and made great use of solo stops and quasi-orchestral effects.

The use of popular transcriptions was quite legitimate in the entertainment field, especially at a time when some of the pieces would rarely be heard by the public through any other medium. Many people had their first hearing of the Overture to *William Tell* or the slow movement from the Mendelssohn violin concerto at the hands of an organist, who played as many notes from the original score as his fingers could manage, and aped the orchestral effects to the best of his and the organ's ability.

All this had its effect upon the composition of American organs. As builders discovered more and more methods of making lush and theatrical effects available to the organist, they began to incorporate some of the devices into church organs. Ranks of pipes voiced to imitate orchestral instruments were added. Super-octave couplers were more used; and, in order that their effect would not be lost when playing on the upper reaches of the manuals, an extra octave was added to most ranks of pipes. Electric action, pistons, couplers, and indicators increased and multiplied.

These additions may be merely gadgets to the player with poor taste, or even to the experienced British organist whose incurable conservatism prevents him from making use of them. But they have not been added indiscriminately to church organs. Our builders, with enviable reputations of craftsmanship to maintain, have not robbed their instruments of fundamentals in order to make way for novelties. The newer tone qualities are not included unless they contribute to and are absorbed by the general ensemble. If these organs are capable of ghastly effects under the fingers and feet of a novice, we must remember that they are the same instruments that made possible the performances of such fine organists as Fisher, Middleschulte, Bingham, Federlein, Yon, Barnes, Sowerby, Creston, MacMillan, and Willan.

There were plenty of organ students in the early part of this century. Even in small communities, very few people allowed themselves to be persuaded to take over the church organ without some instruction. Perhaps the weakness lay in the fact that the students' training was not, primarily, as church organists.

In England, most organists came from the ranks of former choir boys who had first studied with their organists, and then acted as assistants until positions were open for them. They thought of the organ only in terms of the church: their training and background dated from childhood. There were always vacancies, for, in addition to death and retirement, there was a great deal of emigration to the United States and British colonies, where the organist of a small church received a better salary than an English cathedral organist.

English composers and publishers of organ music recognized and met the needs of young organists. Literally thousands of pieces and hundreds of collections were available, and from this mass of organ literature even the tyro could find enough to provide him with the voluntaries and postludes within his capabilities. Much of it was dull, but even the more prominent organists played a great deal of dull music. It is interesting to note that many transcriptions were published; but, whereas in America the organ was made to meet the requirements of the music as nearly as possible, in England the music was adapted to the organ. There was no attempt to imitate orchestral effects.

The tendency in America was to overemphaize the organ's role as a concert instrument. Organists who went to Europe to study looked upon their teachers as virtuosi rather than as church organists. They brought back the technic and the repertoire of virtuosi and passed them on to their pupils. This was all well and good up to a point, but hundreds of young students who never would become virtuosi were studying recital pieces before they had mastered the art of playing hymn and anthem accompaniments. Their ability to play a church service was mistakenly taken for granted. Few of them served apprenticeships with seasoned organists, few of them had a background of youthful service in choirs.

Student organists who spent hours practicing sonatas, fugues, and themes and variations often found themselves with nothing suitable to play for the Sunday service. There were many good, short pieces; but our composers had become accustomed to writing for skilled organists, and there was little worthwhile that the student could learn quickly. There was a scarcity of good, simple music for the organ. Perhaps some organists used English collections, but these were tame to ears that had become excited by brilliant recital pieces and the sentimental arrangements played by popular organists.

At this point, the entertainment factor made itself felt. The market became swamped with transcriptions written in imitation of the style of popular organists and original pieces that followed the same general pattern. Their fault did not lie in the fact that they were easy to play—that was a virtue rather than a fault—but that they were not organ music at all, and that they were not suitable for church services. The temptation to use fancy stops (which the builders had provided in good faith) in combination with *celestes* and tremulants was too great for many young organists to resist. Too many young players, finding that they could produce sensational effects by these means without very much effort, made no serious attempt to improve their technic to a point that would enable them to play something better.

The public's concept of organ music suffered a severe setback after World War I. Large theaters across the country installed organs to be used alternately with their orchestras. Smaller moving picture houses soon followed suit, partly to be up-to-date and partly as an economy measure, for it was cheaper to engage one organist than to maintain a five- or six-piece orchestra. In the 1920's there was scarcely a community without a "movie organ."

In spite of the imposing consoles revealed by spotlights during the intermissions between pictures, most of these organs were poor things. There was none of the fundamental tone considered essential by organists. There were, on the other hand, "pretty" stops, *vox humanas, celestes,* bells, gongs, harps, drums, Chinese blocks, and other novelties. They were, generally, unit organs, with one rank of pipes for every half dozen stop tablets arrayed over the manuals.

Legitimate organ music could not be played on these instruments, nor was it wanted. The players were provided with cue sheets, which told them what type of music was required for so many seconds to follow the changing situations of the picture. (The last movement of the *William Tell* Overture is firmly associated in many people's minds with the galloping of cavalry or a sheriff's posse to rescue someone in a tight spot.) The organist was generally given ten minutes or so sometime during the programme in which to entertain the audience unaided. His offering varied according to his ability. He might play anything from a light overture or march to the latest popular hit. But always there were the *vox humanas, celestes,* and tremulants which made the music shake like a sort of audible jello.

Theater owners who could afford to do so offered large salaries to induce legitimate organists to play for them. Few organists accepted.

Theater work involved long hours, loss of independence, and no opportunity to play the organ as it should be played.

To meet the demand for players, hundreds of people who were clever at the piano keyboard—and hundreds who were not—and could play catchy rhythms convincingly, entered the theater field. They did not learn to play the theater organ: they acclimatized themselves to the instruments and invented showy tricks to cover their technical shortcomings.

No lowering of general musical standards was intended. Theater players did not pretend to play fine music or to be fine organists. They merely wished to make a living by contributing to the fun and amusement of people who were out for an evening's entertainment.

But harm did result—a harm that has outlasted the transitory existence of the theater organ.

In the first place, a large section of the public took what they heard seriously. The music of the moving picture theater became their standard: the theater organ became their ideal. The style of music and playing has survived in popular radio broadcasts and recordings; and is, alas, widely imitated, not by church organists but by people who play church organs.

The second harmful effect of the theater organ on organ music generally was the discouragement of industry and ambition on the part of those who, under other circumstances, might have become good organ students. The young man who studied the organ properly must spend many hours a week developing pedal technic, an organ touch, and other fundamentals. The only opportunity he had to test his progress in public was to play relatively simple pieces to apathetic congregations at Sunday church services, for which he received little or no remuneration. It is not surprising, then, that many young organists chose the quick, and easy way of mastering a few tricks and getting jobs in small or medium-sized theaters where they played for from two to five interested audiences a day and received a pretty good salary for a relatively easy life.

If economic conditions had remained normal, the dearth of organ students in the 1920's might have been overcome when the sound film silenced theater organs. But, by that time, the depression of the 1930's was upon us. Few people could afford music lessons, and there was no incentive, apart from the satisfaction of achievement, to study the organ. Those organists who had positions clung to them, at reduced salaries, as their only reliable sources of income. What vacancies there were offered no temptation to the student to go to the expense of tuition in order to compete for them. The neglect of the organ continued.

In 1934, Laurens Hammond invented what has since become known as the electronic organ, in which sound originated by means of the rotation of metal discs in an electromagnetic field and was amplified electrically. This instrument occupied no more space than was required for a small console and an amplification cabinet, it was capable of a wide variety of tone colors, and it was a good deal cheaper than a pipe organ. What its chances of survival would have been in prosperous times, it is hard to say; but, appearing on the market when money was scarce, it sold in such great numbers that pipe-organ builders were, for a time, seriously concerned.

Since then, several manufacturers have marketed similar instruments. In the hands of capable organists who can recognize and cope with their limitations, electronic organs can be very effective. Certainly they were a boon to congregations who, for economic reasons, had long endured harmoniums, reed organs, and small, worn-out pipe organs. Unfortunately, there are not enough capable organists to go around; and the reputation of electronic organs suffers because they are so often played by people who have neither the ability nor the desire to emphasize their good points.

Some pipe organ builders have met the competition of electronic organs by producing small, compact organs, using the unit principle to some extent, and making provision for variety of tone by the inclusion of soft mutation stops. These organs are not suitable for recital work, but they are quite satisfactory for the music of the church service.

The many instruments with abbreviated keyboards and a dozen sticks to serve as pedals, advertised extensively in newspapers and magazines, are not organs at all. They are expensive toys designed for people who get a thrill from playing the melody of *Old Black Joe* from a foolproof chart. The most accomplished organist would be unable to make a good showing with them.

Most churches today are furnished with instruments of some kind that are suitable for the playing of the services. In fact, church organs are generally larger and more elaborate than is necessary. A great many ranks of pipes and mechanical aids could be dispensed with, not because they are undesirable but because they are not used. The tonal possibilities of even small organs often remain unexplored because the people who play them are not qualified to use them intelligently.

Unfortunately, the plenitude of organs is not matched by the number of people capable of playing them. Although there are as many first-rate organists as there ever were—perhaps more—there are far fewer of modest attainments who are capable of playing church services satisfactorily. The number of students has not increased appreciably over the unproductive 1920's and 1930's.

There are, no doubt, any number of factors that contribute to the lack of interest in organ study; but perhaps the greatest lies in the unattractiveness of church duty.

The organist is often the only person in the church who has any real interest in church music. He may receive no active cooperation, even from the minister. Clergymen who are sympathetic towards the problems of the organist and choirmaster are few; and even these, because of lack of musical training, may be less understanding and helpful than they would like to be. Other ministers are not the least bit interested in the music; still others adopt an attitude that borders on hostility, looking upon the organist and choir as competitors for public attention rather than as collaborators in the service of worship.

The organist, who is also the choirmaster, generally, finds little enthusiasm for music where he might expect to find it—in the choir loft. He may spend a large part of half a dozen rehearsals preparing music for a festival service only to be told, after the last rehearsal, that six or eight choristers cannot be present. They may have known all along that they were going to be absent from the service for which the music was being prepared, but that did not prevent them from wasting the time of the whole choir, and allowing the organist to mount a pinnacle of enthusiasm only to be faced with an abyss of frustration. If the organist fails to control his temper and displays anything but Christian resignation, he is "hard to get along with." If he tries to get rid of these drones, he finds that he has offended not only them but their families and friends and thereby stirred up a minor tempest. The minister has the unpleasant task of taking the organist aside and, in the most saintly and tolerant manner imaginable, bringing pressure to bear on him to reinstate the dismissed choristers. He does not say "or else!" but he implies it. It does the organist no good to explain that the choir is, or should be, a working organization which can accomplish nothing unless the members pull their weight. Peace (even an uneasy peace) must be preserved, though it be at the cost of worship music.

Although church music generally has fallen to such a low level, the organist finds an astonishing number of people in pulpit, choir loft, and pew who know far more about it than he does and who feel qualified to reverse in ten seconds a decision that he has reached after hours of careful consideration. Sometimes, after an innovation to which the minister has given his whole hearted approval and support, the organist is instructed to desist from a repetition because "certain members of the congregation object." Since church officials are seldom democratic or consistent, the organist concludes that he has offended a Liberal Contributor. Even though the majority of regular attendants are quite satisfied with the music, a Liberal Contributor who attends only half a dozen times a year may veto anything he does not like.

For fighting his single-handed, losing battle on behalf of church music, the organist and choirmaster is poorly paid. The church officials measure his time in hours actually spent on the organ bench during services and rehearsals, failing to take into account the hours spent in practicing and planning, which far exceed those spent "on duty."

Even if he is one of the better-paid organists, his salary is only the nucleus of his income. If he chooses to augment it by teaching music to private pupils, he must laboriously build up a class that will enable him to earn a respectable sum in ten months of the year, and his working hours are in the late afternoons and early evenings and weekends, when all his friends are free. He has no security. He may be dismissed from his position just when he has succeeded in bringing his income to a satisfactory level, in which case he must go elsewhere and be prepared to live as best he can on his church salary until he can build up another class.

Some of the worst-paid organists, not being able to augment their salaries sufficiently by teaching, take other positions, regarding their church obligations as a part-time job. Unless they are unusually enthusiastic and energetic, this arrangement does not last long. The duties of an organist and choirmaster, properly performed, are too heavy to undertake in addition to another full-time occupation. Either the organist or the music must suffer.

People of this age appreciate goods and services in proportion to what they pay for them; and the organist who sacrifices his time and energy to serve for a small salary receives far more criticism and less respect than he would if he took advantage of the congregation's position and forced them to pay him more.

Church officials may claim that this picture of conditions under which organists work is a biased one. Or admitting some of these statements, they may argue that they are powerless to improve those conditions. They may or may not be right. The fact remains that this is the picture that organists and prospective organists see and none but the most dedicated of young people want to spend a period of rigorous preparation for the future that church positions offer them.

In the meantime, there are hundreds of churches without organists. Their music is in the hands of people who have little training and who have no intention of improving their qualifications. These substitutes for organists must not be condemned too hastily. Many of them are not playing because they think they are capable or because they want to. They accept the positions and the conditions that go with them simply because there is no one else to do it.

Prospects for churches in small communities are not bright. I know of towns with five or six churches that have no organ students. When their present organists die or retire or move away, it is going to be difficult to replace them; for a salary of six or eight hundred dollars will not attract applicants from other places when no other means of support are offered.

The lack of church musicians is the greatest stumbling block to the progress of worship music. Church governing bodies do not seem to be aware of this problem and perhaps will not become aware of it until their organs fall silent and their choirs disperse for lack of organists and choirmasters. There is a very real danger of this happening within the next decade or two unless preventive steps are taken.

✣ REFERENCES

Hymn Tunes

A list which includes contemporary hymn tune writers is difficult to prepare. Few of their tunes have wide circulation as yet: most of them are found in only one or two of the most lately revised hymnals. Those that are likely to be available to the greatest number of church people have been selected, and I am aware that there may be important omissions.

Since reference to writers of gospel hymns was made at the end of Chapter XIV, no further reference is made here. In that respect, this list is not as representative as the preceding ones, but is restricted to various better types.

Some of the composers mentioned have written many tunes: others have written only one that has been published. Nevertheless, the one tune of any particular composer may, in time, surpass in popularity all the tunes of more prolific writers.

Because dates of the births and deaths of twentieth century composers are not as readily available as those of past generations, the list is necessarily incomplete in that respect.

Bancroft, H. Hugh, b. 1904.
Barnes, E. S., b. 1887.
Barrows, Donald S.
Biggs, Arthur H.
Bode, Arnold G. H.
Bullock, Ernest, b. 1890.
Burt, Bates G.
Coller, Percy E. B.
Conant, Grace Wilbur
Cozens, John
Currier, Everett R.
Day, George Henry
Dickey, Mark

Diggle, Roland
Douglas, Winfred
Evans, David, b. 1874.
Ferris, Theodore P.
Forcier, Robert W., b. 1878.
George, Graham
Glynn, Franklin
Goldsworthy, W. A.
Gray, D. Vincent
Hall, Walter Henry
Hallstrom, Henry
Harwood, Basil
Holst, Gustav

Hopkins, John Henry
Hopkins, John Henry, Jr.
Hopkirk, James b. 1908.
Ingham, H. T.
Ireland, John N., b. 1879.
Iverson, Daniel
Jacob, A. L.
James, Philip
Joseph, Jane M.
Lang, Craig S.
Ley, Henry G., b. 1887.
Means, Claude
Miller, Anne L.
Morris, R. O.
Morse, Anna J.
Mullinar, Michael
Naylor, Edward W., b. 1867.
Nicholson, Sydney H.
Noble, T. Tertius, b. 1867.
Northrop, A.
Oliver, Henry Kemble
Owen, Frank K.
Parsons, Ernest J.
Robbins, Howard C.
Roberts, R. E.
Rooper, J. B.

Runkel, Kenneth E.
Russell, Frederick G.
Russell, Studley, b. 1901.
Scott, J. S.
Sharpe, E.
Shaw, Geoffrey, 1879–1943.
Shaw, Martin, b. 1875.
Silvester, Frederick C., b. 1901.
Slater, Gordon A., b. 1896.
Slathe, G.
Smith, Alfred M.
Sowerby, Leo, b. 1895.
Stewart, C. Hylton, 1884–1932.
Strohm, Albert J.
Terry, Richard Runciman
Thatcher, Reginald S.
Vale, Walter S.
Warrack, Guy
Warrell, Arthur S.
Whinfield, W. G.
Whitehead, Alfred E., b. 1887.
Willan, Healey, b. 1880.
Williams, David McK.
Williams, Ralph Vaughan, 1872–1958.
Wolle, J. Fred
Wood, Thomas, b. 1892.

Anthems, Cantatas

The fact that this list is much shorter than it might be should not be construed as a preference for the works of these composers over the many compositions of equal worth which it has been necessary to omit. The list has been compiled from material made available to me by the generosity of certain publishers. Actually, it is not as restricted as might appear, since the catalogues of the publishers named include works of other publishers for whom they are agents: Carl Fischer for the Oxford University Press, Schirmer for J. Curwen and Sons.

Asterisks denote oratorios and other extended choral works.

Anderson, William H.—
    My Master hath a garden   [F]
Armstrong, Thomas—
    Christ, whose glory fills the skies
    [F]
    Creator Spirit   [S]
Asper, Frank—
    Song of Mary   [F]

Atkins, Ivor—
    Abide with me   [N]
    Behold, I come quickly   [N]
    There is none that can resist thy
    voice   [N]
Avery, S. R.—
    I called upon the Lord   [S]
    *Raising of Lazarus, The   [S]

Bairstow, Edward C.—
*Communion Service in E flat (unison) [F]
Day draws on with golden light, The [F]
Jesu, the very thought of thee [F]
Of the Father's love begotten [N]
Promise which was made unto the fathers, The [N]
Save us, O Lord [N]

Baldwin, Ralph Lyman—
Broken heart for sacrifice, A [B]

Barnes, E. S.—
Behold, I bring you glad tidings [S]
By the rivers of Babylon [S]
Give ear unto my voice [F]
O worship the King [S]
Wilderness, The [B]
Ye that fear the Lord [F]

Bingham, Seth—
Come, thou almighty King [F]
Jubilate Deo [B]
Lord's Prayer, The [F]

Brown, Leon—
Blessed be thou, O Lord [B]
Holy Spirit, truth divine [B]
Thy will for evermore be done [B]

Buck, Percy C.—
God be merciful unto us [N]
Jesus said: "He that hath seen me" [F]
O Lord God [N]
There came wise men from the East [F]

Bullock, Ernest—
Christ, the fair glory [F]
Give laud unto the Lord [F]
O for a closer walk with God [F]

Candlyn, T. F. H.—
*Four horsemen, The [Gray]

Coerne, Louis A.—
Blessed is he [S]
Lift up your heads [B]
Lord is my rock, The [B]
Savior, source of every blessing [S]

Coke-Jephcott, Norman—
Love from Galilee, The [S]
O God, who hast prepared for those who love thee [F]

Coleridge-Taylor, Samuel—
By the waters of Babylon [N]
In thee, O Lord [N]
Now late on the Sabbath day [N]

Cousins, Thomas—
Glorious Everlasting [Brodt]

Creston, Paul—
Devoutly I adore thee [S]
Psalm 23 [S]

Darke, Harold E.—
O brother man [F]
O gladsome light [F]
Sing a song of joy [F]
*Sower, The [F]

Davies, H. Walford—
And Jesus entered into the temple [N]
*Grace to you and peace [N]
O thou that hearest prayer [N]
Spiritual Songs [N]
Walk to Emmaus, The [N]

De Lamarter, Eric—
Choral Responses (6 sets) [F]

Dett, Nathaniel—
Listen to the lambs [S]
O holy Lord [S]

Dickinson, Clarence—
Easter Litany, An [Gray]
O anxious hearts [Gray]
Thy word is like a garden, Lord [Gray]
World, rejoice! [Gray]

Diggle, Roland—
Christ hath a garden [F]
Upon the hills [F]

Dunkley, Ferdinand—
Blessed is the man [F]

Farrar, E.—
Prevent us, O Lord [N]

Federlein, Gottfried—
Behold now, praise ye the Lord [S]
Comfort ye my people [S]
God is my salvation [S]

Fletcher, Percy E.—
  Hark! hark, my soul [N]
  Now is come salvation [N]
  Now once again [N]
  Ring out, wild bells [N]
Gaul, Harvey B.—
  Bread of the world [B]
  Eyes of the Lord, The [B]
  Lighten our darkness [S]
  O Lord God of hosts [S]
  *Son of man [F]
Grace, Harvey—
  Praise to the Lord [F]
  Thanks be to thee [N]
Harris, Roy—
  Sanctus [S]
Harris, William H.—
  From a heart made whole [F]
  Heavens declare the glory of God, The [F]
  Most glorious Lord of life [F]
  O what their joy and their glory must be [F]
  Vox ultima crucis (Tarry no longer) [F]
Hollins, Alfred—
  Be glad, then, ye children of Zion [N]
  O worship the Lord [N]
  Why seek ye the living [N]
Holst, Gustav—
  Christmas Day [N]
  Eternal Father [S]
  Man born to toil [F]
  Of one that is so fair and bright [S]
Howells, Herbert—
  *Communion Service (Unison) [F]
  Let God arise [F]
  Like as the hart [F]
  My eyes for beauty pine [F]
  Spotless rose, A [Stainer & Bell]
Ireland, John—
  Greater love hath no man [Stainer & Bell]
James, Philip—
  Child Jesus came to earth [B]

Christ is born [B]
Hail, dear Conqueror [S]
We pray thee, gracious Lord [S]
Jenkins, Cyril—
  Dawn of peace [S]
  Fierce raged the tempest [S]
  Hymn to the soul [S]
  Lead, kindly light [J. Fischer]
  Light in darkness [N]
Ley, Henry G.—
  Come, thou long expected Jesus [F]
  Eternal Ruler [F]
  Lo, round the throne [F]
  Strife is o'er, The [F]
Lockwood, Charlotte M.—
  All thy works praise thee [Gray]
  How burn the stars unchanging [Gray]
  Our Father and our God [Gray]
  Thy glory dawns [Gray]
Macfarlane, Will C.—
  Beatitudes, The [S]
  Ho, every one that thirsteth [S]
  Like as the hart desireth [S]
  O love that wilt not let me go [S]
  Open our eyes [S]
  O rest in the Lord [S]
Mackinnon, Hugh A.—
  Ballad of Saint Stephen [Gray]
  Give to my restless heart [Gray]
  I saw three ships [Gray]
  O, the holly [Gray]
  Of the light of the dawn [Gray]
Macpherson, Charles—
  Behold, O God, our defender [N]
  If a man die, shall he live again? [N]
  Jesu, Lord of life and glory [N]
  Whom the Lord loveth [N]
Miles, Russell Hancock—
  As the hart panteth [Gray]
  Savior, lead us [S]
Milligan, Harold V.—
  Hear my cry [S]
Naylor, E. W.—
  And there shall be signs [N]

I will cause the shower to come down [N]

O Jerusalem, look about thee [N]

Noble, T. Tertius—
Come, O thou traveller unknown [S]
Fierce was the wild billow [S]
I will lay me down in peace [S]
Let all the world in every corner sing [Harris, Oakville]
Saints of God, The [Harris]
Souls of the righteous [S]

Pritchard, Arthur J.—
All holy Father, Son and Spirit blest [S]
Magnificat and Nunc Dimittis [F]

Rathbone, George—
Every good gift [N]
Not unto us, O Lord [N]
Rejoice in the Lord alway [N]
Strife is o'er, The [N]

Rogers, Bernard—
Lord, who shall dwell [N]
Teach me, O Lord [N]

Rootham, Cyril B.—
Praise the Lord, O my soul [F]

Saar, Louis Victor—
Come in, dear angels [F]
O Jesu, so fair [F]

Sargent, Malcolm—
Second Crucifixion, The [F]

Schumann, William—
Te Deum [S]

Shaw, Geoffrey—
Day draws on with golden light, The [N]
How far is it to Bethlehem? [N]
Praise God in his holiness [S]
Psalm 23 [S]
Worship [N]

Shaw, Martin—
Blessing, A [S]
Hymn of Faith, A [F]
O Christ, who holds the open gate [N]
O Light from age to age the same [F]

Sing we merrily [N]
With a voice of singing [S]

Skilton, Charles S.—
Lord of all being, throned afar [F]

Sowerby, Leo—
Behold, bless ye the Lord [B]
I will lift up mine eyes [B]
Song of immortal hope [B]

Stanton, Walter K.—
Jesu, lover of my soul [F]
Sing we triumphant hymns of praise [F]
Spacious firmament, The [F]

Stewart, C. Hylton—
Christ being raised from the dead [F]
On this day, earth shall ring [F]
Winds of Bethlehem, The [F]

Talmadge, Charles L.—
Jesus, the very thought of thee [S]
We love the place, O God [S]

Thiman, Eric—
Christ hath a garden [N]
Christ the Lord is risen again [N]
Grant us light [S]
Jesu, the very thought of thee [F]
Jesus shall reign [F]
Last Supper, The [N]
Spacious firmament, The [N]

Thompson, Van Denman—
Breathe on me, breath of God [Gray]
Dear Lord, who once upon the lake [S]
Prayer for God's presence, A [Gray]
Thou art my King [Gray]

Voris, W. R.—
Blessed are the pure in heart [Gray]
Come, faithful people [Gray]
Drop, drop, slow tears [Gray]
God's only Son [Gray]
Redeeming love [Gray]

Weatherseed, J. J.—
Lighten our darkness [B]

Webbe, William Y.—
  Day of resurrection [Gray]
  Let now the heavenly host [Gray]
  Praises of God [Gray]
Whitehead, Alfred E.—
  Eternal Ruler of the ceaseless round
    [B]
  Gate of life stands wide, The [B]
  Jesu, the very thought of thee
    [Gray]
Whitlock, Percy W.—
  Be still, my soul [F]
  Come, let us join our cheerful songs [F]
  Glorious in heaven [F]
  Sing praise to God [F]
Whittaker, W. G.—
  Festal Psalm, A [F]
Willan, Healey—
  Before the ending of the day [F]
  Christ hath a garden [Harris, Oakville]
  I looked, and behold, a white cloud
    [N]

  Three kings, The [F]
  While all things were in quiet silence [N]
Williams, David McK.—
  Darest thou, O my soul [Gray]
  Sleep, O sleep, son Jesus [Gray]
Williams, Ralph Vaughan—
  Let us now praise famous men [S]
  Lord, thou hast been our refuge
    [S]
  Magnificat [F]
  Nothing is here for tears [F]
  O how amiable [F]
  O taste and see [F]
  Shepherds of the delectable mountains, The [F]
Wood, Charles—
  I will arise [N]
  Invocation [F]
  Solitary reaper, The [F]
  Try me, O God [N]

16
THE YEARS AHEAD

───

❖ THE NEED FOR IDEALISTS AND REFORMERS

This is not the first period in history in which church music has languished, as we have discovered in our survey of the past. Following each such period there has come, sooner or later, a renascence; but it has not come about spontaneously. It has required patience, energy, faith, and persistence on the part of dedicated men; and only those qualities, coupled with all the resources at our disposal, will effect a new renascence that could surpass all others.

Those church musicians who, through composition and in the preparation of worship music, are maintaining high standards, must be asked to assume the mantles of reformers. It is not an easy role to assume, for they will meet with opposition from the pulpit, the choir loft, and the pew. Yet, it is plainly the duty of those who fare sumptuously to share the good things they possess with others.

Church musicians, whether composers, organists, choirmasters, or choristers, are the beneficiaries of all the musicians that have been mentioned in these pages. Worship music would have been very different from what it is today if no ancient Greeks had experimented with scales, if Ambrose and Gregory had not instituted reforms, if Palestrina and his contemporaries had displayed less genius, if there had been no Reformation, if the works of Bach had been left to gather dust on the cupboard shelves in Leipzig, or if the Victorians had been less active. Our ancestors nurtured and enriched church music according to their abilities and opportunities; and we, to whom it has been entrusted, have the responsibility of passing it on untarnished to posterity. In order to do this, we must not merely preserve: we must re-create.

Music has no permanent existence. A church that was filled with music a moment ago is now silent. One cannot return to the church on Monday morning and hear what he heard on Sunday, although he can *see* the things he *saw* on Sunday. The music will not exist again until it is re-created by the musicians. It cannot be handed on to a next generation by a passive people. There must be active and repeated re-creation.

The music of a service is not confined within the four walls of any church, nor the concern only of the people gathered within those walls. It is part of the expression of praise of all Christendom. Considered thus, the music in a church in North Carolina concerns congregations in South Dakota and Alaska, just as the playing of a flutist in an orchestra concerns the trumpeter and the 'cellist. In both cases, individuals are contributing to a concerted effort. The best work of the conscientious and capable will not prevent the music from being marred by the careless and inept.

In addition to the qualities that have already been mentioned—patience, energy, faith, and persistence—the reformers and restorers of worship music must have vision and idealism, without which all practical measures lose direction and purpose. They must think in terms of worship rather than in terms of music, and in doing so, they will find that the standard of worship music rises. That so much of our church music is poor stuff is not a refutation of this statement, for it has obviously been written and is sung by people who have not had vision, and who have not given much thought to the purpose of worship music.

But the dreaming of dreams and the seeing of visions will not bring about reforms without practical measures to implement them. It is to these practical measures that we must now give some consideration, bearing in mind that we still have not quite answered the question posed at the beginning of this book: What *is* church music?

✤ THE CLERGY

The problem of worship music has baffled and irritated most clergymen for centuries. While some simply do not care anything about it, and others actually encourage the use of poor music, the majority are concerned about its effect upon the services of the church. Perhaps they are not well enough informed to judge the music on its own merits, but they do know whether or not it creates a hiatus in the devotions of the people. They are justifiably annoyed when the atmosphere of reverence is suddenly dispelled by an unsuitable hymn tune, anthem, or organ solo. Some of them may be as much annoyed with themselves as with the organist and choir, realizing that the responsibility rests upon their own shoulders, yet lacking the musical qualifications to discharge that responsibility.

There are two classes of clergy who escape this particular form of frustration.

There are those who are musically educated, who can speak with an authority backed by a profound knowledge of the subject. Some of these, not confining their influence to individual churches, have been among the leaders in the advancement of worship music—Ambrose, Gregory, Luther, the Wesleys, the American divines who combatted fuguing and ornamentation in the late seventeenth century, John Curwen and his associates, many English clergymen of the nineteenth century, Winfred Douglas, and others.

There are those ministers, musical or not, fortunate enough to have organists and choirmasters who are capable, sympathetic and intuitive; who after consultation with the clergyman, can be trusted to provide music that will fulfill all the requirements of the service.

There are many such ministers and many such organists and choirmasters, but, unfortunately, they constitute a small percentage of the whole.

Most clergymen receive no preparation for leadership and direction in the field of church music. There is no one to whom they can turn for advice. Their organists may not be churchmen in the best sense of the word, or even good musicians. Their fellow-clergy are in the same position as themselves—untrained and unsure. They cannot turn to the governing bodies of their churches, for church governing bodies have no policy or programme as far as music is concerned.

Perhaps it is this lack of official interest that is at the root of the matter. (This statement refers, of course, to Protestant church music. The Roman Catholic Church has, on numerous occasions, set more or less vague standards; not because of any particular official interest in the music, but in sheer exasperation because worldly musicians have taken advantage of official neglect.)

Authoritarian measures have seldom been satisfactory. They emphasize the letter, restricting all music to a certain type, and leave no freedom for individuals to interpret the spirit.

Edicts, as far as music was concerned, retarded progress by prohibiting innovations; and that, of course, was a serious matter when musicians could not exist as such without the approval of their work by the church. Moreover, the edicts did not preserve music unsullied. While the gifted were curbed, the ungifted, remote from ecclesiastical censorshop, introduced all sorts of crude music.

Perhaps the most restrictive measures suffered by Protestants were those imposed by the early Calvinists. Their reasons for barring all but metrical psalms, sung in unison and unaccompanied, seemed sound enough at the time; but they should have known that, if the people were permitted to sing at public worship, they would not long confine themselves to such a simple, unimaginative mode of expression. Once these narrow bounds were crossed, there were no more to be observed. The result was chaos.

If authoritarian decrees have failed to produce and maintain a more or less uniform high standard, absolute freedom in the choice of music, as practiced by most Protestant bodies, has been equally unsuccessful. Somewhere between the two extremes must lie the solution.

Most Protestant bodies consider that they do their duty to church music by appointing committees every twenty or twenty-five years to revise their hymnals. These committees, some of whose members are competent and some merely willing, are baffled by the same difficulty which we encountered in the first pages of this book: that there are no definite standards with which to conform. Since their people have never been subjected to a course of education in church music, they have to include hymns of all types in the hope of satisfying all tastes. Some they would rather omit, but dare not for fear of offending people of whom these hymns are "old favorites." To compensate for the presence of such unwelcome hymns, the committee includes some newer ones, and some older ones which have not been familiar to their people, in the hope that they may be noticed, gain favor, and supplant the poor types. The result is often a hodgepodge. Wearily the committee lays its burden down, aware that it has succeeded in completely satisfying nobody. The music continues to be chosen in hit and miss fashion for another twenty-five years until another revising committee is appointed to face the same old difficulties and problems.

Let us consider, not what would happen, but what *should* happen if the committee, submitting its revision to the church governing body, reported in detail the difficulties they had encountered and recommended a campaign dedicated to the improvement of church music.

Surely the governing body could be convinced, by a sincere and eloquent advocate, of two facts that ought to be obvious: that music has an important role in public worship, and that it is not playing that role.

It seems that a permanent committee on church music might well be appointed. The first difficulty would be to find men and women capable of serving as members. If people were appointed simply because it was their turn to serve on a committee—and some committees are thus formed —the whole plan might be better abandoned. It would be as well to canvass the clergy in the hope of finding three or four genuinely interested in worship music who have had some musical training. Perhaps a potential leader and reformer might be discovered. (Luther was both a clergyman and a musician; so were John Curwen and Canon Winfred Douglas. The present Bishop of Toronto ranks among the best organists in his diocese.)

To this small group of clergy might be added an equal number of church musicians—organists and choirmasters of long and varied experience, sound judgment, and good churchmanship. An intimate knowledge of conditions in small and rural areas should be required of at least some members.

Such a committee should be a permanent one. The job to be done is too great for quarterly or even monthly meetings. The members should be paid. If they accomplish their mission, their salaries will be insignificant compared with the results.

The ultimate, but not immediate aim would be the establishment of broad standards for church music. The hasty drawing up of a set of regulations will simply lead nowhere, as it has done in the past.

The first and most urgent need is for a programme of education. Since a committee of eight or ten cannot possibly reach and influence all the members of their denomination scattered across the country, they should concentrate on the training of three groups: (1) men to succeed them on the committee; (2) divinity students; and (3) church musicians.

Perhaps the general excellence of English church music is due to the fact that so many of the clergy and church musicians once served as choir boys, and at an early, impressionable age became steeped in the tradition and practice of church music. Lacking this training ground, as most Protestant churches do, the only alternative seems to be for at least one divinity school of each denomination to make church music a major subject. It would not be necessary for all students to take this course, but certainly some should be encouraged to do so if we are to have clergymen capable of plotting and guiding our future with an intelligent regard to both worship and music. A few of the larger theological seminaries do offer good courses in music, but the students who take them do so entirely on their own initiative, without any official encouragement or recognition from the denominations they represent.

Even a general course should prepare the fledgling minister for assuming some of the responsibility for music that will be his. Most students know no more about the vexing problem when they leave divinity school than they did when they entered. Some seminaries, preparing young men for orders in liturgical churches, do not even teach them to intone their parts of the service. Most newly ordained ministers are first sent to small, struggling churches that cannot afford (or think they cannot afford) competent organists and choirmasters. The sole responsibility for the music is dumped into their laps. It is a situation that they should not have to face untrained. They should not be at the mercy of amateur organists who have no real conception of church music.

Ministers of individual churches are the only constant links between the people and the governing bodies of their particular denominations. If the people are to be educated to better standards of church music, their ministers must assume the direction, if not the leadership. By "leadership" it is not meant fervent exhortations to the congregation to "sing heartily" and the setting of a bad example by shouting the melody at the top of one's lungs. But divinity students should be taught something about ideals, about the choosing of hymns, about the type of music that is most likely to enhance the devotional atmosphere of public worship. Above all, they should be taught to know when music is not fulfilling its purpose as an aid to worship and how to take steps to remedy the condition.

Since the minister, however musical and well informed he may be, cannot hope to accomplish much without well-trained help, the central committee should make every effort to insure that such help will be available. At present, our churches do nothing about the training of church musicians. Their instruction is received entirely in the secular field. Even some of the best ones, who can play organ fugues and sonatas very well and produce thrilling choral effects, do not show to advantage when playing service music or teaching their choirs to sing hymns and simple anthems. And that any musicians at all are available for church duty is purely a matter of chance, not of design.

It is not feasible for church governing bodies to set up music schools all over the country, but there is still much that they could do towards the training of church musicians. There are schools of church music conducted on a small scale here and there and from time to time and even intensive courses in connection with seminaries for special training in church work. But these are conducted unofficially, and excellent though they are, their influence is not wide. Those who enroll in the courses are good musicians to begin with, and they graduate to positions in large churches where the music has never been much of a problem.

What is needed is some encouragement for young people in small towns to study the organ, and the provision of some specific instruction in the performance of church duties.

There are still many local churches that will not permit anyone but the regular organist to use the organ. The instrument is kept locked during the week. They do not realize that, sooner or later, they may have to lock the organ permanently and throw the key away because there will be no one to play it. There are other churches in regions where the winters are severe and the temperature so often extreme that practicing is impossible for either the organist or student. And, finally, there are the pitifully tiny salaries paid to many organists—salaries which are an accurate reflection of the value placed upon church music.

It is only by a programme of education, planned by a central committee and carried far and wide by individual clergymen, that local congregations will begin to attach some importance to church music and provide facilities for the training of church musicians.

Another great help would be the appointment of regional instructors and examiners. The young student who has become fairly proficient should be able to seek instruction in applying his skill to church music from an experienced colleague appointed by the central committee. If such representatives were authorized to issue certificates of approval, young organists would be eager to achieve certain minimum standards, and their congregations would encourage them to do so.

Although regimentation is foreign to the doctrines of Protestantism, some organization is necessary, and there is an urgent need for organization in the field of church music. Freedom in the choice of music ought to be respected; but freedom without judgment can be, and has been, harmful. Judgment can be acquired only through education, and an educational programme can be successfully planned and inaugurated only by the clergy through their governing bodies.

✤ ORGANISTS AND CHOIRMASTERS

Whether or not the clergy provide leadership, inspiration, and ideals for a renascence of worship music, it is the organist and choirmaster who will have to bear the burden of the task.

It is difficult to speak in generalities about organists. When we speak of violinists or pianists, our minds turn at once to artists who have established themselves in the top rank by their performances and with the general consent of critics and public. When we speak of organists, most people think of the men and women who play organs in local churches. Comparatively few people have heard first-rate organists, or even know them by name. The standard of organ playing accepted by the public varies from place to place and is often set by performers of a degree of skill that would not justify the performer of any other instrument to play in public.

The lives of most reputable organists are quiet, and their routine circumscribed. As a class, they are far more conventional than other musicians. Having built up repertoires that serve for their church duties and occasional recitals, and worked out curricula for their teaching, they are inclined to let matters rest there. They are not restless, exploratory, and progressive as other artists are.

There are few concert organists today. It is true that a concert tour is not a very profitable undertaking, but that is largely the fault of organists. In the early part of the century, organ recitals by eminent organists attracted large audiences. North American artists, and those from Europe who made American tours, became widely known. An examination of some of these old programmes shows that the organists were far less stuffy than their modern successors. They played Bach and Buxtehude and a great deal of other solid, serious music, but they were not afraid to meet the audiences on their own ground. People loved to hear brilliant, showy pieces like Lemmens' *The Storm* and Batiste's *Quatre Grandes Offertoires de Saint-Cécile*. A Guilmant *Sonata* or a Saint-Saëns *Rhapsody* interested them. They liked short French pieces, variations and fantasias by Lemare and Faulkes, marches and overtures. Perhaps they should not have liked them, but they did, and it was far better fare than was served to them after the legitimate concert organist retired from the field in favor of the theater organist.

The public did not tire of the organ. Municipal and theater organs were not built to provide the people with something that was unpopular. It is true that many civic and most theater organists pandered to uncultivated tastes in music, but so did the dance bands and jazz orchestras and blues singers. Elman and Kreisler, Rachmaninoff and Rubinstein did not retire as a result. The Boston Symphony Orchestra did not disband or the Metropolitan Opera House close its doors. But organists made no attempt to meet the competition: they withdrew into their shells. They abandoned all attempts to please the public. Their repertoires became more and more austere, designed to please organists more than anyone else.

In a way, one cannot blame organists for withdrawing from the highly competitive concert field. Their chief sources of income were their church positions and their teaching, and they could carry out both these duties quite satisfactorily without concert work—more satisfactorily, indeed, since concert work made necessary interruptions in their normal schedules. They had an obligation to their churches and to their pupils and no obligation at all, strictly speaking, to a public that was satisfied with something less than they were prepared to give.

And yet, we cannot but regret that they remained aloof and permitted the public's conception of organ music to deteriorate without raising a finger to stop it. Whereas other musicians recognized the need for a certain amount of light and bright music to coax the attention of the public to better things, organists dropped from their repertoires anything that might please the audiences. Their music remained good —so good that it repelled the average listener. Organ recitals are sparsely attended today because the programmes bore the public. They bore musicians, too.

The effect upon organ students has been bad. There are hundreds of people playing church organs who have never heard an organ played properly. Their standard is that which prevails in their localities; and that standard is, as often as not, the product of the popular conception of organ music during the past thirty years or more—tremulants and vibratos, sticky stops, left-footed pedal parts, and easy arrangements. If they play hymns for congregational singing with combinations in which *celeste* stops are prominent, with the tremulant pulled out and most of the bass notes pedalled bumpily an octave lower than written, it is because they know no better. It is no good shrugging off this situation with the supercilious remark that these people should not be playing organs at all. They *are* playing organs, and if they were not, many churches would be without music. They must be taken into account in any plan for the improvement of worship music.

More serious students are often discouraged rather than inspired by hearing a recital by a good organist. They may or may not appreciate the music they hear, but they realize that it is far beyond their ability and their congregations' comprehension. They may form the ambition to play Bach fugues some day, but their real problem is what to play *now*. The recitalist does not help them.

If we are to raise the standard of organ playing, which is a condition to raising the standard of worship music, the first step is to find people who are willing to study the organ. Perhaps that is the greatest problem of all. Young people cannot be drafted into service, although many are persuaded to play church organs against their inclination and better judgment.

The prospective church organist must be devoted to music and to his church. It is not likely that anyone who is not fond of music will even think of playing the organ, but it is quite another matter to find people who are willing to subordinate music and themselves to the needs of the church. It is, indeed, difficult to find people with enough loyalty to the church to make sacrifices for it.

Devotion to the church is something that must be inspired by the clergy. That is clearly their business, and how they go about it is for them to decide.

Ideals in church music should be shared by everyone—clergy, organists and choirmasters, choirs and congregations—but where ideals do not exist, it is difficult to see how they are to be fostered except through an educational programme sponsored by an official body. Such a programme should inspire not only ideals but generosity and patience in regard to the music.

Generosity must not be confined to a tolerant attitude towards the organist and his work: it must include a willingness to set a respectable monetary valuation on his services.

It is likely that most congregations feel that the organist is pretty well paid, even if he receives only five or ten dollars a Sunday. As far as they can see, all he has to do is to walk into church, play two or three pieces and three or four hymns, and the accompaniment to the anthem or solo. He is only there for a little over an hour, and he is doing nothing for at least half that time.

Since most young organists begin playing in public much too soon, they have to spend hours practicing those pieces and hymns and accompaniments. If they play two services a Sunday, their work adds up to some twenty pieces, thirty hymns, and at least eight accompaniments every month. What young pianist who has been studying two years (and many of our organists have not been studying their instrument that long) has a repertoire of twenty pieces which he can play in public? Even concert artists are not required to learn pieces at that rate!

Even organists who, through years of experience, have built up substantial repertoires, cannot practice as much as they would like. They have to read much of the music, and there is little time for the memorizing that would permit them to give their undivided attention to playing.

The beginning organist, too, must play much of the music at sight, or after trying it over only once or twice. He is seldom capable of doing this satisfactorily, yet there is simply not time for him to study any of his work thoroughly. If he is the choirmaster as well as the organist, he cannot devote more than a few minutes now and then to planning his choir work.

There are still young organists willing to give most or all of their spare time to the preparation and performance of the service music, but when they have to earn a living in some other way, there is not enough spare time to do the job properly. It is a mistake to suppose that the organist of a small church requires less time for his work than his colleague in a large, splendidly equipped church. He requires more time, actually, because he has to work harder to improve his own playing and to train an inexperienced choir.

It would be well, then, after a young man has signified his willingness to play the church organ, to pay him as much as the congregation can afford in order that he may spend as much time as possible in the preparation of his work. This might be called subsidizing organ study to a certain extent; but students are subsidized in other fields through scholarships. The church people are receiving a return for their investment through the organist's services, and they will be the ones who will benefit by his improvement.

When and if satisfactory arrangements are made, the young organist should not be expected to play pieces for a while. The practicing of organ pieces will consume most of his time, and that is the very phase of his work least essential to public worship. He would be better to spend whatever time he can improving his technic, playing pieces only as he learns them thoroughly, and concentrate on the accompaniment to choral and congregational music. If the services he is to play are liturgical, he will require some time to acquire a *feel* for his work.

It is, after all, not unreasonable to ask the congregation to sit in silence before the service begins, and to leave in silence after it has ended. It was once quite common in Protestant churches, and some denominations still dispense with the organ with no deterioration of worship. If the people feel that they must have music before the young organist has built up a modest repertoire, there could be no harm in using good phonograph records. Surely a well selected record by E. Power Biggs or the Philadelphia Orchestra would be less distracting than the fumbling of an organist trying to play something he has not had time to prepare.

A programme like this would mean less organ playing in public for two or three years, but what there was of it would be better.

Some advice and assistance in the matter of playing the service and interpreting anthems should be available to the young organist. These accomplishments are too often taken for granted by teachers and students. The church organist is, primarily, an accompanist, but not an accompanist only. The choir and congregation depend on him for leadership and inspiration. If he is skilled, he can *make* the congregation want to sing. Part of his particular church's educational programme should be the appointment of regional instructors who would advise him concerning the all-important duties of service playing, either privately or by means of a clinic.

There is a great need for organ music that is good, yet not difficult to play. It is interesting to compare the thousands of pieces published for young pianists with the meager supply available to student organists. There are many books of organ pieces on the market, but few of them are organ pieces in the sense that they were written for that instrument. They are largely transcriptions, with no legitimate pedal part, and offering nothing to assist the student in developing his organ technic. It might be a good plan to revive some of the older organ collections. If our best organists are shocked at the notion of their young colleagues playing Faulkes, Batiste, and Shelley, many of them are capable of writing other pieces that will serve the same purpose.

No organist should be satisfied to play the service merely adequately, with only a few easy organ pieces. He should strive to meet the standards of the American Guild or the Canadian College of Organists, and *part* of his practice period should be dedicated to that end. At present, the aim of most serious students is to attain those standards while taking time off to prepare from four to six pieces for the Sunday services. He does neither well. Of course, he may be a pretty fair church organist without possessing Guild qualifications, and he may be an associate or fellow of the Guild without being a good church organist. His study should be divided into two parts: the first devoted to improving his organ playing under the best instructor he can find, the second to learning how to apply what he has learned to his immediate needs as a church organist.

It is generally assumed that the ability to play the organ goes hand in hand with the ability to teach and conduct the choir. Few young organists have the opportunity to test this assumption. The playing of the organ occupies so much of their attention that they can spare none for the choir. They simply play along and hope that the choir will follow them.

As a matter of fact, many good organists are not good choirmasters. Choirs have sometimes declined quickly after the appointment of eminent organists who had not the ability or the knowledge to train and lead them.

A contributing factor to the decline of choirs in general may be the shortage of leaders who can make choral work instructive and interesting. This is not always because the young organist has no talent for conducting the choir. He may have quite a bit of talent, but he cannot exercise it if his abilities are not such as to permit him to divide his attention between playing and conducting. A good many choirs are capable of better work than they are doing. Anthems which they could sing lie unused on the shelves because the organists are unable to play them, or unable to play them and conduct the choir at the same time.

It is desirable that the duties of organist and choirmaster be combined whenever practicable; but in many cases far better results would be obtained by appointing a separate choirmaster who would be responsible (under the minister) for all the music of the church.

Instruction in choral conducting is not easily come by. Not one in a thousand people who conduct choirs has had any systematic training in the art, and there are very few places where he could receive that training.

The advantages enjoyed by church musicians who have served as choir boys under good choirmasters have already been cited. Without any conscious intention of doing so, the choir boy absorbs a great deal of his choirmaster's methods. The majority of boys who sing at school or in "junior" choirs at church have no such training. Less hinges upon their efforts than those of the church choir boy. The standards of music and performance are lower, and the instructors are not as good.

Yet, there is no better training for a choirmaster than singing in a choir under a good conductor. A young man who contemplates taking up this work would be well advised to join the best choir he can find for a year or two. If he has a poor voice (and choirmasters are notoriously poor singers themselves) he might ask to join the choir as an observer. Most choirmasters would be glad to have someone with whom to discuss their plans and methods. They might even permit the student to put the choir through its paces at rehearsal and offer constructive comment on his work later.

If the choirmaster who is serving as his model does not spend much time on voice production, the student might take a few lessons from a good singing teacher, not with the idea of improving his own voice, but to learn methods.

Listening carefully to recordings by excellent choirs can do much for the young choirmaster's education. It is helpful to follow the score of the work being sung, noting how the conductor interprets the composer's intentions and trying to determine how he produces his effects.

The studying of hymn tunes and the scores of anthems, trying to hear in imagination the music as he wants it to sound, will enable the choirmaster to approach rehearsals with clear-cut objectives.

Very little has been said about the many capable church musicians to whom we owe so much. They need no advice except, perhaps, to be more sympathetic and encouraging towards the less capable. An educational programme such as has been suggested would die burgeoning without their cooperation.

The future state of worship music depends on whether we make strenuous efforts to train and encourage church musicians or allow the species to become almost extinct.

✤ WORSHIP MUSIC

The recognition by the clergy of the need for some organized effort to improve church music, and the improvement of facilities for the training of organists and choirmasters, are important, but still only preliminary steps towards raising standards.

A great deal of fine church music of the past was not worship music in the best sense of the term, since the people were not able to participate even vicariously, and it did not assist them in their devotions. For the clergy, organist, and choir, the anthems and motets and masses may often have been sincere expressions of religious fervor. But people do not go to church to watch and listen to others worship. A church service should be a corporate act of worship: everything that happens there should be designed to affect everyone present. Whenever that has not been the case, interest in the church has declined.

The task of clergy and church musicians is to lead the people in and to worship. Having prepared themselves for the task, they must, before approaching the people, consider ways and means of accomplishing their purpose. They must, in short, find an answer to the question, What *is* church music? And so must we.

It is generally agreed that any offering made to God should be as nearly worthy as we can make it. Certainly it should not be inferior to what we consider worthy for secular purposes.

A shack would not be erected for a church even in a poor community where the people lived in shacks. A crudely built communion table would not be considered acceptable even if it was the best effort of its builder, who had sought to make it sacred by roughly carving on it the words: "Holy, holy, holy." No unskilled artist would be permitted to draw or paint murals on the church walls, however reverent his intention. These unskilled contributors might be commended for the spirit in which they made their offerings, but the offerings themselves would be rejected, tactfully if possible, but rejected in any case.

Yet, poorly written verses set to almost any kind of tunes are accepted as hymns, solos, and anthems. They are not only accepted, but are considered to be sanctified by some reference to the Divinity or to some vague, spiritual experience. If the church organist labels these things as rubbish, he arouses the congregation's ire and resentment to the point where they may consider dismissing him.

The majority of people are able to recognize at least elementary standards of architecture, woodwork, and painting. Their environment includes so many good examples of those arts that crudities become obvious. Examples of good poetry and good music are no less plentiful, but they form part of the environment of only those people who seek them out. Not many do seek them out; and for that reason, the crudities of verse and music are not obvious to most of our church people and many of our clergy.

The problem then arises whether to allow the people freedom to sing anything they like, which has already lowered the standards of church music, or to impose a censorship which, in addition to being hateful, has not accomplished any spectacular results in the past.

Fortunately, it is possible to make provision for the congregation to sing what they like without having them sing *everything* that they like.

It must be remembered, too, that poor hymns and tunes are not the unanimous favorites of all the congregations that sing them. Ministers and organists who bend over backwards to please people who like poor music may not realize how unfair they are to other members of the congregation who would prefer something better (including those who stay away from church because they cannot stand the music).

If it is agreed that only good music should be heard in church (by "good" music it is meant that which carries some evidence of craftsmanship and inspiration) and if it can be proved that such music does not deprive the people of any part of their enjoyment and participation in the service, there seems no good reason why the use of inferior and tawdry music should not be discontinued. It would be a mistake to discontinue it gradually. Ten poor hymns or anthems or solos can retard progress as effectively as a hundred.

Since a ban on poor music would cause resentment, its use could be discouraged by omitting it from recommended lists—which would cause less resentment. The revision of hymnals, which would sweep out the unworthy hymns, might be postponed until the people become reconciled to their disuse. The whole purpose of the general committee, which should be made known, would not be to deprive the people of enjoyment, but to provide more. Unless strenuous efforts were made to arouse as much enthusiasm for good music as exists for bad, the battle would be lost from the start.

If, by common consent, only music that would bear critical scrutiny was allowed in church, at least fifty percent of what is now sung would be disposed of.

But in seeking standards, we become aware that not all good music is suitable for worship music. Some, indeed, is most unsuitable in that it does not contribute to the purpose for which the congregation is, or should be, assembled. In short, it does not turn hearts and minds Godwards. There is music that will turn the hearts and minds of *some* people Godwards; there is some that will have the same effect on *most* people; but there is no music to which one can point, and say with certainty that it will promote the devotions of *all* people.

Musicians in the secular field are under no obligation to try to please everybody. They play for certain sections of the public only. When an orchestra or an artist advertises a concert, people know pretty well what type of music will be played; and those who do not care for it remain away.

The church, on the other hand, must be all-embracing. It is not intended to serve only sections of the community. The literate and the illiterate, the cultured and the uncultured, the musical and the non-musical, the saint and the sinner, all worship under one roof. Those charged with the preparation of church services too often lose sight of the fact that it is their task to unite these groups in common worship.

Attempts to reform church music generally fail because the reformers' horizon is too narrow. The tendency is to concentrate on music acceptable to one section of the people, frequently the reformers themselves, and to disregard the tastes and appreciation of the rest.

Perhaps the most vigorous reform movement at present is that which would restore plainsong for the people, Elizabethan choral music and German organ music of the baroque period. Some of our foremost writers and church musicians are taking an active part in this movement, and many of the clergy are supporting it.

Musicians favor this type of music because it is good music. That does not mean that there was not bad modal music or bad baroque music. There was; but time has permitted it to pass into oblivion, and only the best remains.

The clergy support it because they associate it with "the good old days" when the church spoke with authority, when church life was simpler and, supposedly, beset with fewer problems than in the present.

The revival of anything archaic for the purpose of making it an integral part of modern life must always be doomed to failure. The archaic loses much of its meaning and effectiveness in the setting of the present day. Only if all the conditions of the period to which it belongs are revived can it regain its original significance.

Hand in hand with the movement for a return of plainsong is a revival of the so-called baroque or classic or German organs. Their relationship to twentieth-century organs may be compared to the relationship of the harpsichord to the piano. As reconstructions of museum pieces, these instruments are interesting, but their introduction into American and Canadian churches is to be deplored. They lack altogether the warmth and majesty that organ builders have been slowly and painfully developing in the past three hundred years. To the uninitiated they sound like a combination of whistles and somewhat harsh reeds. It is significant that their proponents are not consistent in their revival. They do not scorn electric blowers, pistons and all the other conveniences that were unknown in Bach's time. They do not seem to realize, either, that Bach would have hailed with delight improvements in tonality as he would have welcomed mechanical improvements.

Because so many eminent clergy and church musicians favor plainsong, classic polyphony, and baroque organs, many church bodies are showing a tendency to look upon these types as ideal worship music. They are; but only for those who understand such music and for whom it fulfills the requirements of worship music. It is in an idiom strange to the ears of most people and has no associations for them. Used sparingly, it has its place in modern worship; used exclusively, it will deprive the people of participation and drive them to something worse. They are about as likely to forsake familiar idioms for plainsong as they are to have their water pipes removed and begin drawing water from wells.

If the archaic is to be ruled out as a norm of worship music, the ultramodern must also be ruled out, and for much the same reason. It is not an idiom through which people are accustomed to worship. That is not the fault of the music, but of the hesitancy of churches to emerge from the past and realize in what century they are operating. The *Twentieth Century Folk Mass* by Geoffrey Beaumont, used recently and experimentally, might, like plainsong and polyphony, serve as a medium of sincere expression of devotion for some people. No one can say certainly what was the inner reaction of those who heard it. But the majority of church people are not ready for it.

For that matter, no one knows just what the majority of church people are ready for, as far as music is concerned. I have said that the ideal music is that which assists the people in their worship, but one might be associated with a congregation for a long time without knowing what music fulfills that condition, simply because they have long since lost sight of the fact that music is intended to assist them in their devotions. When they fail to sing a hymn, it is generally because they do not like the tune or are not interested enough to learn it. When they sing another hymn heartily, it does not necessarily mean that it is helping them in their worship, but simply that they find the tune attractive.

Not until the purpose of worship music is fully and carefully explained to churchgoers can their reactions be judged. Possibly some of the things that they now sing lustily and thoughtlessly would lose some of their appeal when considered thoughtfully. If a congregation understands that the hymns are not merely opportunities for exercising the lungs, and that anthems and organ music should have much the same significance as prayers—if, in short, they can be persuaded to adopt the correct attitude towards worship music—then various types of music can be tried and the reactions noted.

The results might be surprising. It might be found, for instance, that some people who have been given credit for a taste for poor music would react favorably to something better.

The level of the people's appreciation must be found before any forward movement can begin. Nothing will be gained by setting a standard of music beyond their comprehension and expecting them to struggle up to it unaided. The level will vary among congregations and individuals; and, for that reason, the standards of music will also vary. Three important factors must be kept in mind when selecting music for public worship: first, it must enable the congregation to express themselves in an idiom with which they are familiar; second, it must be the best music which they are capable of appreciating; third, it must assist in turning their minds Godwards.

Perhaps late nineteenth- and early twentieth-century music is likely to meet all these requirements at present. People who argue the merits of plainsong, and others who show a decided preference for gospel hymns, forget their differences when they are asked to sing "The Church's one foundation," "How sweet the Name of Jesus sounds," "Abide with me," or "When I survey the wondrous Cross." It is on such common ground, and in such a spirit of unity, that the people must meet if they are to go forward together. In what direction they move, musically speaking, will depend on their inclinations, and the success of cautious experiments conducted by those charged with the responsibility for church music.

Clergy and church musicians will require infinite patience in any programme for the betterment of church music. It takes years to change the habits and tastes of a congregation, and two or three false moves can cancel out months of progress.

If the highest common level of appreciation can be found and maintained for a time, some progress will already have been made. The level might not be as high as the organist and choirmaster would like it to be, but if the people can be kept interested in the best music they can appreciate for the time being, they are less likely to bemoan the omission of the worst. If they hear a great deal that they like and understand, they develop a receptive attitude towards all music that they hear in church, and their interest may be aroused rather than otherwise by the introduction of music of a different and better type at long intervals. The intervals between the injections of different types of music may be shortened very gradually, and the taste of the congregation raised correspondingly.

On the other hand, the overly optimistic choirmaster who interprets the congregation's awakened interest as an indication that they are ready for sweeping and drastic reforms will find the whole carefully planned programme crashing about his ears. Content to forget about poor music while they are enjoying better music that they can understand, the people are apt to suffer a sudden and complete relapse if they are forced to listen to a great deal that is foreign to them.

This sort of programme may sound discouragingly slow to those who compare the present state of church music with what it ought to be. It must be remembered, however, that one can fall over a cliff in a matter of seconds, but it is a long, laborious, and sometimes seemingly hopeless, task to climb up again. It is better to persuade a congregation to sing one plainsong tune, to listen to one Bach choral-prelude and one anthem of Vaughan Williams every six weeks or so (if those are the types of music which the organist and choirmaster favor) than to have them accept none at all. At least some progress is being made; and, having climbed that little, there is reason to hope that they will climb farther.

The problem of association is one that cannot be avoided. Perhaps the best plan would be to use as much music as possible that has no association with secular things. Since pure music may fail in its purpose because it awakens no association in the minds of the listeners, it should be played often enough to create an association with public worship.

Where printed service lists are made available to the congregation, it might be well to omit the titles of pieces that the organist plays. If a piece is played a dozen times a year and appears on the service list as *Morning*, it will simply serve to divert the people's thoughts a dozen times a year to scenes and experiences outside the church. On the other hand, if no suggestive title is furnished, the people may begin to associate that particular piece with the reverent atmosphere of public worship. Even a neutral sort of title, such as *Prelude* or *Andante*, would be better omitted, since it can mean nothing without an identifying coupling with a composer's name; and a church service is no place for reflections concerning the careers, successes, and temperaments of individual composers.

It is not suggested that the organist play only pieces which the people will not recognize; and in playing more familiar pieces, it is inevitable that at least some members of the congregation will recognize them and be aware of associations suggested by titles, programmes, a knowledge of the composers' lives and methods, and any number of other extraneous factors. It would be foolish and detrimental to his purpose for the organist to avoid familiar music on that account. But nothing should be done to accentuate extraneous associations; and if the people have had explained to them the real purpose of worship music, they may listen to a piece played in church with a somewhat different reaction than they would hear the same piece played elsewhere.

The association of music with words to which it is frequently sung is strong. For that reason, it is not wise to borrow the music of secular songs for hymns and anthems. Sooner or later, while singing or recalling the tune, one's mind will be enticed away from the religious words to the secular. Even some good music that could be played effectively on the organ must be avoided for the same reason, for it loses its value as an aid to worship if it brings to mind the words of songs which are very definitely not religious.

Since the association of words and music is so important, people should be given good words to sing, and encouraged to give the meaning of those words some attention. Much of our hymnody is mediocre verse. It has no distinction. It restates thoughts that have been stated many times before in much the same way. People pay very little attention to the words they sing. They thoughtlessly make statements in hymns that they would not make otherwise. Think how perturbed they would be if, just before the collection, the minister reminded them that they had just sung

> Take my silver and my gold,
> Not a mite would I withhold,

and told them that they were expected to make good that promise.

When a congregation sings

> So vile I am, how dare I hope to stand
> In the pure glory of that holy land;

> or

> False and full of sin I am,

how often is the meaning of the words reflected in their faces?

Certainly the music cannot mean very much if it is a medium through which people express thoughts that have no meaning for them.

Part of the unreality of our hymnody lies in the fact that so much of it reflects the thoughts and environment of the past. There is a definite place for old hymns and old music in our religious life; but there must be opportunities for the expression of modern thought, both in words and music, if hymnody is to have reality for the people.

It is desirable that new hymns should have new tunes. Old tunes which have strong associations with old hymns are apt to detract from the new.

Sentimental associations, the power of certain music to recall occasions and circumstances which made deep impressions, cannot be controlled; nor would it be kind to deprive people of those tender memories were it possible to do so. Nevertheless, retrospection can amount to distraction if it causes one to forget the present moment of worship.

Ideally, every service of public worship should make a deep enough impression to make retrospection unnecessary and unlikely. If worship is a present, sincere reality, it will occupy the whole attention of the congregation. That is the end towards which services should be planned. All services should be on the same plane as the so-called special services. Once they are allowed to degenerate into a religious routine, all aspects of church life, including the music, suffer.

The compilation of good hymnals is not at a standstill, by any means. In recent years, some significant new ones have appeared, sponsored by many denominational groups. Excellent examples are: *The Hymnal* (Protestant Episcopal), *The Hymnbook* (Presbyterian-Reformed), *The Brethren Hymnal*, *The Pilgrim Hymnal*, *The Lutheran Service Book*, and *The Hymnal for Schools and Colleges*.

It is not hard to realize that two teams of clergymen and organists, sharing the same views about music and aiming for the same goal, might find it necessary to use quite different types of music in their churches. It is the effect of the music on the people, rather than the music itself, that is important; and we must always take into account the diversity of response mentioned in our first chapter, and the policy of adaptation which makes Christianity and everything connected with it flexible enough to meet the needs of various types of people. The highest common level of music appreciation differs, but it is never as low as the prevalence of poor church music might lead one to believe.

The highest existing level of appreciation of any congregation should not, of course, be considered as the ultimate goal. In very few churches could the best music of all times, schools, and types be used with equal effect; and as long as music is being written and trends are changing, the catalogue of church music cannot be said to be complete. The church must examine, experiment, accept and reject if the best music suitable for the purpose is to be made available for Divine worship.

Perhaps we have come as near to a definition of church music as we are likely to come.

Ideally, it should be good music, acknowledged as such by musicians and worthy of being played and sung anywhere. It must, however, have this qualification: that it elevates the mind, and assists the people to turn their thoughts Godwards.

Practically, it should come as near the ideal as the musical appreciation of the people will permit. Certainly it must not fall below the highest level of the secular music they are accustomed to hearing. The qualification remains, of course: it must condition the congregation for worship.

✤ CONGREGATIONAL SINGING: THE CORE OF PROTESTANT CHURCH MUSIC

If interest in worship music is to be renewed and higher standards set, if will be necessary to start where every renascence of Protestant church music has had its beginnings—with the congregation.

The apparent lack of interest on the part of church people is not necessarily evidence that they would not welcome opportunities for fuller participation in church services. They did not, after all, relinquish that participation of their own accord.

It is a moving experience to stand outside some small churches that possess neither organs nor choirs and hear the congregations singing hymns to piano accompaniment. It is too bad that they do not sing better hymns but, from the point of view of church life if not of church musicians, it is better that they sing what they do sing than not at all.

Most people enjoy group singing. That some stand silent in church because they are not encouraged to sing does not mean that they are different from their forefathers or from their friends who belong to singing churches. I have never been present at a session devoted to hymn singing that has not been successful—so successful, in fact, that one wonders why such sessions are not held more frequently. The success of an attempt to interest the people in hymn singing can almost be guaranteed.

How such an educational programme should be inaugurated will depend partly on the general temperament of the congregation, but chiefly on the personality of the minister or the choirmaster who is conducting it.

If attention was given to congregational singing at the church service, rather than at a special session devoted to that purpose, the people would be more deeply impressed with the fact that it is part of, rather than apart from, public worship.

The minister might, briefly, stress the importance of music in the history of the church and, particularly, the importance of congregational singing in the Protestant churches. If he could say that, without underrating the contribution of instrumental and choral music, all the musical resources of the church would be dedicated for a certain period to the restoration of congregational singing to its rightful place, the people would be even more deeply impressed. The minister would have to be careful not to appropriate the time usually taken by organ and choral music for an extension of his sermon, unless his motives were to become suspect. He could not omit hymns, or stanzas or hymns, if he hoped to convince the people that hymn singing is important.

Congregational instruction would be better limited to one hymn at each service; first, because the instruction should not be hurried, and the consideration of more than one hymn would interfere with other essential parts of the service; second, because it is better to stop while the people are still interested than to continue until their attention begins to waver.

The minister, or someone whom he chose for the purpose, might begin by inviting the congregation to consider the words of a fairly familiar hymn. He might read the words, interpolating comments of his own, or he might simply restate the sentiment and meaning of the verses in his own words. Many hymns are not so profound that they should require an analysis of their content, but when it is remembered that most people take in the words with their eyes rather than with their minds, the need for educating them to read and sing thoughtfully will be realized.

Nothing is to be gained by eulogizing the writer of the hymn or describing the circumstances under which it was written. Extraneous associations are better avoided and the hymn considered solely on its merits and its suitability for public worship.

The person who is interpreting the hymn should point out the necessity of observing principal punctuation marks and of carrying phrases right through without breaks that distort the meanings. In five minutes, he can transform the hymn from something that has been sung woodenly and mechanically to something living and meaningful.

When the congregation has caught the spirit of the hymn, a stanza should be sung for them by the choir or a soloist who can be relied upon to do it well. From there on, the people will do the rest. Even the hymns which have received no special attention will improve as the congregation begins to apply some of the principles learned during the brief instruction period.

There are several important points to be considered when planning instruction in hymn singing.

At first, both hymns and tunes should be familiar. If the people find out how much they have to learn about hymns that they have known all their lives, they are more likely to be alert when asked to sing a less familiar hymn.

Many writers stress the desirability of using only simple music for congregational singing. While it is not advisable to introduce tunes that are difficult to learn and sing, one must not underrate the intelligence and musical ability of the congregation. People who have learned to sing parts at school are better equipped to tackle a hymn that requires a little musical intelligence than their grandparents were.

The range of tune melodies should not exceed a minor tenth, those lying between middle C on the piano and the second E flat above being preferable. Many tunes are unsingable by the average congregation because the composers seem to have overestimated their voice range.

If some of the people can sing parts, by all means encourage them to do so, in spite of the advice of some experts that congregational singing should be in unison. No one should be deprived of that enjoyment, and it is unfortunate that few denominations furnish their congregations with music editions of the hymnals. The congregation should share a prearranged signal, such as is customarily given to the choir, when unison singing is desired—when, for instance, a varied accompaniment or a descant is to be used for a stanza.

The stressed syllables should appear in the same places in every stanza. A number of English hymns require a bit of juggling for some stanzas in order to avoid weak syllables on strong beats. I do not know how English congregations react to this, but Americans and Canadians do not want to be bothered with it.

The mood of the tune should match the mood of the hymn. A tune in a minor key or with modal harmonies that have much the same effect on the congregation will not help to bring home the reality of a hymn of praise.

In order to emphasize the differences in sentiments and moods of hymns, it might help to have the congregation stand for hymns of praise, such as "Praise, my soul, the King of heaven"; sit for reflective or contemplative hymns like "Jerusalem the golden," and sit or kneel for prayerful hymns like "Breathe on me, breath of God."

In playing hymn tunes during instruction periods, the organist should avoid the muddiness of tone that so often marks accompaniments. A preponderance of diapasons and flutes will best serve the purpose.

When the congregation has begun singing well, the organist might try varying the harmonies of the accompaniment a little, first as a quiet background, later, when he sees that it does not disturb the congregation, a little more boldly.

The choir could play an important role in the development of hymn singing, either by remaining in the choir loft and setting an example, or by mingling with the congregation to lend leadership. If the time comes when the organist can play varying harmonies to familar hymn tunes, the choir might sing some descants or faux bourdons.

Even more unifying than singing hymns is the experience of chanting together. One may sing a hymn well by listening to the organ or watching a conductor, and without paying a great deal of attention to what his neighbors are doing. In chanting, it becomes very important to know what the people around one are doing. There must be an interdependence among the members of the congregation, the sharing of feeling and rhythm which create a certain togetherness. (The same is true of plainsong hymn tunes.)

In Protestant churches with liturgical services, practice in hymn singing should certainly lead, before long, to practice in chanting those canticles and psalms which are regularly chanted at church services.

Whether or not chants are introduced into nonliturgical churches where they have not been used before rests upon the discretion of the ministers. Possibly a loss as to how to go about it prevents many churches from using them. Actually, a congregation that has no experience in chanting, that knows nothing of the rules and has acquired no bad habits, may reach a higher standard than other congregations that have been chanting badly for years. If chanting is done, it should certainly be regarded as something that belongs to the whole congregation and not to the choir only.

How far instruction in congregational singing could be carried is hard to prophesy. Continued as part of the church service, it could be of inestimable benefit. Some congregations, or sections of congregations, might ask for special sessions for the purpose of singing hymns. It is just possible that there might be some interest created in a course in part singing. No one quite expects that development; but then, no one quite expected it when the preliminary ground was being prepared for singing schools. Even if only a few asked for instruction beyond that received by the congregation in general, prospective members for the choir would have been uncovered.

However far it is carried, the development of congregational singing is the only foundation on which a successful renascence of worship music can be built. Only through their own participation will the people be able to appreciate and participate vicariously in the larger and more complex forms of church music.

✣ THE CHOIR

Choirs are not essential to public worship. They were probably unknown in the primitive Church, there was no place for them in the Calvinistic wing of Protestantism for a long time after the Reformation, and even today many churches manage quite well without them.

Although lovers of church music would like to see more and better choirs, certainly nothing would be lost if many of those in existence were to disband. The time and effort spent in their organization, maintenance, and training are not nearly justified by the results.

Perhaps part of the trouble lies in the fact that church people, like some of their predecessors in certain periods of history, have lost sight of the function of the choir. Most people, asked to define the duty of the choir, would say that it is to "lead the singing." Nothing could be farther from the truth if, by "leading the singing," we mean that the choir takes a prominent part in music that should be sung by the congregation.

In hymns and chants, the choristers function as part of the congregation. With four hundred people in the congregation singing as they ought to sing, forty people in the choir loft will not influence them very much.

Another reason for maintaining choirs in some churches seems to be to avoid the embarrassment of empty choir lofts. As long as the seats are filled, even by incompetent people, appearances are kept up and the delusion of a choir is complete.

In many churches, the choir is used as a medium for giving as many people as possible opportunities to take a prominent part before the churchgoing public. There are senior choirs, intermediate choirs, junior choirs, teen-age choirs and many other variations, none of them very good. There may not be enough real talent in the church for one fair choir, and the choirmaster cannot possibly do a good job if he has to divide his limited time between two or three groups. There is singing, to be sure—lots of it—but it does nothing for the service.

The "junior choir" is almost invariably designed for the sake of fond parents rather than for the children. It is composed of little girls who, in fairness to their voices, should not be singing loudly enough to be of much use to a choir; and boys who might be valuable if they were properly trained and incorporated into the main choir, but who, untrained, have nothing to offer. Of course, the parents and their friends are not interested in what sounds the children make. Their pleasure is visual, rather than aural, as they watch the freshly scrubbed and groomed youngsters garbed in vestments calculated to lend a religious atmosphere to the scene. Remarks after the service concern the appearance, not the performance, of the junior choir. The children are generally well aware of the reasons for which they are being exhibited; aware, too, that what they are singing and their manner of singing it are far below the standards of their grade choirs at public school.

There are places for entertainment, places where amateur singers may parade their talents, places where ambitious parents can show off their bright children. The church is not one of those places—at least, it should not be.

The purpose of the choir is to lead the people to planes of music which they would not be able to reach by their own efforts. The congregation should not have to depend on the assistance of the choir in singing their own portions of the service, nor should the contributions of the choir be made at the expense of congregational singing.

The four principal qualifications of a chorister are a good voice, some training (or a willingness to receive training), a spirit of dedication, and the ability to submerge personality for the common good.

Perhaps, in view of the difficulty in persuading people to accept the responsibilities of choir duty, one is rather optimistic in insisting upon such a combination of qualities, but one cannot have a choir with anything less.

Membership in choirs is altogether too easy to achieve. Ministers and choirmasters make a great mistake in begging people to join, and choirmasters accept candidates far too readily. There are too many churches where the choir is used as a means of maintaining interest in the church. We keep our young people—or try to—by getting them into the choir; a young married couple may be invited to join because, in that way, they will meet other young married couples.

By all means keep the young people and make newcomers feel at home, but do not use the choir for that purpose. Problems that belong to the minister should not be foisted upon the choirmaster, spoiling his chances of building the choir into a singing organization.

Choir membership should be reserved for those who express a desire to serve. Perhaps not many will signify their desire, even after the minister has announced that applications are invited; but six, eight, or a dozen willing and more or less capable people can make some headway, whereas a larger group made up chiefly of dead-heads will cause the choral music to remain at or sink to a low level.

Efforts to promote congregational singing, such as were just outlined in the discussion of that subject, will almost certainly result in at least a few people expressing a desire to carry the training farther, and these might be good choir material.

What if no one volunteers for choir work? Well, there can be no choir in that case. One does not learn to play a violin without first obtaining an instrument.

In considering candidates for the choir, the choirmaster need not insist upon exceptionally good voices, although he should choose the best available, having regard to the balance of parts. A voice of fair quality or promise that will blend with the others should be acceptable. Voices that will be prominent, either because of some peculiar quality or because their owners cannot control them, must be passed over.

It is a good thing to remember that vocal qualities change somewhat as people grow older; and for that reason it is desirable to enroll members of different ages. Girls in their late teens and twenties sing with a freshness of tone that is delightful at first, but may prove tiresome as a steady diet; the voices of women in their forties lose a great deal of that freshness, although retaining pleasant mature qualities that, combined with younger voices, help to round out a satisfying ensemble.

Almost the opposite is true of males. Young men in their late teens have scarcely had time to develop their adult voices. If they have sung while their voices were changing, they will probably have acquired a roughness that will be hard to overcome; and, in any case, their voices lack the resonance that should come later. Enough older men will be required to bring the tenor and bass sections up to strength and quality.

It is a pity that most Protestant churches allow their boys' voices to go to waste. A large percentage of boys between the ages of seven or eight and fourteen have voices capable of being trained for choir work. Yet there are many choirs badly in need of voices for their soprano sections while their Sunday schools are full of potential boy choristers.

Whether there was ever any prejudice against the use of boys' voices in the choirs of nonliturgical churches, I do not know; but certainly there can be none now in view of the large number of boys who are admitted to junior choirs.

Admittedly, the choirmaster who has had no experience in the training of boys' voices will have a lot to learn, but he can find assistance in books, by careful study of recordings, and by consultation with more experienced colleagues. The boys will respond better than they do in a junior choir, for they will realize that they are doing something worth-while.

If boys are used in the soprano section, a little different policy will have to be employed in selecting people for other parts. There must be enough voices of light quality to balance the boys. There is no reason why the choir should not be divided into two sections; one consisting of women sopranos and more robust altos, tenors, and basses; the other of boys and lighter supporting parts. Each section could be used alone for certain effects, as a conductor often uses only a section of his orchestra.

A greater use of boys could easily result in the revival of the once commonplace but lately neglected male alto or counter-tenor. The records by the choirs of King's College Chapel, Cambridge, and St. Paul's Cathedral, London, which were mentioned earlier, demonstrate convincingly the desirability of combining male altos with boy sopranos. The blend of voices is perfect.

An insistence upon balance of voices may mean limiting membership in the choir. If one has twelve basses and only three tenors, for instance, the situation is bad enough without adding more basses. Unless more tenors can be found, the remedy is to cut the bass section—and the so-prano and alto sections too, perhaps—to balance the tenors. Strangely enough, most choirs are concerned with adding members to achieve bal-ance; it does not seem to occur to anyone that the same result can be reached by making the choir smaller.

So much for the choosing of the voices.

Most voices will need training, and it is to be hoped that the choir-master will have prepared himself for this task. Even choristers who can produce their voices well will have to learn to sing with the other choris-ters to produce a full, rounded tone.

Choirs that are already established, as well as newly organized ones, could afford to spend a great deal of time in developing tone quality. Almost any group of people can learn to emit sounds of certain pitches in combination and succession, but that is not necessarily pleasant music. It is not technic alone that makes a great pianist, violinist, singer, or-chestra, or choir: it is beauty of tone. A choir with good tone quality stands out for that reason alone in this age of raucous singing.

Learning to read parts should go hand in hand with voice produc-tion. If the majority of the choristers are indifferent readers, group in-struction may be given; otherwise, the weak readers may be taught singly or in small groups. Fortunately, instruction in part-singing given in schools prepares most people for choir work.

Once the choir can produce a good tone and read pretty well, it is time to begin singing something. There is not much point in attempting to produce music until the instrument—in this case, the choir—is ready.

The first music to be prepared is that of the service—the hymns, the chants. There are choirs that have not practiced hymns for years, and anyone not aware of the fact would soon suspect it after hearing them sing. There is nothing better than hymn tunes for developing balance and accurate reading. The choir should be trained to sing hymns well in four parts, in unison and, later, in descant and faux bourdon arrangements.

Where chants are used, they should be a principal part of the choir's training until the chanting becomes as free and flowing as conversation.

In the field of choral music—that is, music in which the congregation does not participate—a programme must be planned.

The choir should sing nothing in church that it cannot sing well. We read in many books that the music sung by the average church choir should be simple. That is not as true today as it once was, for most choristers have far more basic training in music, apart from their instruction at rehearsals, than used to be the case. Simplicity is a relative term, of course; and whether or not an anthem is simple from the point of view of the singers depends upon their capabilities. Perhaps it would be better to say that the music should be such as the choir can sing easily.

At rehearsals, the choir should be working on something that presents difficulties to be overcome, for only in that way will it improve and be able to gauge its progress. It is interesting to try over an anthem now and then which is currently too difficult, analyze the difficulties, set aside a part of each practice for tackling them one by one, and make the singing of that particular anthem on a certain date (six months or a year later) an objective.

The type of choral music to be sung must be governed to some extent by the congregation's level of appreciation. An anthem does not fulfill the purpose of worship music if it leaves the people cold. No doubt there are clergymen who could preach good sermons in Greek or Latin or Hebrew, but their efforts would be entirely wasted on congregations that understood only English. In the same way, a choir must speak to and for the people in an idiom that they understand, even if the choirmaster has to forego music that he considers better. As in the case of hymns, the highest level of the congregation's appreciation should be sought; and that will probably be the choir's level as well, since choristers are drawn from the ranks of the congregation.

Of course, every effort should be made to raise and extend that level; and in order to do so, it may be necessary to introduce occasionally anthems that will sound a little strange to the people. They will not mind if it is not overdone. The choirmaster's goal should be approached very slowly and subtly. There is no quick method that will not exclude the congregation from a vicarious participation in choral music.

If it is always remembered that choral music must be worship music from the points of view of both singers and listeners, a wide variety of styles of music may be used. The ideal repertoire would be one that included some of the best church music of all centuries since the fifteenth, and the ideal choir one flexible enough to adapt itself to all styles and schools.

The revival of large choral works—such as oratorios or cantatas—either by church choirs or by choral societies composed chiefly of singers from various choirs, is greatly to be desired.

Some of the shorter cantatas may be made part of a service, as they were in Bach's time, and as Stainer's *The Crucifixion* is still presented in many churches on Good Friday. Preceded and followed by hymns and prayers, such works retain all their significance as worship music, especially if the choristers sing them reverently.

Larger works are more difficult to present in church because facilities for their performances are not always available. However, even when presented in a concert hall, there is no reason why they should not fulfill the purpose for which they were written. Unfortunately, they seldom do.

Perhaps the most frequently performed oratorio is Handel's *Messiah,* which is generally conceded to be the most inspired of all oratorios. Almost invariably a great deal of its religious significance is sacrificed to the conventions of the concert.

It is not difficult to understand the papal disapproval of the masses of Haydn and Mozart as parts of the liturgy in church. In the first place, they did not, and were not intended to, fit into the framework of the service; and the music was of a type associated with the concert hall. Yet they could be inspiring and uplifting even in a concert hall if they were sung and heard in an atmosphere of reverence.

Similarly, Rossini's *Stabat Mater* and Verdi's *Requiem* were written in the composers' operatic style because that was their method of expression. The intentions of both composers have been frustrated by a failure on the part of the public to realize what those intentions were.

The choosing and training of voices and the planning of a progressive programme for the choir, are matters that can be brought under the control of the choirmaster. Beyond his control are the instilling and developing of a spirit of dedication in his choristers. He can do much to hold the interest of choir members by making their work attractive, but the developing of character and the awakening of a sense of duty are not in his field.

Lack of loyalty, and unwillingness to accept responsibility that entails sacrifice, are problems that trouble the church today. Only the church can solve those problems.

bibliography

AIGRAIN, REV. RENÉ, *Religious Music* (London: Sands and Company, 1931; New York: J. Fischer & Brothers).

ARNOLD, J. H., *Plainsong Accompaniment* (London: Oxford University Press, 1927).

BAILEY, ALBERT, *Gospel in Hymns; Backgrounds and Interpretations* (New York: Charles Scribner's Sons, 1950).

BAUER, MARION, and PEYSER, ETHEL, *How Music Grew, from Prehistoric Times to the Present Day* (New York: G. P. Putnam's Sons, 1939).

——, *Music Through the Ages* (New York: G. P. Putnam's Sons, 1946).

BEKKER, PAUL, *Story of Music* (New York: W. W. Norton & Company, 1927).

BENSON, LOUIS F., *The English Hymn* (New York: Doubleday & Company, Inc., 1915).

BLACKWOOD, ANDREW W., *The Fine Art of Public Worship* (New York: Abingdon Press, 1939).

BLOM, ERIC, *Music in England*, rev. ed. (Baltimore: Penguin Books, 1947).

BONAVIA–HUNT, N., *The Church Organ* (London: The Faith Press).

BOX, REV. G. H., *Judaism in the Greek Period* (London: Oxford University Press, 1932).

BROWN, THERON, and BUTTERWORTH, HEZEKIAH, *The Story of the Hymns and Tunes* (New York: George H. Doran Company, 1906).

BURGESS, FRANCIS, *The Rudiments of Plainchant* (London: Office of Musical Opinion, 1923).

CHRISTY, VAN A., *Glee Club and Chorus* (New York: G. Schirmer, Inc., 1940).

Church Music Society Papers. Oxford University Press, London.

   About Hymns (Robert Bridges)
   Song Schools in the Middle Ages (H. Thompson)
   Church Music Today (Thomas Armstrong)
   Organ Voluntaries (M. P. Conway)
   Restoration Church Music (Heathcote Statham)
   The Use of Small Church Organs (S. H. Lovett)
   Music in Village Churches
   Music in Parish Churches (Harvey Grace)
   Congregational Hymn Practices (C. E. Daly)
   Organ Playing (M. P. Conway)

CLEALL, CHARLES, *Voice Production* (London: Novello and Company).

CLOKEY, J. W., *In Every Corner Sing* (New York, Morehouse-Goreham, 1945).

COLEMAN, HENRY, *Hymn Tune Voluntaries* (London: Oxford University Press, 1930).

DARRELL, R. D., *Guide to Books on Music and Musicians* (New York: G. Schirmer, 1951).

DAVIES, H. WALFORD, *Church Choirs* (New York: Carl Fischer, Inc.).

——, *Music and Christian Worship* (London: Humphrey Milford, 1913).

DAVISON, ARCHIBALD T., *Church Music: Illusion and Reality* (Cambridge, Mass.: Harvard University Press, 1952).

——, *Protestant Church Music in America* (Boston: E. C. Schirmer Music Company, 1933).

DEARMER, P., *Short Handbook of Public Worship* (London: Oxford University Press, 1931).

DICKINSON, EDWARD, *Music in the History of the Western Church* (New York: Charles Scribner's Sons, 1902).

DIX, DOM GREGORY, *The Shape of the Liturgy* (Glasgow: Dacre Press, 1945).

DOUGLAS, WINFRED, *Church Music in History and Practice* (New York: Charles Scribner's Sons, 1955).

ETHERINGTON, CHARLES L., *The Organist and Choirmaster* (New York: The Macmillan Company, 1952).

EWEN, DAVID, *Music Comes to America* (New York: Allen, Town & Heath, 1947).

FARMER, H. H., *Servant of the Word* (New York: Charles Scribner's Sons, 1942).

FINNEY, THEODORE M., *A History of Music* (New York: Harcourt, Brace & World, Inc., 1947).

FISKE, GEORGE WALTER, *The Recovery of Worship* (New York: The Macmillan Company, 1931).

FLEMING, GEORGE T., *The Music of the Congregation* (London: The Faith Press, 1923).

GARDNER, GEORGE, *Worship and Music, Suggestions for Clergy and Choirmasters* (New York: The Macmillan Company, 1918).

—— and NICHOLSON, SYDNEY H., *A Manual of English Church Music* (New York: The Macmillan Company, 1923).

GRACE, HARVEY, *The Complete Organist* (London: Oxford University Press, 1920).

—— and DAVIES, H. WALFORD, *Music and Worship* (New York: The H. W. Gray Company, 1935).

GRATTON–FLOOD, W. H., *Early Tudor Composers* (London: Oxford University Press, 1925).

GROVE'S *Dictionary of Music and Musicians* (New York: The Macmillan Company, 1935).

HADOW, W. H., *Church Music* (London: Longmans, Green & Company, Ltd., 1926).

HISLOP, D. H., *Our Heritage in Public Worship* (New York: Charles Scribner's Sons, 1935).

HOWARD, JOHN T., *Our American Music* (New York: Thomas Y. Crowell Company, 1946).

IDELSOHN, A. Z., *Jewish Music* (New York: Holt, Rinehart and Winston, Inc., 1929).

JONES, ARCHIE N., *Techniques in Choral Conducting* (New York: Carl Fischer, Inc.).

JULIAN, JOHN, *Dictionary of Hymnology* (New York: Charles Scribner's Sons, 1915).

KETTERING, DONALD D., *Steps toward a Singing Church* (Philadelphia: The Westminster Press, 1948).

LANG, PAUL HENRY, *Music in Western Civilization* (New York: W. W. Norton Company, 1941).

MAXWELL, W. D., *Concerning Worship* (London: G. Cumberledge, 1948).

McDORMAND, THOMAS B., *The Art of Building Worship Service* (Broadman, 1942).

McKINNEY, HOWARD D., and ANDERSON, W. R., *Music in History* (New York: American Book Company, 1940).

MELLALIEU, NORMAN W., *The Boy's Changing Voice* (New York: Carl Fischer, Inc.).

METCALF, FRANK J., *American Writers and Compilers of Sacred Music* (Nashville, Tenn.: *Abingdon Press*, 1925).

MOODY, C. H., *The Choirboy in the Making* (London: Oxford University Press, 1923).

Music in Church, rev. ed., Report of the Committee appointed by the Archbishops of Canterbury and York (London: The Church Information Board, 1957).

NICHOLSON, SYDNEY H., *Church Music* (London: The Faith Press).

——, *Quires and Places Where They Sing* (London: G. Bell & Sons, 1932).

NOBLE, T. TERTIUS, *The Training of the Boy Chorister* (New York: G. Schirmer, Inc.).

OESTERLEY, REV. W. O. E., *The Jewish Background of the Christian Liturgy* (London: Oxford University Press, 1925).

OSBORNE, STANLEY L., *The Strain Upraise* (Toronto: The Ryerson Press, 1957).

PALMER, ALBERT W., *Art of Conducting Public Worship* (New York: The Macmillan Company, 1939).

PATRICK, M., *Four Centuries of Scottish Psalmody* (London: Oxford University Press, 1949).

PRICE, CARL F., *The Music and Hymnody of the Methodist Hymnal* (New York: Eaton and Mains, 1911).

REESE, GUSTAVE, *Music in the Middle Ages* (New York: W. W. Norton & Company, 1940).

RILEY, ATHELSTAN, *Concerning Hymn Tunes and Sequences* (London: Mowbrays).

ROBERTSON, A., *Sacred Music* (New York: Chanticleer Press, 1950).

ROMA, LISA, *The Science and Art of Singing* (New York: G. Schirmer, Inc.).

ROUTLEY, E., *The Church and Music* (London: Gerald Duckworth & Company, Ltd., 1950).

——, *Hymns and the Faith* (Greenwich, Conn.: The Seabury Press, Inc., 1956).

SAMINSKY, LAZARE, *The Music of the Ghetto and the Bible* (New York: Bloch Publishing Company, 1934).

SCEATS, GODFREY, *Plainchant and Faburden* (London: The Faith Press).

——, *The Liturgical Use of the Organ* (London: Musical Opinion, 1922).

SCHOLES, PERCY A., ed., *The Oxford Companion to Music*, 8th ed. (London: Oxford University Press, 1950).

STEVENSON, ROBERT M., *Patterns in Protestant Church Music* (Durham, N.C.: Duke University Press, 1953).

STEWART, G. W., *Music in Church Worship* (London: Hodder and Stoughton, 1926).

TERRY, CHARLES SANFORD, *Bach's Chorales* (New York: G. P. Putnam's Sons, 1915).

——, *J. S. Bach's Four-Part Chorales* (London: Oxford University Press, 1929).

——, *J. S. Bach's Original Hymn Tunes* (London: Oxford University Press, 1932).

THIMAN, ERIC H., *Varied Harmonies to Hymn Tunes* (New York: Carl Fischer, Inc., 1934).

WOOLDRIDGE, H. E., and ARKWRIGHT, G. E. P., *Musica Antiquata* (New York: Carl Fischer, Inc.)

ZANZIG, AUGUSTUS D., *Music in American Life* (London: Oxford University Press, 1932).

iNDEX

(See also reference lists at the ends of various chapters)